"What a powerful read! Clear, cc [T0028693] moving, this book should be on ~~the shelf of every~~ every parent, and every Christian of good conscience who wants to engage the conversation around gender and sexuality with integrity. With the patience of a teacher and the humility of a fellow traveler, Austen Hartke carefully unpacks the terminology, sociological studies, and biblical and theological perspectives that most impact transgender Christians, and he combines them with compelling personal stories—including his own—to point us toward truth. It's rare to find a book that manages to be this intellectually rigorous and this readable at the same time. But then, Austen Hartke is a rare talent, one we are so blessed to call part of the body of Christ."

—Rachel Held Evans†, author of
Searching for Sunday and *Inspired*

"Far too often in the conversations at the intersections of LGBT+ identity and Christian faith, the trans community has been ignored. Now, with stunning clarity, scholarly insight, and extraordinary vulnerability, Austen Hartke explores trans identity through the lens of Scripture in a poignant and accessible way that challenges, convicts, and inspires everyone to lean more fully into their God-created identity. This resource challenges false narratives about gender so often promoted in nonaffirming spaces and offers a richly biblical path forward in our understanding and embrace of trans individuals into the life of the church. *Transforming* is truly a game changer and one of the most important theological books to have been written in recent memory."

—Brandan Robertson, pastor, activist, and
author of *Filled to Be Emptied: The Path
to Liberation for Privileged People*

"Austen Hartke brings such compassion, grace, and love to his ministry and advocacy. In this timely book, he gives the church a wonderful gift by amplifying the diverse voices of transgender Christians. He also issues an important, much-needed invitation, calling us all to faithful reexamination of what Scripture has to say about identity, gender, and community."

—Jeff Chu, author of *Does Jesus Really Love Me? A Gay Christian's Pilgrimage in Search of God in America*

"Austen Hartke has become a major interpreter of transgender Christian reality. This book will be recognized as a very important early contribution to an essential conversation, with so much at stake for the precious, vulnerable people whose well-being should be at the center of Christian concern."

—David P. Gushee, author of *After Evangelicalism* and *Still Christian*

"The authentic, intimate stories of transgender Christians in this book unveil an image of the divine that is not monolithic but rather wonderfully multifaceted. By highlighting these stories as an important part of the trajectory of Christianity, *Transforming* reveals a truth about the body of Christ: that it is incomplete without the inclusion of God's transgender children. This is a seminal book that must be read by anyone seeking to understand what it really means to be the church."

—David and Constantino Khalaf, authors of *Modern Kinship: A Queer Guide to Christian Marriage*

"For people who are trans or nonbinary people, the Bible can sometimes feel like a weapon that is used against us. At the same time, for those of us who are Christians, the Bible is utterly important to our faith. So what's a trans Christian, or their friends and allies, to do? Austen Hartke's book answers that question. Hartke combines careful biblical exegesis with helpful education around gender and gender identity, all wrapped in a conversational tone and packed with practical advice. This book will be a must-read for trans Christians, pastors,

lay leaders, parents, and all who believe in God's creative and transforming love."
—E. Carrington Heath, Senior Pastor, Congregational Church (UCC), Exeter, New Hampshire, and author of *Called Out: 100 Devotions for LGBTQ Christians*

"Hartke's *Transforming* is an important work of understanding, compassion, and storytelling. Hartke not only possesses great theological and biblical knowledge but has a deeply compassionate and conversational approach to a topic that is hard for many in the church. Not only will trans Christians find their own struggles reflected in these pages, but parents, allies, and people wishing to understand and know God's transformative story for *all* God's people will find a safe home in this book."
—Dianna Anderson, author of *Damaged Goods: New Perspectives on Christian Purity* and *Problematic: How Toxic Callout Culture Is Destroying Feminism*

"I am encouraged by brave individuals who have challenged old, harmful interpretations of Scripture in favor of a more loving and inclusive Christianity that more fully reflects our Jesus. Through story and Scripture, Hartke does just that, sharing the pain of exclusion and the joy of following God to becoming more fully himself. This is an important read for any Christian who believes in celebrating the diversity of creation and the value of all people."
—Rachel Murr, author of *Unnatural: Spiritual Resiliency in Queer Christian Women*

"In *Transforming*, Austen Hartke makes a vital contribution to theologies both queer and Christian. This book will be invaluable to anyone seeking to understand trans lives and show respect to trans people. But Hartke is up to something more, something important: Hartke wants dialogue to take place among Christians, and he wants trans voices to be recognized as authoritative in that conversation. Hartke manages to engage evangelical perspectives respectfully, without sinking into apologetics. The

trans voices in this book speak boldly, engaging Christian tradition and Scripture with refreshing insight. On its face, *Transforming* invites readers to perceive the marvel of trans identity; but it is also a powerful call to perceive anew what is surprising and life-giving in an authentic read of Christian faith."
—Elizabeth M. Edman, author of *Queer Virtue: What LGBTQ People Know about Life and Love and How It Can Revitalize Christianity*

"There has been need for a book by a young transgender Christian. Seminary-trained transgender man Austen Hartke is the right person to answer the call and fill the need. Hartke begins his book with basic terminology and expands to scriptural support for transgender persons not just being in the church, hiding unnamed in the back row, but serving in openness and authenticity. Whether you do not know any or know many transgender people of faith, you'll learn from Hartke's accessible, humble, and informative writing."
—Kathy Baldock, Executive Director, Canyonwalker Connections, Reno, Nevada

"Hartke's *Transforming* is gentle but uncompromising, humble but smart, just as I have come to know Hartke to be. The power of this book is that it has a clear pastoral heart while resting on a foundation of helpful scholarship."
—Jared Byas, cohost of *The Bible for Normal People* and author of *Love Matters More*

"*Transforming* is a foundational text for pastors and congregations seeking to authentically welcome and affirm transgender, nonbinary, and gender-expansive people in their ministry. The study guide in the back of the book invites readers to embody what they've learned in approachable and practical ways."
—Court VonLindern, NextGen & Inclusiveness Ministries, Mountain Sky Conference of The United Methodist Church

Transforming

Updated and Expanded Edition

with Study Guide

Transforming

The Bible and the Lives
of Transgender Christians

*Updated and Expanded Edition
with Study Guide*

Austen Hartke

WJK WESTMINSTER
JOHN KNOX PRESS
LOUISVILLE · KENTUCKY

© 2018, 2023 Austen Hartke
Foreword © 2018 Westminster John Knox Press
Foreword to new edition © 2023 Jamie Bruesehoff and Rebekah Bruesehoff

Updated and Expanded Edition
Published by Westminster John Knox Press
Louisville, Kentucky

23 24 25 26 27 28 29 30 31 32—10 9 8 7 6 5 4 3 2 1

All rights reserved. No part of this book may be reproduced or transmitted in any form or by any means, electronic or mechanical, including photocopying, recording, or by any information storage or retrieval system, without permission in writing from the publisher. For information, address Westminster John Knox Press, 100 Witherspoon Street, Louisville, Kentucky 40202-1396. Or contact us online at www.wjkbooks.com.

Unless otherwise indicated, Scripture quotations are from the New Revised Standard Version of the Bible, copyright © 1989 by the Division of Christian Education of the National Council of the Churches of Christ in the U.S.A., and are used by permission.

Scripture quotations marked NIV are from The Holy Bible, New International Version. Copyright © 1973, 1978, 1984, 2011 by Biblica, Inc.* Used by permission. All rights reserved worldwide.

Book design by Drew Stevens
Cover design by Allison Taylor

Library of Congress Cataloging-in-Publication Data

Names: Hartke, Austen, author.
Title: Transforming : the Bible and the lives of transgender Christians / Austen Hartke.
Description: Updated and expanded edition. | Louisville, Kentucky : Westminster John Knox Press, [2023] | Includes bibliographical references. | Summary: "Offers insight into Scriptures often used to enforce a fixed and binary conception of gender and highlights the narratives of both gender-expansive biblical characters and transgender Christians living today. This new, expanded edition includes even more tools to equip churches, pastors, and allies to better welcome and care for their trans and nonbinary neighbors"-- Provided by publisher.
Identifiers: LCCN 2022058855 (print) | LCCN 2022058856 (ebook) | ISBN 9780664267865 (paperback) | ISBN 9781646983100 (ebook)
Subjects: LCSH: Gender nonconformity--Religious aspects--Christianity. | Christian transgender people--Religious life.
Classification: LCC BR115.T76 H37 2023 (print) | LCC BR115.T76 (ebook) | DDC 261.8/35768--dc23/eng/20230103
LC record available at https://lccn.loc.gov/2022058855
LC ebook record available at https://lccn.loc.gov/2022058856

Most Westminster John Knox Press books are available at special quantity discounts when purchased in bulk by corporations, organizations, and special-interest groups. For more information, please e-mail SpecialSales@wjkbooks.com.

For every trans Christian who feels alone;
for every parent caught between a rock and a hard place;
for every church and every ministry professional
committed to holding the door open—
this book is for you.

Contents

Foreword to the New Edition by Rebekah Bruesehoff
and Jamie Bruesehoff   ix
Foreword to the First Edition by Matthew Vines   xiii
Introduction: Did God Make a Mistake?   1

Part One

1. Standing on the Edge   9
2. The Beginner's Guide to Gender   23
3. Sin, Sickness, or Specialty?   39

Part Two

4. And God Said, Let There Be Marshes   53
5. Biblical Culture Shock   67
6. What's My Name Again?   83
7. God Breaks the Rules to Get You In   95
8. All the Best Disciples Are Eunuchs   109
9. Nothing Can Prevent Me   121
10. Even Jesus Had a Body   137
11. Life beyond Apologetics   151
12. Does Gender Matter Anymore?   163

Conclusion: The Trans-Affirming Toolbox   175
Afterword: Spiritual Care for Gender-Expansive
Christians: A Conversation with Professor Susannah
Cornwall   187
Small Group Study Guide   205
Sermon Series Guide   217
Acknowledgments   225
Notes   229
Further Reading   245

Foreword to the New Edition

Being transgender in the church, especially as a young person, can be scary. The people doing the most harm to the transgender community are overwhelmingly people of faith. They're so loud that it's easy to think all Christians think that way, but that's just not true. I want people to know that being transgender and being Christian are *not* mutually exclusive. Because so much of what we hear in the world today pits these two communities against each other, it can feel really weird to be part of both of them.

I am transgender, and I am Christian. I know not all churches are good and safe places, but I wish more people knew that there are churches that affirm and celebrate the beautiful diversity of God's creation, including transgender people. When you find one of those churches, that's when you finally feel how good it can be to be part of a community that sees you and loves you both as a transgender person and as a Christian: a community where you truly belong.

I've been really lucky to be a part of that kind of community all my life. My dad is a pastor, and my mom is a church professional. Together, they have four degrees in religion. For them, it was never a question of whether loving and supporting me was the right thing to do. They saw the difference in me when I stopped pretending to be someone else and stepped into who God made me to be. My church community saw that too. Knowing me helped them move from thinking about transgender people as an "issue" to seeing us as human beings. I was just a little girl in a flowery purple dress, twirling on the church lawn. After that, my parents did a lot of work to help educate the congregation about what it means to be transgender and what that means for the church. It took time, but two years after I transitioned, on the tenth anniversary of my baptism, we gathered with our congregation, my godparents, and my family to bless me and my forever name. My grandfather, who baptized me as a baby, presided over the service. Being loved and supported so deeply by the people around me is what allows me to thrive.

That's not to say it was all sunshine and rainbows. It still isn't today. I have been excluded from some communities because of who I am. Some of the most hurtful and hateful things said about and to my family come from people of faith. They threaten to hurt me or my parents or tell us we're going to hell, in the name of Jesus. It seems about as unchristian as you can get, but I continue to find hope in the church.

When I was eleven years old, I spoke at the Evangelical Lutheran Church in America's 2018 Youth Gathering in Houston, Texas. I stood on stage in front of 31,000 high school youth and their adult leaders and shared my story as a transgender person, and my hope for the church and the world. It felt incredible to know that my church cared enough about kids like me to put me on that stage, but it was even better to see the reactions of the people who were there and hear the stories that came after. I heard about youth who saw themselves celebrated in the church for the first time, young people who came out to their families and congregations, and pastors who came out to their youth groups. The ripples of impact that went out from that day continue to give me hope that people of faith can do this work and evolve their understanding just as they embraced the story of a transgender young person like me through the lens of Christianity. I don't have to give up part of who I am. I can be both transgender and Christian.

In 2021, I was confirmed in the Evangelical Lutheran Church in America. As a confirmed member of the church, I can vote on important matters, and my presence counts like that of every other adult in the room. It meant a lot to me to be confirmed in a church that sees me for who God made me to be, that proclaims that I am a called and claimed child of God, and that lifts up my voice as a transgender young person. Now my hope is that we can build a church and world where all transgender people can feel safe and loved.

REBEKAH BRUESEHOFF

Our daughter Rebekah shows us what is possible when a transgender young person is surrounded by love, affirmation, and celebration long before they ever hear any messages to the contrary.
We work with a top-notch team at the Children's Hospital of
Philadelphia for Rebekah's gender-related care. She was eight
years old for her first appointment at the Gender Clinic, where
we began building relationships with their psychologists and
social workers, years before hormones or any other treatments
would be introduced. Dr. Hawkins, a psychologist and codirec-
tor at the clinic, spent some time talking to me and my husband, and then she spent some time with Rebekah. When she
came back after talking with Rebekah, Dr. Hawkins confessed
she was a little teary-eyed. Dr. Hawkins had asked Rebekah how
she might explain what it means to be transgender to someone
who didn't understand. Rebekah's answer was simple and honest: "Being transgender means being who God made me to be."
     Rebekah has been told from the very beginning of her
gender journey that she is a called and claimed child of God,
created to be exactly who she knows herself to be. That's her
foundation. When people tell her that God doesn't make mistakes, she says, "I know. I'm not a mistake." Of course, over
time Rebekah has learned the ugly truth about the church's
past and present when it comes to transgender people. She's
seen the harm that people of faith continue to do to people like
her, personally and politically. But because she is so secure in
her identity and in her faith in the God that created her, she's
able to hope and work for a world where that's not the case any
longer. She's helped me find that hope too.
     When Rebekah transitioned, the church was the place my
husband and I most feared. We weren't afraid of God. We
were afraid of human beings and of the institution to which
they belonged. Rebekah's dad was the pastor of a small congregation in a rural, conservative area. While we knew there was
room in our denomination for the affirmation and celebration
of LGBTQIA+ identities, we didn't know how our congregation would respond. The first time Rebekah showed up at
church as herself, one parishioner found my husband afterward
and said, "I don't really understand this whole transgender

thing. But she used to hide behind you and refuse to say 'Hi' to me on Sunday mornings. Today, she ran up to me, twirled in her dress, and gave me a high five. What more is there to know?" By being herself and by showing up as God created her to be, Rebekah opens hearts and changes minds in a way I never imagined possible. That's true of every transgender person I've ever met. That's where I find hope.

Of course, there is a lot more to know, but we in the church don't have to have all the answers. Things in our congregation weren't perfect all at once, but people learned and grew alongside us. There will be mistakes and missteps. We have to learn and do the work, but there is grace for the journey. First and foremost, the church must understand and unequivocally proclaim that transgender people are whole and holy parts of the body of Christ. That's where this book and Austen Hartke come in. I can't think of a better place to start as we seek to understand what it means to be transgender and Christian, what the Bible says, and how it can inform our relationships and our ministries.

To some people, Rebekah's experience of being loved, supported, and affirmed as a transgender young person of faith seems like an anomaly, but she's not alone. There are families and congregations just like ours in communities all over the country. These families and congregations are loving and affirming the transgender young people in their midst, not in spite of their faith, but because of it. Transgender young people need those congregations. Families need pastors who can walk with them on this journey. Our communities are richer and the body of Christ is more fully present when transgender people are a part of them. I have the deepest gratitude to Austen for writing this book and to you for reading it. Together, we can make the church a safer and more welcoming place for all God's children.

Jamie Bruesehoff
January 2022

Foreword to the First Edition

This book is a gift to the church, and it couldn't come at a more urgent time.

As more transgender people have come out in recent years, many cisgender people like me have begun to recognize the daunting scale of discrimination and hostility that trans people have to face every day. It's not overstating the matter to say that our society's mistreatment of transgender people is an ongoing humanitarian crisis.

According to the landmark National Transgender Discrimination Survey published in 2014, in the United States, 41 percent of transgender adults have attempted suicide. Just think about that: forty-one percent. (The overall rate for the general population is 1.6 percent.) But as horrifying as that statistic is, it's not surprising in light of these other numbers: 90 percent of transgender people have experienced harassment or discrimination at work, 57 percent have experienced significant family rejection, 26 percent have been fired for who they are, and 19 percent have experienced homelessness because of their gender identity. In recent years, too, the number of transgender people who have been murdered has gone up, and transgender women of color are usually the victims of these widely ignored attacks.

Where has the church been amidst this barrage of harassment, discrimination, and violence against transgender and gender-nonconforming people? All too often, the church has been part of the problem. For many transgender people, some of the most painful rejection they've experienced has been in church. After being mocked and bullied in school, they've been told by their pastors on Sunday that who they are at a fundamental level is a disgrace to God. Unless they can change something that cannot be changed, transgender people are frequently told that there is no place for them among God's people, and a few verses from Scripture are casually deployed as tools of exclusion by those who've barely gotten to know the people they're excluding.

In the face of that kind of hostility, it would be perfectly defensible for transgender people to want nothing to do with Christianity—and indeed, if Jesus were here, I think he'd be turning over tables to protest the church's inhumane treatment of them. But that only makes the faith and testimonies of transgender Christians all the more powerful. I've met faithful transgender Christians all over the world, from Mississippi to Minnesota and as far away as Budapest. I've been inspired by their stories, and I've grown and changed as a result of them. I've also learned a great deal about theology and biblical interpretation from transgender Christians, and in this book you'll get to learn from one of the best teachers I know.

Austen Hartke is an ideal person to write this profoundly important book. I first got to know Austen a few years back through his wonderful YouTube series "Transgender and Christian," where he breaks down theological issues related to gender identity with grace, warmth, and expert skill. A graduate of Luther Seminary's Master of Arts program in Old Testament/Hebrew Bible Studies and the winner of the 2014 John Milton Prize in Old Testament Writing from Luther Seminary, Austen has a keen theological mind and an infectious love for Scripture. He's taught at The Reformation Project's conferences, and I've seen firsthand how his work has helped countless transgender people reconcile their faith and their gender identity.

But as powerful as Austen's own story is, he isn't just interested in letting you learn more about him. Austen has a huge heart for other transgender people, and in this book he shares with you the stories of other extraordinary transgender Christians, like the Reverend M Jade Kaiser, a nonbinary believer, and Nicole Garcia, a trans Latina minister. Austen is passionate about amplifying the voices of trans people of color, trans women, nonbinary people, and others who experience multiple layers of marginalization in the church. That commitment shapes and enriches every page of his book.

I have a story to share about Austen that will show you some of his character and heart for others. When I was in Budapest recently, I spent an evening with about twenty LGBTQ Christians and allies. One young man who came that night had recently come out as transgender. He told me he'd found Austen's work online and that it had helped him in his journey as a transgender Christian. But even more than that, Austen had actually struck up a friendship with this man, answering his messages and going out of his way to provide encouragement and support to him from halfway across the world. This trans Christian expressed his amazement to me that Austen, an American with a growing platform and reputation, would take the time to befriend and support someone who was coming out as far away as Hungary. I was thrilled for him, but not surprised. That's just who Austen is.

It's out of that same servant's heart that Austen wrote this book. There is a desperate need for more pastoral and theological resources to help transgender and gender-nonconforming Christians, and through this book Austen is taking a significant step toward filling that need. He easily could have walked away from the church. He could have scorned those who haven't accepted him for who he is. But he didn't. He stayed out of his love for the church, and his writing and teaching are changing lives around the world. This book will only increase his impact, and it will be the first resource I recommend for transgender Christians and those seeking to love—and learn from—transgender and gender-nonconforming people in the church.

So pull up a chair and get started. This is a conversation that cannot wait, and Austen is the best of guides.

MATTHEW VINES
Founder and executive director of The Reformation Project,
and author of *God and the Gay Christian:
The Biblical Case in Support of Same-Sex Relationships*
July 2, 2017

Introduction

Did God Make a Mistake?

Whenever I go to speak with Christians who are unfamiliar with transgender folks, it seems as if we spend the first few minutes dancing around the question they really want to ask. Not "Have you had the surgery?" or "What's your real name?" (Though I've heard those too, and I always take a moment to remind people that those questions aren't appropriate or a good way to start a conversation.) No, the question I get most often sounds more like this: "So, if God made you female, but you know yourself to be male, does that mean that you think God made a mistake?"

I asked myself that same question for a long time before coming out as transgender. As a teenager I believed strongly in the idea that everything happens for a reason, and if that was true, then there must have been a reason God had made me with a body that was designated female when I was born. Even though I'd known for most of my life that I didn't feel like a girl, I did my best to ignore that fact and push it down deep where I didn't have to think about it. The biggest hurdle I faced in addressing my gender identity was that it seemed like saying God was wrong.

So imagine my relief when I started coming across Scripture passages that appeared to have something to say about gender identity and the way God made the world! In seminary I read the Bible cover to cover and spent hours in the library poring over books about creation narratives, clothing in the ancient world, and the meaning of the incarnation. I learned from Job that sometimes things happen in the world that don't make much sense to us human beings. I learned from Abraham what it's like to have your name changed. I learned from the apostle Philip that sometimes you have to say yes to God even when you have no idea what God is doing. And of course I learned from Jesus, who after his resurrection chose to show his body to the disciples—a body that was scarred and transformed, and yet still his own.

The more I learned, the more I felt compelled to open up myself to the world. I wanted to take out the parts of myself that I'd packed away out of sight, and to let them breathe in the sunshine. It almost felt as if my heart was trying to escape my chest, pulling in the same sort of way it had when I began considering a seminary education. I decided to follow that call, and when I started talking with other transgender people and describing my experiences, I heard them speaking parts of my own story back to me. When I discovered that there were other transgender Christians (who knew?!), I felt as if I'd stumbled across buried treasure.

Before long, I was finding my own answer to that original question: "Did God make a mistake?" Personally, my answer is no. I don't believe God made a mistake in creating me just as I am. God created me with a body that was designated female when I was born—a body that I struggled to connect with for the first twenty-six years of my life and that I now finally feel at home in—but God also created me with a capacity for change and with a mind that knows that I'm male. I believe God made all of me—gender identity included—and intended for me to be a transgender person who sees the world through a different lens. I don't think God made a mistake. I think God made me transgender on purpose.

After I graduated from seminary I wasn't sure what to do next. I really wanted to keep talking with other trans Christians and to keep exploring the Scripture passages that had given me so much life! I began making videos about gender-related theological topics and posting them on YouTube, and before long people started leaving comments. Some were wonderful, and some were mean-spirited, but the ones that got to me the most came from transgender teenagers and young people who had desperate questions. Questions like, "Does God still love me if I'm trans?" and "My pastor says I'm going to hell. What do I do?" I did my best to point toward helpful resources (many of which you'll find in the Further Reading section in the back of this book), but in the end I couldn't find a written, accessible place where all kinds of different trans-affirming theologies came together. I wanted a book written by transgender people and for transgender people and the faith communities that care about them.

That's why I began talking with friends of mine who also identified as transgender Christians, asking them if they'd be willing to share some of the things they've learned. I certainly don't have all the answers! As a white, bisexual, transgender man, I have no idea what it's like to navigate Christian faith as a person of color, or as a nonbinary person, or as a trans woman. I wanted to include some stories that end happily—and some others that don't end on such an upbeat note. Trans Christians face incredible obstacles in churches around the world. While some of us find ways to make it back into affirming communities with a faith that's still strong, not all of us have found that fountain of healing yet.

I'm so thankful to the people who agreed to sit down and gift me with their time and their knowledge, as this project was coming together. When I talked with the people you're about to meet in these pages, I always ended each interview with the same big question: "Do you think God made a mistake?" Strangely enough, even though we're all very different, we seem to agree on this subject.

Here are a few of their answers:

If there's a mistake at all, it's that we've created this understanding of gender that is so deeply limiting of God's creation. That's the mistake. We've always been diverse people.
We've always recognized that using tools, for lack of a better word, to best support our bodies is a good thing. Certainly those of us who change our bodies physically because
of our gender identity are not the first people in the world
who have needed assistance to be our best selves.

—M

God created us with the ability to also be creators, and some
of those creators created surgical procedures and medical
procedures and concepts and ideologies and systems and
communities that do wonderful things! If we aren't taking
part in that creative process, then we're going against our
very created nature.

—Lawrence

God doesn't make mistakes; she just makes things easier or
a bit more difficult to find. Transitioning doesn't mean that
God made a mistake, just that I need to work a bit harder to
find the fullness of life God has for me.

—River

I think that God knit me together in my mother's womb,
but has also been knitting me together every day since. I
think God knit together my body and my identity. I'm not
just a woman. I'm not just a man. I'm transgender. That's
what God intended.

—Asher

I can't wait for you to read more about each of these wonderful people in the coming chapters, and to get a glimpse inside
their faith and their lives. One quick note before we get going:
In this book I sometimes use the word "queer" as a synonym
for people with LGBTQI2A identities. Not every gay, lesbian,

bisexual, transgender, intersex, Two Spirit, or asexual person uses this word to describe themselves, because even though it's in the process of being reclaimed by LGBTQI2A communities, historically it has been used as a slur. In the interviews in this book I use the word "queer" only to describe someone who has already affirmed that they use this word for themselves. If you are unsure whether it's right to use a word to describe a person's identity, it's always best to ask first!

We'll talk more about language and definition in chapter 2, but for now let's wade a little deeper into these theological waters. Christians these days have questions about what the Bible has to say regarding clothing, changing bodies, new names, and the way God created human beings to exist in this world. I am thankful that trans Christians, who have been living and studying these questions for years, have come up with some pretty fascinating answers! Let's begin by asking ourselves why theology for and about transgender people is important.

PART ONE

1
Standing on the Edge

"Do they even let . . . people like you . . . in?"

This was the first thing my sister Madelyn asked when I told her that I was applying to seminary. Of course, she didn't mean it in a derogatory way—she was and continues to be one of the most supportive people in my life—but she was curious and concerned. In 2011, when I submitted my application to a degree program in youth ministry, I had not yet come to grips with my gender identity. I had been open about my bisexuality for about seven years, though, and I didn't relish the idea of having to get back into the closet.

This meant that when I started considering a seminary program, my discernment process didn't begin with "Is God leading me toward ministry?" or even "Would this degree give me a leg up in my career?" No, when I arrived on campus for visit days, I was seeking some more basic answers. For instance, if I brought my whole self to the study of Scripture and the building up of the church, would I be welcomed? If I opened myself to honest and authentic communion with others in the classroom and in the sanctuary, could I count on being physically safe?

Most Christians in the United States today don't have to choose between being open about their relationships or being excommunicated. Most Christians don't have to risk being assaulted on their way to services for wearing their favorite dress, only to arrive and hear a sermon condemning them to eternal punishment. But some do.

That is why, to this day, I feel just a little bit nervous when I walk into any unfamiliar church building. It's a response reinforced by years of necessary self-defense, which too many LGBTQI2A Christians have to cultivate. The landmark 2013 Pew Research Center Survey of LGBT Americans tells us that 29 percent of LGBT-identified folks have been made to feel unwelcome in religious spaces.[1] When we consider the fact that in 2021 Gallup estimated that 7.1 percent of adult Americans (approximately eighteen million people) identify as LGBT,[2] this means that roughly five million people have been treated poorly by those who share their faith, simply because of their sexuality or gender identity.

That negative treatment—whether it manifests itself as hostile stares, a direct order to leave, or physical violence—doesn't exist in a vacuum. As Christianity continues to be the dominant religious force behind much of American culture, people outside church walls have begun to express frustration with the faith's attitude toward LGBTQI2A people. A 2014 study revealed that 70 percent of millennials and 58 percent of Americans overall now believe that religious groups are alienating people by being too judgmental about issues like same-sex marriage.[3] One-quarter of the people who were raised in religious families, but have left their tradition, admit that negative treatment or teachings about LGBTQI2A people was a factor in their decision to leave. With organized Christianity in America already facing a steady decline,[4] we might well ask how the church could possibly afford to push anyone out, especially persons who desperately seek to be recognized and accepted as part of the faith.

And that's the strangest part about these recent studies: despite Christianity's reputation for anti-LGBTQI2A sentiment, half of queer-identified adults claim a religious affiliation, and 17 percent consider their faith very important in their lives.[5] What's more, these percentages appear to be getting larger every year.[6]

How does it feel to be caught in the crosshairs between your faith and your identity, which has been declared part of "the culture wars"? For some LGBTQI2A Christians, it's a refining fire that brings about an even greater passion for mercy, justice, and a relationship with God. Gay and lesbian Christians like Rev. Dr. Horace L. Griffin and Rachel Murr have even written about their experiences and their journey to a greater understanding of the "clobber passages" related to sexuality. In recent years, cultural and political issues like same-sex marriage have brought lesbian, gay, and bisexual issues into the cultural limelight.

Up until recent years, however, transgender people have been more or less ignored, both within society at large and more obviously within Christian circles. The writers at *Christianity Today*, an evangelical magazine, expressed low-level apprehensions about trans issues beginning in 2008, but it wasn't until 2012 that the T in LGBT found its first big Christian news headline. A Girl Scout troop in Colorado allowed a young transgender woman to join; this prompted swift retribution, in the form of a cookie boycott by some Christians. In 2013, Dr. Donovan Ackley III, a professor at the evangelical Azusa Pacific University, came out as transgender and was subsequently asked to leave. In May 2014, *Time* magazine declared the year "the transgender tipping point" and predicted that trans issues would be "America's next civil-rights frontier." This was followed by the introduction of a record number of trans-exclusionary bills in state legislatures in 2015.

While transgender visibility has increased rapidly since 2012 (the number of people who personally know a trans person jumped from 30 percent in 2016 to 42 percent in 2021),[7] visibility itself has not always had a positive effect. As more trans people come forward and share their stories and the struggles that they face, those who find trans identities distasteful or morally corrupt feel that they must also come forward with their own opinions, policies, and theological pronouncements. In October 2015, just three months after Olympic superstar Caitlyn Jenner came out as transgender on the cover of *Vanity Fair* magazine, the Association of Certified Biblical Counselors (ACBC) put together an event that they billed as "evangelical Christians' first-ever conference on transgender issues."[8] No transgender people were asked to speak at this event. Instead, the largely Southern Baptist–identified speakers agreed beforehand to a statement that rejected the idea that "a human being could possess a gender other than the one indicated by biological sex." Members of the ACBC argued that gender dysphoria is a result of original sin, and Owen Strachan, the executive director of the Council on Biblical Manhood and Womanhood, declared, "Even if we have never intended to choose a transgender identity, if we embrace this impulse, we are following, chasing a sinful instinct. We are in fact sinning against God."[9]

Then, in 2016, what had previously been a predominantly theological debate, between conservative Christians and those who supported transgender justice, became an all-out battle that exploded onto the national legislative scene. On May 13, the US Justice Department and the US Department of Education sent out a joint guidance letter to all public schools, clarifying that Title IX protections against discrimination based on sex now functionally included discrimination based on gender identity. The letter stated that, in order to be in compliance with Title IX, public schools must not discriminate based on gender identity when it comes to gender-segregated spaces like restrooms, locker rooms, single-sex classes or schools, fraternities, or sororities. All schools that wished to continue receiving federal monies must be in compliance with Title IX.[10]

The movement toward protection for transgender people in the United States was becoming, in the opinion of some Christians, a threat to religious liberty. Dozens of schools began the process of requesting religious exemption waivers so that they would not have to comply with the clarified ruling[11]—a move reminiscent of the religious exemption from providing birth control won by Hobby Lobby in 2014 and the exemption from service to same-gender couples requested by a bakery in Colorado in 2013.

The May 2016 guidance on Title IX was eventually rescinded in February 2017, citing the problem of "significant litigation," and as it turned out, the individual corporations, small businesses, and schools who had brought forward that litigation were not working alone. Three powerhouses of conservative Christian social action—the Alliance Defending Freedom, the Family Research Council, and Focus on the Family—have been instrumental in providing funding and legal counsel in support of what they consider to be religious freedom. When it comes to transgender issues specifically, each of these three organizations has had a hand in stirring the pot.

While it claims not to lobby government officials or promote legislation, the Alliance Defending Freedom—whose mission statement is "To keep the doors open for the Gospel by advocating for religious liberty, the sanctity of life, and marriage and family"—has created a policy template barring transgender students from school bathrooms and has offered to defend any school district that implements such a policy.[12] This "Student Physical Privacy Act" was then used as a model upon which several state legislatures built proposals banning transgender people from the public bathrooms that aligned with their gender identity.[13]

The Family Research Council, a public-policy organization whose mission is to "advance faith, family and freedom in public policy and the culture from a Christian worldview," has also been instrumental in influencing legislative efforts against transgender Americans. Their political action committee, the Faith Family Freedom Fund, ran advertising campaigns against Houston's proposed Equal Rights Ordinance in 2015, claiming that if the nondiscrimination measure passed, Houstonians could be fined for blocking a man from entering a women's bathroom. Peter Sprigg of the Family Research Council argued that including gender identity as a protected category in civil rights laws would "threaten the public safety of women and children by creating the legitimized access that sexual predators tend to seek."[14]

This has not proven to be the case. In the twelve states that had included gender identity in their nondiscrimination laws as of March 2014, no one had assaulted anyone else through access gained to these spaces as a result of this type of policy.[15] Moreover, the same study done on nondiscrimination laws showed that there had never been an incident where a transgender person harassed or attacked anyone in a gendered facility, debunking the idea that transgender people are a danger to others. In fact, according to a 2013 study conducted by the Williams Institute, 70 percent of transgender people have themselves at some point been the victim of either verbal or physical assault in gendered restrooms.[16]

Focus on the Family is arguably the most well-known Christian ministry organization in the United States. In 2015 they updated a position statement on their website to contain an entire series on transgender issues, which included the assertion that transgender identities "violate God's intentional design for sex and sexuality." The statement continues,

> We believe that this is a cultural and theological challenge that we must engage and win. The modern "transgender" movement is systematically working to dismantle the reality of two sexes—male and female—as the Bible and the world have always known this to be. If the transgender lobby succeeds, there will be striking consequences for individuals, marriage, family and society at large.[17]

In this spirit of engaging to win, Focus on the Family's policy division, the Family Policy Alliance (formerly known as CitizenLink), helped implement House Bill 2 in North Carolina in 2016. This bill was the first piece of state legislation signed into law that specifically required transgender people to use the bathroom or other gendered facility that corresponded with the gender marker on their birth certificate, and blocked any nondiscrimination policy that included gender identity or sexual orientation from becoming law anywhere within the state.

These two stipulations may seem inconsequential to those who don't identify as transgender, but the stress caused by the realization that you might be arrested for entering one bathroom and harassed or attacked if you enter the other can hardly be overstated. In an interview with Greta Gustava Martela, one of the founders of the transgender crisis hotline Trans Lifeline, it was discovered that incoming calls to the crisis center doubled in the three weeks after HB2 was signed into law.[18] This law, which was later found by the US Justice Department to violate the Federal Civil Rights Act, was put in place through the direct efforts of Focus on the Family and the Family Policy Alliance. According to the most recently released IRS documentation, the FPA contributed over a third of the operating budget for their affiliate, the North Carolina Family Policy Council.[19] The NCFPC, in turn, pressed North Carolina governor Pat McCrory to call a special session,[20] which passed HB2 through the entire state legislative process in one day.

Many Christian denominations hold similarly negative views when it comes to transgender identities, though the actions they take may not be as recognizably detrimental. Some take a more moderate stance or promote a form of conditional acceptance. The Southern Baptist Convention passed a resolution in 2014 that declares "gender identity confusion" to be the effect of a fallen human nature, and something that must not be encouraged or normalized. Toward the end of the same document it is resolved that the Convention "love our transgender neighbors, seek their good always, welcome them to our churches and, as they repent and believe in Christ, receive them into church membership."[21] Though the statement calls for a loving response, the emphasis is placed on a required repentance, which presupposes three things: that transgender identities are themselves sinful, that a trans person can reject their identity if they try hard enough, and that trans identities are incompatible with faith in Christ.

Other Christian groups, like the Lutheran Church–Missouri Synod (LCMS), have focused not so much on transgender identities as on a person's physical transition. The LCMS Commission on Theology and Church Relations released a statement in 2014 that advises pastors to discourage any form of transition for transgender congregants, and instead suggests that pastors refer trans people to a Christian therapist.[22] In the same year, the Assemblies of God churches adopted a statement "discouraging any and all attempts to physically change, alter, or disagree with [a person's] predominant biological sex—including but not limited to elective sex-reassignment, transvestite, transgender, or nonbinary 'genderqueer' acts or conduct."[23] While these statements do not give much direction on how to treat a transgender person who has already transitioned, they create an environment that would give any current member some significant second thoughts before coming out.

The extent to which a transgender member might be allowed to be involved in the life of the church has also been a point of dissent for many Christians. Some denominations welcome transgender people looking for a church home but deny them official membership. Others allow membership but won't elect a trans person into any leadership position. The Roman Catholic Church made the news in 2015 after the Vatican's policy-enforcing arm, the Congregation for the Doctrine of the Faith, determined that transgender people are not eligible to become godparents. After Alex Salinas requested to become his nephew's godfather, the church stated that being openly transgender "reveals in a public way an attitude opposite to the moral imperative of solving the problem of sexual identity according to the truth of one's own sexuality."[24] The statement went on to say that Salinas was not fit to become a godparent because "it is evident that this person does not possess the requirement of leading a life according to the faith and in the position of godfather."

This was a blow to Catholics who had hoped that the church under Pope Francis's leadership would be a more welcoming place for LGBTQI2A Christians. Francis himself faced criticism for what many saw as a comparison between transgender people and nuclear weapons during an interview with authors Andrea Tornielli and Giacomo Galeazzi in their book *This Economy Kills: Pope Francis on Capitalism and Social Justice*. During a part of the interview in which he talks about things that destroy the order of creation, Francis uses the following examples: "Let's think of the nuclear arms, of the possibility to annihilate in a few instants a very high number of human beings. Let's think also of genetic manipulation, of the manipulation of life, or of the gender theory, that does not recognize the order of creation."[25] The phrase "gender theory," when used in this sort of context, usually refers to the way that people have come to see all aspects of gender along a spectrum, rather than as a binary. Francis appears to be articulating his opinion that these ranges of human experience are outside God's created order and may even be dangerous. This sentiment seemed to be echoed by the Vatican's document "Male and Female He Created Them," which was put out by the church's Congregation for Catholic Education arm in 2019 and used similar language.

What effect must it have on young transgender Catholics to know that their church community considers them unnatural and dangerous? What does a transgender member of an Assemblies of God church do when they're told transitioning is not an option? When James Dobson, the founder of Focus on the Family, goes on record encouraging men to "defend your wife's privacy and security in restroom facilities" against "a strange-looking man, dressed like a woman," and lamenting the fact that it's no longer acceptable to shoot the transgender person in this situation, what effect does this have on our country?[26]

The year 2020 was the deadliest on record for transgender and gender-expansive people.[27] At least forty-four transgender people were murdered in the United States that year, alongside at least 375 of our trans siblings in other countries around the world—and these are just the murders that we know about.[28] Oftentimes transgender people are misgendered by law enforcement and news agencies after their death; as a result, their true identities and their stories are lost to us. Additionally, it's crucial to note that the majority of transgender homicide victims in the United States are women of color—specifically, Black trans women—who must deal with the triple threat of sexism, transphobia, and racism in the specific form of anti-Blackness. The number of transgender and gender-expansive people killed nationally and worldwide in 2021 nearly met—but did not exceed—the previous year's totals. Given the fact that more of our trans siblings have been killed each year since organizations began tracking these tragedies in 2008, we remain on edge as we wait to see whether the plateau reached in 2021 is just a statistical anomaly. Regardless of overall trends, we know that numbers don't tell the whole story and that each life lost means a light snuffed out and whole world destroyed to the victim's loved ones.

The National LGBTQ Task Force (then the National Gay and Lesbian Task Force) and the National Center for Transgender Equality put forward a report in 2011 that attempted to understand the reasons behind the current murder epidemic. They found that, when all other factors were accounted for, transgender people were disproportionately affected by homelessness, poverty, job discrimination, bullying in school, and harassment by law enforcement.[29] Essentially, the mental and emotional bias that American culture holds against transgender individuals leaks out into real-world actions against trans people, whether that action is turning down a nonbinary applicant for a job or shooting a trans woman in a bathroom.

When our churches support or even organically formulate the idea that transgender people are morally, intellectually, or theologically inferior, we feed right into the hatred that leads to death for an already marginalized group. The 2011 discrimination report found that 41 percent of trans individuals have attempted suicide, compared to 1.6 percent of the general population of the United States. Nearly half of trans folks attempt suicide, not because there's something inherently wrong with them, but because they experience a phenomenon called "minority stress."[30] Minority stress describes the friction that occurs between a person who holds a marginalized identity and the hostile environment in which they live. Transgender people live with a continuous expectation of rejection, and many experience an endless underlying current of fear because of the threat of physical or emotional violence. This constant stress can lead to depression, anxiety, substance use disorders, and suicidal thoughts and actions. A study coordinated by the Williams Institute and the American Foundation for Suicide Prevention found direct evidence of minority stress when they discovered that suicide rates among transgender and gender-nonconforming adults jumped from the base 41 percent to 59 percent among those who were harassed at work, 61 percent among those who were harassed by law-enforcement officers, and 78 percent among those who experienced physical or sexual violence.[31]

The strain on transgender people has increased with the advent of bathroom bills and the legislation of gendered spaces. Williams Institute manager of transgender research Jody L. Herman confirmed that experiences in gendered restrooms are significantly affecting levels of minority stress. She states unequivocally that "policies to protect transgender people's access to restrooms can be understood as policies that are connected to the health and well-being of transgender people."[32]

Living every hour of your life with your guard up can take its toll on anyone, but for trans and gender-expansive people, the stress can be deadly. Yet Christian churches and organizations continue to advocate and fund policies that make this state of being inescapable.

If the high rates of suicide and murder for transgender people can be traced to legitimate fears of harassment, discrimination, and rejection, then the obvious solution is to create an environment in which the injured, the worn-out, and the hopeless feel safe and loved. In fact, the number one predictor of health and well-being in LGBTQI2A youth is family acceptance and the creation of a safe haven at home.[33] Over half of the LGBTQI2A young people who were rejected by their families reported having attempted suicide, compared to only 32 percent of those who had supportive families. Family acceptance is also a protection against depression, substance use disorders, and other negative mental health issues that are usually seen in those who experience minority stress.

The problem is that family acceptance itself is intricately tied to religious affiliation. Many parents who try to follow their faith and do what's best for their child's soul may end up doing irreversible harm to their child's physical and mental health. As Caitlin Ryan, director of the Family Acceptance Project, put it, "Most families, including very religious families, are shocked to learn that behaviors they engage in to try to help their LGBT children fit in and be accepted by others instead contribute to serious health risks, such as suicide attempts."[34] What the Family Acceptance Project and others have found is that high religiosity in families is directly connected to high levels of family rejection.

When parents attend churches that teach that being transgender is sinful, they are much more likely to reject their child if that child comes out; in turn, a child who is rejected is more likely to suffer from mental health issues and to die by suicide. This sad fact was made visible for many in the death of Leelah Alcorn, who stepped out in front of a truck in December 2014 after experiencing negative faith-based reactions from her parents and being forced to attend Christian conversion therapy to "cure" her of her gender identity.

Christianity has been dominated by the voices of those who speak out against the existence, the well-being, and the humanity of transgender people. These voices have sunk into the fabric of American culture, and the result has been a rash of murders that causes no religious outrage, no demand for justice from those who should have cared for the wounded ones on the side of the road. We have closed our ears to the cry of the parents who have lost their children because of toxic theology; we have turned away from the tears of the youth who ask if Jesus can love them just as they are. Too many of those questioning their gender identity have been made to feel that they must choose between God and an authentic and healthy life. Not all of the people forced into that decision make it out alive.

This is where transgender Christians have been forced to live: out on the edges. They walk the fine line between acceptance and rejection, between God's love and the church's judgment.

But this is also where God begins to bring life out of death, because although religious affiliation in families has been connected to rejection of LGBTQI2A children, faith can also be one of the largest contributors to well-being in youth if their religious community supports them.[35] We know that family acceptance and the creation of a refuge in homes and communities is incredibly important to the health of transgender people, and so we must ask, is it time for God's house to truly become a house of prayer for all people? Will we hear the words of Scripture, and the stories of the trans Christians in our midst, and allow our sanctuaries to become the spaces they were always meant to be?

2
The Beginner's Guide to Gender

Maybe you're a pastor with a new transgender congregant. Maybe you're a faithful parent whose child just came out as genderfluid. Maybe you're trans yourself and just coming to understand the connections between your faith and your identity. Maybe you're a casual reader who's curious about this trans thing that everyone's talking about! Whoever you are, you probably have some questions. Before we get started on answers, though, it's important that we share some common language.

Imagine we are two people who speak different languages preparing dinner together. How could we talk about what kind of meal to make if we had different words for the veggies and pasta we were preparing? Realistically, we'd probably do a lot of pointing—picking up a carrot here and a sprig of thyme there, and giving the other person a questioning look as if to say, "What do you call this?" That's what this chapter's all about: getting us on the same page and speaking the same language, so that we can have the deeper conversations over the meal later on.

It's good to keep in mind two general rules when we're talking about language in LGBTQI2A communities. First, while it can feel comforting to have strict definitions for words that are the same always and everywhere, the truth is that language is constantly changing. As we discover new things about the universe and about ourselves, new words are created, and as we learn more about those discoveries, the definitions shift in order to become more accurate or to make sense in different contexts.

For example, take the word "planet," which comes from the Greek *asters planetai*, which means "wandering star." The ancient Greeks thought that perhaps all the heavenly bodies were essentially the same thing, just farther from or nearer to us. It wasn't until Copernicus published his theory that the earth was just one of several planets orbiting the sun that astronomers started being more specific. Pluto was famously added to the number of planets in our solar system in 1930, and then demoted to "dwarf planet" in 2006. During this time the definition and usage of "planet" was changing, and the same can be true of much of the language used with LGBTQI2A communities. Just as astronomers no longer call a planet a wandering star, most intersex people today don't call themselves hermaphrodites, because the word just isn't accurate and language has changed. Context matters, however. A poet might call a planet a wandering star, because poets are in the business of images and emotions rather than scientific fact, and a person with differences in sex development may call themself a hermaphrodite if that is the word that's used most consistently and recognizably where they live.

This leads us to our second general rule when talking about LGBTQIA language: always prioritize the definition given by the person standing in front of you. If you watch a documentary or read a book (including this one!) that gives you one definition for a word or identity, but then you meet someone in your school or your knitting group who holds that identity but understands it differently, don't try to correct them. That person understands their own identity better than anyone else, and it's a gift to be able to learn from them.

There's a huge variety in the way LGBTQI2A people describe who they are, just as people describe colors many different ways. Much like there are many shades of red, there are many shades of what it means to be transgender. I might look at a rose and call it scarlet, while another person might call it magenta, and a third might say vermilion. While we might argue about who's technically correct about the color, the truth is that each pair of eyes is receiving and processing that color differently, and none of us knows for sure what the flower looks like to the person standing next to us. In the same way, I don't know what someone else's internal experience of gender is like. They're the only human being who can know that. If they have a nuance to their identity that's different from how I understand or experience it, that's OK. In fact, it's beautiful.

So, having laid those ground rules, let's get into some overall definitions:

There's one big misconception about gender diversity that we'd better address right away: the difference between gender and orientation. Your *sexual* or *affectional orientation* is about whom you are sexually and romantically attracted to. A person may be gay, lesbian, bisexual, pansexual, asexual, or another orientation, and that all has to do with their sexual and/or romantic relationship with other people. Historically, gay people have tended to buck gender norms; because of this, and because gay people are more visible in many societies, transgender folks may initially come out as gay, because that's the only language they've been exposed to that seems like it might explain their differences. However, orientation and gender are two separate things, and being gay does not lead to being transgender. You can think of orientation as a horizontal line, and gender identity as a vertical line; though these two things aren't the same, they can sometimes intersect, as you'll hear in some of the stories in later chapters.

If being transgender isn't about who you're attracted to, what is it about? Well, part of what's so fascinating about gender is that it's biopsychosocial, by which we mean that it has aspects that have to do with our biology, aspects that have to do with our psychology, and aspects that are socially constructed, and all these aspects interact with each other.[1]

The biological part of this equation has to do with your body, and is often referred to as your *assigned sex*, or *sex assigned at birth*, which stems from the moment the doctor declares, "It's a boy!" or "It's a girl!" These days, of course, many parents find out the assigned sex of their baby when the ultrasound technician reports what they see on a screen a few months earlier. Someone's assigned sex is determined by a quick glance at the new baby's external genitalia, and that glance sets each of us up for a lifetime of gender expectations. Most people don't know much about other biological parts of their gender, like their chromosomes or hormone levels, and unless something isn't developing or working as expected, you might not even know very much about your internal reproductive organs!

By focusing only on external reproductive organs, you end up getting your assigned sex based on just one piece of your body, which is itself just one piece of your gender. Even though we tend to want to categorize bodies into two groups, male and female, that doesn't work for everyone, even on a biological level. It works for most people—and if a person's physical characteristics are easy to classify as either male or female, we say that person is *endosex*—but some people are *intersex*, which means they have differences in their reproductive organs, chromosomes, or ability to produce or receive gender-related hormones.

The psychological part of gender is your *gender identity*, which is your internal sense of being male, female, both, or neither. Almost every person on earth has a gender identity (read on for the one exception!), although we may have a hard time explaining why and how we know what gender we are. We don't choose our gender identity; rather, it's something that has innate seeds within us and develops as we grow. This internal sense happens in the brain, which is of course part of our body and thus biological, and that means it can be difficult to draw a hard line between psychological and biological aspects of gender. Gender identity can't be changed by other people. So in this way it's similar to orientation, in that attempts at "conversion therapy," also known as Gender Identity Change Efforts (GICE), do not work. In fact, they can cause incredible harm.[2]

The sociological part of gender shows up in our lives in both individual and communal forms. Individually, each person has a *gender expression,* which has to do with the way you act out gender through things like clothing, hair, voice, and mannerisms. We may try to match our gender expression to our gender identity as closely as we can, like a businessman in New York who wears a suit and tie to work. Or we may be a little more playful with it, like a man who puts on makeup and a dress for a drag show.

Our gender expression is often influenced by our cultural norms and by the situation we're in as much as by our own wishes, so it's important to remember that you shouldn't make assumptions about someone's gender identity based on their gender expression. You might assume that a man doing drag might really be a trans woman, but the important contextual distinction is that drag is a performance of gender for entertainment, rather than a revelation of our everyday selves. So someone performing in drag doesn't really tell you anything about who they are the rest of the time. That would be like seeing a person dressed up as Cinderella at Disney World and assuming that she lives the rest of her life as a princess! She might be a princess, and the person doing drag might be trans, but you won't be able to figure that out based solely on their gender expression, especially in an entertainment context.

The communal form of the sociological aspect of gender has to do with the gender roles that your particular culture has constructed. *Gender roles* govern the way we're expected to be and act depending on our gender. For instance, when you try to picture a doctor or a nurse, which one do you expect to be a man, and which do you expect to be a woman?

In the United States we tend to adhere to the *gender binary,* a social system in which it is assumed that all people can be divided into one of two genders, and we've set up male and female gender roles to mirror that. Gender roles have been broken down considerably in the past hundred years, and of course we do see women who are doctors and men who are nurses, but gender roles are still enforced in many other ways. It's important to note that while the gender binary and male and female gender roles are the norm in white, Western contexts, other cultures around the world may distinguish between up to seven different genders, and therefore may have as many different gender roles. We'll talk about some of these cultures throughout this book, and we'll explore the cracks in the gender binary as it exists in the United States today, especially for people who hold multiple identities related to race, ethnicity, nationality, class, and ability.

Now that you've got a sense of these three aspects—the biological, the psychological, and the social—let's talk about the variety of ways gender is lived out.

A *transgender person* is someone whose gender identity does not match the sex they were assigned at birth. Because of this broad definition, "trans" or "transgender" is often used as an all-encompassing term to cover many different kinds of gender-expansive identities, although not everyone finds this umbrella structure useful.[3] "Transgender" is generally used as an adjective, or a descriptive word. So in a sentence you'd say, "Mary is a transgender woman," not "Mary is *a* transgender," or "Mary is transgender*ed*." Some trans people intentionally choose to refer to themselves as "transsexual,"[4] but of the two words, most young people prefer "transgender"[5] and may find "transsexual" offensive. As always, this is why we should take care to find out which words people use for themselves, and then honor that in our own speech. There are also some people who prefer to highlight their specific gender identity first, before connecting it to transness, and so you might hear someone refer to themself as "a woman of trans experience" or "a man of trans experience."

Statistically, most of the people you know probably aren't transgender. It's more common to be a *cisgender person*—someone whose gender identity matches the sex they were assigned at birth. The prefix "trans-" means "across" or "beyond," and the prefix "cis-" means "on the same side"; so what these words are telling you is whether or not your gender identity lines up with your assigned sex. A cisgender person may express themself in ways that aren't typical for their gender, but their gender identity and assigned sex are not incongruent.

We sometimes call people who dress or act in a way that is not typical of their assigned sex in their particular culture *gender-nonconforming* or *gender-expansive*. These are especially helpful terms to use when we're looking at people throughout history whom we can't categorize well with our modern language. Gender-expansive people, through their very existence, tend to broaden their culture's gender norms.[6] However, someone expressing their gender differently doesn't necessarily mean they're transgender. You might be considered gender-nonconforming or gender-expansive if you are a cisgender man who enjoys baking cakes and painting his nails, or a cisgender woman who shaves her head and rides a motorcycle. Not all cisgender people conform to gender roles and norms, and not all transgender people defy them.

Gender dysphoria is the sense of incongruence, anxiety, dissonance, or distress that can be caused by the conflict between a person's gender identity and their assigned sex. Not all transgender people experience dysphoria, but it is common. (There's some evidence to suggest that dysphoria stems more from the external backlash trans people face in strictly gendered contexts than from their own internal experience.[7])

For some transgender people, gender dysphoria is just an occasional nudge in the back of their mind, but for others it can be completely debilitating. For years, doctors and psychologists attempted to "fix" gender dysphoria by trying to get transgender people to identify with their assigned sex—attempting to rewire the brain to match the social expectations placed on the person's body. Over time it's become clear that the only proven remedy for dysphoria is to allow the transgender person to transition—to allow the body and related social expectations to change to match the person's brain.[8]

Transition can include a variety of processes by which a person achieves congruence and alignment of all aspects of their gender. In older documents you'll sometimes see this called a "sex change," but because there's not one single way to transition and because that phrase tends to be connected specifically with surgical changes, it's not the best descriptor. *Social transition* can include things like changing clothing, hairstyle, name, and/or the pronouns you use. *Medical transition* can include things like hormone replacement therapy and different kinds of gender-affirming surgeries. *Legal transition* covers things like changing your name and/or gender marker on documents like a driver's license, passport, and birth certificate.

Not all trans people transition—sometimes because they don't find it necessary to change these things in order to be themselves; sometimes because they don't have the money to access medical and legal transition, which can be incredibly expensive; and sometimes because health conditions or safety concerns make specific kinds of transition impossible for the moment. Because of these complexities, it's important to remember that someone's ability or desire to transition does not make them any more or less trans.

For a long time in the United States, the assumption was that there were two kinds of transgender people: trans men and trans women. A *transgender man* is someone who was assigned female at birth but who has a male gender identity. Similarly, a *transgender woman* is someone who was assigned male at birth but whose gender identity is female. Because of the gender binary, we are used to assuming that all people must be either male or female, and so it's not surprising that we assumed that must be true of trans people as well! In reality, while about one third of trans-identified people in the United States are trans women and one third are trans men, the final third is made up of people who have a gender identity that doesn't fit within the binary.[9]

A *nonbinary* person is someone who isn't either a man or a woman, and who instead has a gender identity that's between or beyond those definitions. Sometimes it can be difficult to understand what a nonbinary gender identity might be like, so let's use another color example. Within the gender binary we assume that all people are either pink or blue, but when we look around at the world, we notice that there are definitely more than two colors out there! Some nonbinary people understand their gender as a mix of male and female, as purple is a mix of pink and blue. Other nonbinary people understand their gender as something beyond the binary altogether, in the same way that green can't be categorized within the definition of either pink, blue, or purple. When we think of gender as a color wheel, rather than as two distinct boxes, it gets easier to understand the vast range of gender possibilities. When learning from nonbinary folks, you may come across the acronym "NB" or the phonetic spelling "enby," a shortened version of "nonbinary."

Much as the term "trans" has been used to cover anyone who has a gender identity that doesn't match their assigned sex, the term "nonbinary" also sometimes functions as an umbrella term for anyone whose gender identity doesn't fit within their culture's definitions of either man or woman. For instance, there are *agender* people—the one exception to our "everyone has a gender identity" rule—who may not have a sense of gender identity at all, or who may understand it cognitively but not experience it themselves. There are also *bigender* and *pangender* people who are more than just one gender, and who may experience their gender identity as a multifaceted thing that combines or holds multiple genders at the same time.

Two of the most common identities outside the gender binary are held by people who are *genderfluid* and people who are *genderqueer*. Someone who's genderfluid may have a gender identity that fluctuates between male, female, or another gender over time. Their experience of their gender identity and their choice of gender expression may change from day to day or month to month, but it's all a part of the person's singular sense of self.

The term "genderqueer," much like the term "queer" itself, is complex in both definition and usage. Because the word "queer" has historically been used as a slur, some people feel very strongly about not using it, and that can extend to use of the word "genderqueer" as well. Other people love the ambiguity of both words, and are part of a wide-ranging movement to reclaim "queer" and all its variations. Because of this difference in feeling about usage, a good general rule is to use the words "queer" or "genderqueer" only for a person who you know uses those words for themself. The great thing about the word "genderqueer" is that it's purposefully ambiguous. A genderqueer person may use this word specifically because their gender is equally hard to pin down! Other genderqueer people see it as an identity that is political as well as personal, and that specifically challenges and pushes back at harmful gender stereotypes and norms in their culture. At the end of the day, the only way you'll be able to find out what a genderqueer person's identity means is by asking that particular individual.

Alongside all the identities we've talked about above, some people also have culturally and ethnically specific gender categories. These identity categories aren't solely about gender, and usually integrate aspects of sexuality, class, vocation, and spirituality as well. Here in North America, many Indigenous nations recognize more than two genders, such as the *aranu'tiq* of the Alutiiq people, the *nádleehi* of the Navajo or Diné people, and the *winkte* of the Lakota people.[10] In order to come together across many languages, gender-expansive people in North America often gather under the label *Two Spirit*, which you'll hear more about in chapter 12.

This isn't just a North American phenomenon—you can find gender-expansive people in Indigenous cultures around the world, including the *fa'afafine* of Samoa, the *hijra* of India, the *sekrata* of Madagascar, and the *muxes* of Mexico.[11] All of these cultures have historically recognized more than two genders, and people in these gender categories are sometimes considered spiritually gifted or powerful, because of the way they can navigate between and beyond binaries like man/woman, sacred/profane, or body/spirit.

The presence of genders beyond just man and woman in societies all over the world tells us that the gender binary isn't the only or the best way to understand gender. The existence of people throughout history who lived as a gender that didn't match their assigned sex tells us something else: that gender-expansive identities are far from a popular new trend. It would be anachronistic to say that people in history were transgender as we understand that word today—especially because we can't go back and ask them about their gender identity—but we can compare the way they interact with their bodies, gender expressions, and gender roles with the experiences of modern gender-expansive people. For example, Ashurbanipal, an ancient king of Syria also known as Sardanapalus, was known for dressing in women's clothing, adopting feminine ways of speaking and acting, and spending time spinning and making clothing.[12] Hatshepsut, one of the most famous pharaohs, was assigned female at birth, but took on the male kingship of Egypt and was immortalized in statues and wall art with a beard and the short skirt typically worn by male Egyptians.[13]

One of the very first written descriptions of gender-expansive people in North America comes from the writings of Álvar Núñez Cabeza de Vaca, a Spanish conquistador who in the 1530s traveled through what became the colonized American Southwest. In his journals he described his stay with the Coahuiltecan people who lived in the Rio Grande valley. He noted that they accepted a third gender made up of individuals whom Cabeza de Vaca himself identified as men, but who acted and dressed like Coahuiltecan women. While the Coahuiltecan culture accepted these differences, Cabeza de Vaca, a Catholic, condemned these gender-nonconformers and described the whole experience as "a piece of devilry."[14]

This was par for the course when it came to Western interactions with the Indigenous peoples of the Americas. Vasco Núñez de Balboa, who in 1513 was the first European to cross the isthmus of Panama, set dogs on forty gender-expansive individuals of the Panamanian Cueva people, because he categorized them as "sodomites" for presenting as women. As historian Genny Beemyn put it, "Europeans did not agree on what to make of cultures that recognized nonbinary genders. Lacking comparable institutional roles in their own societies, they labeled the aspects that seemed familiar to them."[15] This generally meant labeling anyone who expressed their gender in an unconventional way as either a sodomite or a hermaphrodite—terms that were inaccurate then and now—and using gender diversity as a further excuse for genocide.

In the 1600s, in the British colonies that would eventually become the famous thirteen, several people were tried for presenting as a gender other than the one they were assigned at birth. In Massachusetts, Mary Henly was charged with dressing in men's clothing in 1692 after a complaint was filed that she was "seeming to confound the course of nature."[16] By the 1800s so many people were expressing their gender in unconventional ways through clothing that laws were written specifically to prevent it! Presenting oneself in "dress not belonging to his or her sex" became a criminal offense, first in Columbus, Ohio, in 1848, and then later in Chicago, San Francisco, Dallas, Denver, Detroit, Miami, and at least thirty-three other cities—with the most recent legislation enacted in 1974.[17]

Transgender people gained more national visibility in 1953, when Christine Jorgensen returned to the United States after having received gender-affirming surgery in Denmark. Christine had been in the military, and on December 1, 1952, the *New York Daily News* ran a front-page story on her experience titled "Ex-GI Becomes Blonde Beauty," which launched her into the public eye. Christine, who was seen by the media not as a threat so much as an interesting experiment, published bits of her story in several magazines and newspapers and made appearances on national talk shows, always advocating for the acceptance of other people like her.

Another milestone came on June 28, 1969, when police attempted to raid the Stonewall Inn in New York City on the grounds that the inn did not have a valid liquor license. Stonewall was known as one of the only places in the city where members of the blossoming LGBTQI2A community could come together and be themselves, despite the fact that the city currently had laws on the books that criminalized both homosexuality and gender-nonconforming expression through clothing. During this time, liquor licenses were intentionally revoked from bars that were known to be LGBTQI2A hangouts, so that law enforcement would have a reason to arrest the customers and close the bar.

Raids all over the city were becoming increasingly common, and on that early morning in June a few members of the community decided that they'd had enough. Among those who fought back were two self-described drag queens, Marsha P. Johnson[19] and Sylvia Rivera,[20] and a transgender woman named Miss Major Griffin-Gracy.[21] All three were women of color—both Marsha and Miss Major were and are Black, and Sylvia was born to Venezuelan and Puerto Rican parents—and these intersections were reflected in their activism.

During this time, labels for gender-expansive people were evolving rapidly, and there has been some debate about whether Marsha P. Johnson and Sylvia Rivera identified as transgender, or whether that label could be relevant today. We do know that they worked together to form the Street Transvestite Action Revolutionaries (later renamed the Street Transgender Action Revolutionaries), an organization that helped feed, clothe, and shelter hundreds of homeless gender-expansive people in New York City. Miss Major, for her part, is possibly the most revered transgender elder still living, and she continues to advocate for justice on behalf of incarcerated transgender people worldwide, especially for low-income individuals and people of color.

Seeing gender-expansive people in history can help us put societal reactions in context, as well as give us a sense of the true range of human variation, but it does bring up another question. We know that gender has biological, psychological, and social elements, but is there a root cause for gender as a whole? Is it determined by nature or nurture?

We can agree that nurture plays a big part, since gender roles and gender expression are different from culture to culture and change over time. The Aka men of the Central African Republic and Republic of the Congo are expected to be nurturing and gentle, and spend more time holding and caring for children than men in any other society in the world.[22] The women of the Mosuo, or Na, people in China, the largest matrilineal society on earth, own all the property, lead the family businesses, and pass on inheritance from mother to daughter.[23] One example of gender expectations changing over time is hidden in plain sight in many Western countries, where in early 1900s we saw a change in the way we dress babies. Up until World War I it was common to dress all children under age six, regardless of gender, in white dresses, because they were easy to bleach. Then, around 1918, department stores began to suggest that parents dress their girls in blue and their boys in pink, because "pink, being a more decided and stronger color, is more suitable for the boy, while blue, which is more delicate and dainty, is prettier for the girl."[24] It wasn't until the 1940s that the preferred colors switched genders in the United States; to this day, baby boys are still dressed in pink in some European countries, including Belgium.

While gender expression and gender roles are at least partially socially constructed, it's generally been thought that our biology is strict and uninfluenced by things like culture. Surely, when it comes to our biology, nature is the deciding element. Some researchers, like sexologist Anne Fausto-Sterling, disagree. She argues that culture affects the way we view biology, because there's nothing in nature that decides whether XX and XY chromosomes or testicles and ovaries should be categorized as male or female or something else altogether. It's humans who create categories and then decide what is within the range of normal for a particular category.[25] This fact is made most clear when we consider the ways in which intersex children have historically been surgically manipulated to make their differences in sex development fit our own comfort levels—a problem we'll talk more about in chapter 4.

We also know that the connection between biology and behavior isn't a one-way street. While it's easy to believe that testosterone causes competition and estrogen causes cooperation, neuroendocrinologists have found that the way we act can increase or decrease our hormone levels! Studies have shown that if cisgender women have access to social power and behave competitively, their testosterone production goes up,[26] and if cisgender men become fathers and help care for an infant, their testosterone production goes down.[27] This tells us that our behavior can change biological aspects of our gender.

These kinds of studies help to disprove a kind of ideology called gender essentialism. *Gender essentialism* is the belief that there are innate, unchangeable differences between men and women, that a man has a certain male essence that makes him who he is, and that his essence is the biological and spiritual opposite of the essence that a woman has that makes her who she is. This position crops up in think pieces about the differences between men's and women's brains, with headlines like "Why Your Husband Won't Ask for Directions: The Surprising Brain Structure behind Men's Ability to Think Spatially." We've all seen the articles suggesting that men's brains are more adept at math and science, while women's brains are better at relating to other people and caring for children. The problem with these kinds of studies is that they often don't take into consideration the social factors that play a part. For instance, maybe your husband doesn't ask for directions, not because he's more spatially aware, but because he's afraid of looking weak or "unmanly" in front of you. Maybe women are better at childcare because they've been forced into the role of babysitter and mother their whole lives, and they've had to become good at it, to keep from being shamed for not being "feminine enough."

Of course, there are some differences that can be seen between the brains of cisgender men and cisgender women; for instance, a certain amount of white matter or the number of neural connections in a particular region may be more common in one gender than another. Overall, though, researchers are coming to the conclusion that the brains of cisgender men and women are more similar than they are different, and that previous studies have been either skewed or based on too small a sample.[28] Indeed, a recent study on a large number of MRI brain scans showed that, although there were differences between the brains of cisgender men and women, only 6 percent of the brains were consistently on one side of the male-female spectrum, while most brains looked stereotypically male in some regions and stereotypically female in others, with a substantial bell curve right in the middle.[29]

Even though these studies tend to exaggerate differences, let's go ahead and ask one more science question: where do the brains of transgender people fit along this spectrum? As it turns out, the white matter in three key regions of the brains of transgender men was more similar to those in brains of cisgender men than those in brains of cisgender women.[30] Similarly, the white matter in four regions of the brains of transgender women was more similar to those in brains of cisgender women than those in brains of cisgender men.[31] It's important to note that both of these studies were done on transgender people before they had any kind of hormone therapy. What we can take from all this is that parts of the brains of transgender people seem to match their true gender, rather than their assigned sex, though we don't yet know if this difference is something that exists when the person is born or something that develops over time.

For now, it appears that science can tell us something about how transgender people experience their own identity, and sociology and anthropology can help give us context when it comes to the overall human experience. But what can theology tell us about gender diversity? Is there a doctrine that could help us understand why transgender people exist in the first place?

3

Sin, Sickness, or Specialty?

We don't know why people are transgender. That is, we don't yet know the scientific reason behind the fact that a percentage of humans on earth—at least 1.4 million adults in the United States alone[1]—have a gender identity that doesn't match the sex they were assigned at birth. Could it be the hormones we're exposed to in the womb? Could it be caused by some rogue genetic material? Maybe it has to do with the way our brains are wired in the first two years of life, when we're learning so much so fast. Or perhaps there's some kind of learned component that has to do with the way we perceive gender as we grow. Maybe it's a combination of all of these things. The fact is that right now it's a mystery.

But just as we had the story of God's flood-ending rainbow before we understood prisms and light refraction, the fact that we don't yet understand the science behind gender hasn't stopped us from trying to understand our identities theologically. Some Christians see transgender identities as sinful in some way. Others see people who experience gender dysphoria not as morally good or bad, but merely as a group experiencing a kind of mental illness. A third group sees being transgender as just another expression of diversity in creation. So which is it? Is being transgender a sin, a sickness, or a specialty?

In 2015, Christian psychologist Mark Yarhouse published a book in which he dug deeply into these differing points of view. In *Understanding Gender Dysphoria: Navigating Transgender Issues in a Changing Culture*, Yarhouse formalized a three-part structure for understanding each of these beliefs, in the hope that people who hold different positions might be able to have more productive conversations. Let's take a look at each of Yarhouse's three frameworks—and the proponents and theology behind them—to try to get a better sense of where we are in this discussion.

Yarhouse calls his first way of understanding trans identities "the integrity framework."[2] Someone who holds to this framework would consider conflict between one's assigned sex and gender identity sinful because it messes with what they believe to be the strictly male or female nature God gives each of us. In this view, transgender people exist because people are bound to go astray, and proponents of this view tend to see any attempt to move away from one's assigned sex as rebellion against what God has ordained. Yarhouse lifts up Robert Gagnon, a theologian who is well-known for his work condemning same-sex relationships and marginalized sexualities, as an example of someone who believes that one's gender is predetermined and set in stone.

For Gagnon, the root of the problem with trans identities has to do with gender complementarity. He believes that "there are only two primary sexes, 'male and female' or 'man' and 'woman,'" and that "sexual intercourse represents the merger of the two halves of the sexual spectrum. What a man brings to the table, so to speak, of a sexual union is his essential maleness; a woman, her essential femaleness."[3] Gender complementarians believe that "distinctions in masculine and feminine roles are ordained by God as part of the created order, and should find an echo in every human heart."[4] Therefore, someone whose gender identity differs from their assigned sex presents a problem.

Or, rather, they present two problems. The first issue, according to the integrity framework, is that the transgender person is not fulfilling their ordained gender role, as decided by their assigned sex, in everyday life. Men should be protectors, providers, and leaders; women should be nurturers, helpers, and submissive to the leadership of the men in their life.

The second issue is that gender complementarity requires that each person sexually pair up with a person of the "opposite sex." But what is the opposite of a nonbinary person's gender? And should a trans man be dating a cisgender man (in which case their relationship might be seen as gay) or a cisgender woman (in which case the trans man must be recognized as fully male)? The minute a trans person tries to exist within the structure of gender complementarity, things start to get tricky.

The answer, from the perspective of the integrity framework, is that anyone who has a gender identity that doesn't match their assigned sex needs to find a way to get that gender identity to fall in line. The trans person is encouraged to see dysphoria and the internal struggle between their gender identity and their assigned sex as their particular cross to bear, or as part of the flesh that must be crucified in order to become a new creation in Christ. Diversion from the assigned role is considered sinful, and repentance is necessary.

It's not surprising that transgender people who live within this context, whether by choice or because no other options are available, often find themselves full of shame and self-hatred.[5] You can roll the boulder up the hill only so many times before you realize that, no matter how hard you push and how hard you pray, that boulder's going to roll back down again. This kind of theology is the backbone of Gender Identity Change Efforts (GICE), also known as conversion therapy, and we know that trans people who are exposed to GICE are twice as likely to take their own lives, and four times as likely if the GICE takes place before the trans person is ten years old.[6]

The real strength of the integrity framework is its focus on biblical authority and the desire to follow God's will in our lives. For most Christians, trans Christians included, those two factors are incredibly important. But what if the Bible does not actually portray humankind as neatly divided into cisgender men and cisgender women (a topic we'll discuss at length in chapter 4)? What if the gender roles that the integrity framework prizes are not so much divinely ordained as they are human-made (something we'll discuss in chapter 5)?

The second framework Yarhouse introduces is called "the disability framework." He explains that in this framework "gender dysphoria is viewed as a result of living in a fallen world in which the condition—like so many mental health concerns—is a nonmoral reality."[7] In his 2015 book, Yarhouse is hesitant to refer to people as transgender. As a psychologist and major proponent of this view, Yarhouse does not see people as having a trans identity, but rather as individuals who are currently struggling with a mental-health condition in the form of gender dysphoria. He explains, "The person may have choices to make that are associated with their response to symptoms or overall treatment approach . . . and those choices may have moral and ethical dimensions, but their condition is not one they chose; that is, they are not morally culpable for having it."

This change in moral status is the main difference between the identity framework and the disability framework. In the former, the transgender person is deliberately disobeying God; in the latter, they're merely a victim of original sin like every other human being. This distinction can cause a radical shift in attitudes toward trans people, because it means that they can receive compassionate pastoral care that doesn't shame them for their thoughts, feelings, and internal experiences. Yarhouse works hard to create a bridge to help move Christians from an accusatory view to a compassionate view, and for some trans people that shift may ultimately be life-saving.

In relating gender dysphoria to the fall, Yarhouse says, "I think the fall can be seen in the lack of congruence between birth sex and psychological sense of gender identity, particularly when this is strong enough to cause distress and impairment."[8] Theologically, it makes sense to consider things that cause pain and suffering in our world to be a result of the fall and humankind's disobedience after creation, but not all suffering is the same. For instance, if a tornado blows through your town and flattens your house, the suffering you experience is not your fault or anyone else's fault. Disasters do happen, and, as Jesus said when the tower at Siloam fell, those who are injured in such instances are not worse sinners than anyone else.[9] Then there's the kind of suffering you might experience if you try throwing a punch at a brick wall. That kind of suffering is your own fault, and in a case like that, there might be an internal issue you could use some counseling over. Historically we've understood hate and rage to stem from sin, and so if you were motivated by one of those feelings when you hit the wall, then we could theoretically tie your suffering to the fall. You would experience a third kind of suffering if a stranger came up to you on the street and clocked you in the jaw without any provocation or prior interaction. In this case you did nothing wrong, and even though sin might be involved, it would be strictly on the part of the stranger. This last type of suffering— the kind that comes at us from an external source—is the kind transgender people tend to experience most often.

Transgender populations do experience high rates of depression, anxiety, substance use disorders, and suicide. Because of this, some people have attempted to argue that trans identities are inextricably and inherently linked to mental illness. As we learned in chapter 1, however, these issues are directly tied to minority stress—events or conditions that minority populations experience that exceed the average person's ability to endure, and that can then cause mental or physical illness.[10] These events and conditions can include things like a lack of social structures that include other people like you; being denied access to institutions and resources because of your identity; experiencing verbal, physical, or mental abuse because of your differences; being subjected to stereotypes; internalizing other people's negative views; and the lack of hope for these conditions to change in the future. In all cases, the problem is not the identity the person holds, but the response to that identity from others. We can see a distinct example of this kind of stress in studies of LGBTQI2A youth that find "the greater the young person's expectation for rejection based on their sexual/gender identity, the more likely they are to report symptoms of anxiety, depression, and suicidal ideation."[11]

While minority stress is a factor that all marginalized people experience, different groups experience it in unique ways. For transgender people, minority stress can be grouped into four general categories: rejection, nonaffirmation, victimization, and discrimination.[12] Those experiences bleed into a person's inner sense of who they are, and lead to internalized transphobia, expectations of negative reactions from others, and the feeling that the person must hide who they are and what they're feeling. Considering all this pressure, it's not surprising that transgender people are suffering, but the suffering we experience is not original sin manifesting within us. It's the effects of the fall manifesting in the way human beings treat each other.

But what about the internal struggle that a transgender person feels between the sex they were assigned at birth and the gender that they know themselves to be? For some trans people it's only the gendered expectations that other people hold them to that cause a problem. These expectations begin when a sex is assigned at birth by another person, and continue throughout life, as that assigned sex is insisted upon by the people around them. For these folks it really is an external problem caused by others, which is then internalized.

For another group of trans people, the gender dysphoria they feel would exist even if you picked them up and set them on a deserted island. In these cases the distress usually has to do with the person's body and how that body doesn't match up with that person's own sense of self. This is the only point at which it might possibly be justifiable to think of gender dysphoria as a product of the fall—the point at which the trans person experiences suffering that is neither self-inflicted nor caused by others. However, just because this suffering may be caused by original sin does not mean that the person's movement away from suffering and toward affirmation of their gender identity is sinful. While we may believe that imperfections in eyesight are related to the fall, for instance, that doesn't mean that getting fitted for glasses is wrong (we'll talk more about this in chapter 11).

The main failing of the disability framework is that it refuses to recognize the different kinds of suffering that transgender people experience. By assuming that all the suffering trans people experience is a result of that trans identity, the disability framework lets the individuals and institutions that don't affirm transgender people off the hook for the harm they cause. Instead, by looking at transgender people through a clinical lens, it suggests that trans persons must change to fit the mold, rather than changing the mold that constricts them.

Because Yarhouse begins with the assumption that binary male and female genders are mandated by God, the treatment he suggests in the disability framework has to do with alleviating the trans person's dysphoria, while also trying to get them to fit back into the expected gender mold. "I see the value in encouraging individuals who experience gender dysphoria to resolve dysphoria in keeping with their birth sex," Yarhouse explains in his chapter on prevention and treatment. "Where those strategies have been unsuccessful, there is potential value in managing dysphoria through the least invasive expressions (recognizing surgery as the most invasive step toward expression of one's internal sense of identity)."[13]

For those who wish to manage gender dysphoria by finding a way to identify with their assigned sex, Yarhouse's methods may be welcome and helpful. Obviously a therapist who works compassionately with a patient to help them deal with difficult experiences is better than a therapist who tries to motivate and change the patient by using guilt and shame. But for the trans folks who do wish to transition—socially, medically, or legally—this framework can be frustrating at its best and harmful at its worst. Though Yarhouse himself may not actively discourage anyone from transitioning, if that's what they want, the disability framework inherently treats the transgender person's identity as an illness that should be cured, and in the hands of other mental health practitioners it can quickly become an excuse for deadly Gender Identity Change Efforts.

But what if there's another option? The "diversity framework" is Yarhouse's third example of the ways in which we might view transgender identities. He explains that this model "highlights transgender issues as reflecting an identity and culture to be celebrated as an expression of diversity."[14] Rather than seeing transgender folks as sinful people rebelling against God, or as mentally ill people who need treatment that helps reorient them back toward their assigned sex, the diversity framework suggests that differences in gender identities might be a natural variation in a vibrant world.

Before we get into the specifics of how this framework understands trans identities, it is worth noting the outcomes of this affirming third structure. Unlike the results produced by the two other frameworks—where nonaffirming religious views are tied to suicidal behaviors in transgender youth—the supportive results that come out of the diversity framework have been shown to reduce levels of depression and anxiety in transgender kids.[15] This alone makes the diversity framework worth taking seriously as an option.

Let's talk about theology and biology. The Psalms often describe all of creation as a testament to God's existence, love, and power—from the stars in the sky, to the mountains, fruit trees, birds, and small crawling creatures. We can see God at work throughout the cosmos, from the spirals in our fingerprints to the circling galaxies existing light-years away. When we observe the world we live in, it's hard not to notice the incredible differences across species and over space and time. Psalm 104 is known for being a hymn to this kind of biodiversity, in which the psalmist rejoices in the way God has made storks, rabbits, lions, and even sea monsters, and has given each of them a home in their particular environment.

As we observe creation we also find a huge range of physical and social differences when it comes to gender. In fact, when biologists talk about the physical part of gender—assigned sex—they often mean something different than sociologists and theologians mean. For those studying animal physiology and behavior, "sex" refers to how an animal produces gametes, or sex cells. A biologist will take a look at the gametes an animal produces and categorize it accordingly—as male if it makes small gametes, as female if it makes large gametes, and as hermaphroditic if it makes both large and small gametes. In humans those small gametes are called sperm, while the larger gametes are called eggs, though as we learned in the last chapter, we don't consider the production of either of those things to be the only determining factor in our sex assignment.

Throughout creation there are many different kinds of plants and animals that switch back and forth between male and female—or between the creation of small and large gametes—over their lifetimes. The bluehead wrasse, for example, is a type of fish that appears to have three distinct sexes.[16] When the fish are young, they are all essentially sexless; but as they mature, about a third of the fish become males and another third become females, while the last third defies our usual categorization. That last third begins life in a non-gamete-producing or sexless state, then matures into female fish that bear eggs, and then finally switches sexes and begins producing sperm cells, taking on the blue male color and growing larger than the unchanged original males! Scientists have noted that differences in the habitat of the blue wrasse mean that sometimes the unchanged males have an easier time breeding, while at other times the changed males are more successful. When a wrasse school is living in the midst of a patch of sea grass, where the small, unchanged males can hide better, they tend to fertilize more eggs; but when the school is living in the midst of a coral reef, where everything is open and above board, the larger, changed males will fight off the unchanged males and win the ability to father their own children. This form of gender diversity means that the wrasse can live in several different environments, and that wherever they live, they thrive!

Of course humans are not fish, and transgender people don't have the option to change the kinds of gametes their bodies produce, but scientists are beginning to suspect that there's an inherited component to orientation and gender and that the diversity we see in humans may also be beneficial for our species. In 1975 a biologist named E. O. Wilson wrote *Sociobiology: The New Synthesis*, in which he put forward the kin-selection hypothesis that was first used to explain why so many gay and lesbian people exist when most weren't passing on their own genes directly through procreation. The kin-selection hypothesis stems from the finding that more children survive and thrive when they have gay and lesbian aunts and uncles. This is because many hands make light work, as the saying goes. Parents raising a child often benefit from having a third person around to help out, and that third person will be most available to help if they don't have children of their own. In exchange, the gay or lesbian person who is not passing on their own genes is helping to pass on the genes they share with their sibling. Ultimately, families that include gay and lesbian members can afford the time and attention it takes to raise and nurture more kids, which benefits the whole group!

These same benefits now appear to apply to gender-expansive people and their families within cultures that support and affirm them. Several studies done with the fa'afafine—one of the two groups of gender-expansive people in Samoa—bear out what the kin-selection hypothesis first suggested: that gender-expansive people who are accepted in their families but who don't have biological children of their own are more willing to invest in their nieces and nephews than their cisgender relations.[17] This in turn means that families that accept and include their gender-expansive children and siblings are more likely to thrive together.

So if we recognize the diversity in creation, and we see that trans people whose identity is accepted have better mental-health outcomes, and we also see that groups that accept transgender members tend to succeed, why doesn't everyone agree

with the diversity framework? In his description of this view-
point Yarhouse says,

> Evangelical Christians are understandably wary of the
> diversity framework. Evangelicals see among those who
> adhere to the diversity framework a small but vocal group
> that calls for the deconstruction of norms related to sex and
> gender. I describe those efforts as a strong form of the diver-
> sity framework (as contrasted with a weak form that focuses
> primarily on identity and community). . . . Such claims
> challenge not only gender norms that have been widely
> understood to be socially constructed but also a sex binary
> as something fixed and stable, tied to an essentialist view
> with biological foundations.[18]

Without oversimplifying the argument too much, it seems
that the biggest stumbling block for many Christians when
it comes to the diversity framework is the belief that biological gender categories are both cut-and-dried and also divinely
decreed. Yarhouse goes on to say that while the "strong form"
of the diversity framework is unacceptable to most evangelical Christians for this reason, the "weak form," which gives
trans people a sense of identity and community, may be worth
considering. In the end he advocates for an "integrated framework" that takes the best each category has to offer and creates
a space in which people who subscribe to each of the three
lenses can have a conversation.

In the following chapters, we will hear stories from transgender
Christians whose lives today are very much affected by these
lenses and the conversations that surround them. We'll look at
Genesis and the first illustrations of gender, and we'll explore
God's reaction to the people who color outside those lines.
We'll journey alongside the Israelites in the wilderness; we'll
meet one of the first converts to Christianity, and we'll dive
into Paul's letters. We'll ask whether or not gender really is
set in stone, and whether God commands any specific kind of
gender conformity.

I hope that, as you enter these conversations, you'll keep asking questions. Keep wondering about what it means to be a part of a faith that has such a rich history, and what it means to be part of a faith family that includes so many different kinds of people. When do we hold on to cherished ideas about the world, and when do we let go? When do we plant ourselves by the river of truth, and when do we admit that, for now, we only see through a glass darkly? Most importantly, how can we best love God, our neighbor, and ourselves?

To find out, we'll need to go back to the very beginning.

PART TWO

4

And God Said, Let There Be Marshes

In the beginning God created the heavens and the earth.
—Genesis 1:1 NIV

As a kid I would read these first words in my children's Bible over and over again—not because I found them particularly interesting, but because I was the kind of person who always started books from the beginning, and I could never seem to get any further into the Bible than Noah and the ark before I lost interest.

I also liked the first story in my picture Bible because it had some of the best illustrations. On one page you had a friendly orange sun, and on the opposite page a shining yellow moon and twinkling stars. Next came an ocean with big waves, across from a page depicting mountains and forests. Even in a children's Bible the distinctions God made when creating the universe were obvious. Each bit of the world was broken into pairs and opposites. For a kid who liked order and organization, the story of creation in Genesis 1 was just about perfect. There was a place for everything, and everything was in its place.

This kind of structure in Scripture was something that I appreciated up until my teen years, when I began to get a better sense of the way life sometimes fell outside black-and-white boundaries. Biologically, I learned that the world isn't separated distinctly into land or sea; there are also marshes, estuaries, and coral reefs. Personally, when I began to figure out more about my own sense of gender identity, I wondered if all people were really divided into male and female, as Genesis 1 seemed to say they were. For a long time I thought I was the only person worried about this biblical gender separation. Little did I know there was another person halfway across the country asking very similar questions.

Rev. M Jade Kaiser was born and raised in Pensacola, Florida, which was, as they* describe it, "practically southern Alabama." M grew up in The United Methodist Church, but wasn't particularly invested in the politically and theologically conservative ideals they saw around them. "The idea of queerness or transness was not even remotely on my radar," they explained as we talked one night. "I felt different, but I didn't even know any gay people. Nobody talked about it."

When M was in high school, they joined some friends who attended a youth group at a large nondenominational church in town. Rather than pews, M found comfy chairs and couches. Rather than hymns, there were praise songs. It felt as if faith was springing up fresh and new, and M took to it like a duck to water. Near the end of high school they began to discern a call to ministry, but the church M was now attending didn't approve of women in ministry; so, as someone assigned female at birth, M hit a brick wall. "I was told, 'Women can't be ordained.' So it took me two years, even when I was read as a cisgender straight woman, to overcome that basic gender barrier."

Even though M wasn't fully cognizant of their trans identity at this point, the roadblock they were facing would become all too familiar. "That was the constant struggle—that I felt so called to ministry, but people said that Scripture says my call isn't accurate."

---

*M Jade Kaiser uses the pronouns "they," "them," and "theirs" to help signify their nonbinary identity, rather than "he/him/his" or "she/her/hers." For more information on "they" as a singular pronoun, check out "Singular 'They,'" Merriam-Webster, https://www.merriam-webster.com/words-at-play/singular-nonbinary-they.

So M found their way back to the Methodist tradition, where women have been preaching for centuries, from Sarah Mallet in 1787 and Sojourner Truth in 1827 to Maud Keister Jensen, the first woman to receive full clergy rights, in 1956.[1] "There were more people in the Methodist Church who were helping me struggle through that," M explained. "There were Methodist women who were pastors, and I really wanted to engage with them, so that's part of what brought me back."

M's faith deepened in college as they began digging into theology, and as they met people from outside their conservative Christian bubble. They started studying the Bible through a historical-critical lens, which seeks to understand the biblical world and the intentions behind the text in the original language, rather than taking every word literally as we read it in English today. As they read the works of scholars and clergy through the ages, it became clear that there was more than one way to read and interpret the Bible. This was a wonderful and confusing discovery for M, as they realized that not everything they had been taught as a young person was undisputed fact. It also opened their eyes to the possibility that God's acceptance or rejection of LGBTQI2A people might not be an open-and-shut case, as they had once thought.

Shortly out of college, M embarked on their seminary training. Their calling to ministry was as strong as ever, but internally they were struggling with their beliefs about queer identities in the midst of a life of faith. M explained,

One of the most important shifts for me in terms of understanding identities came when I was in seminary. I remember a key moment, watching my best friend come out. He's a gay guy, and I was almost there when it came to fully accepting LGBT people, but I hadn't quite worked it all out yet, theologically. But watching him come to life over the course of his coming-out process just sealed the deal for me. My friend's coming out wasn't opposed to my understanding of God as love, as the One who creates, as the One who brings forth life in each of us.

After witnessing this, M's metric for measuring a life of faith was changed. "My understanding of Scripture became filtered through this question: 'Does this behavior, or identity, or way of being in the world create life? Within a person or within the community?'"

When we read about the way God creates life in Genesis 1, it begins with the separation of light and darkness and, by extension, the creation of day and night. Next, God divides the waters of the deep into two categories: the waters above the sky and the waters below the sky. Then those waters below the sky are parted and gathered together to create two separate domains: the land and the sea. God populates the sky with birds, the sea with fish and other ocean creatures, and the earth with plants and land animals. With each act of creation, from verse 1 to verse 25, God is separating, categorizing, and bringing order out of chaos.

For the Hebrew people of the ancient world, these acts of separation and ordering were intimately familiar. The Torah laws that defined them and identified them as God's people were based on these acts of separation between the sacred and the profane, and between the commendable and the abominable. In Deuteronomy 14, a chapter full of examples of this kind of separation, we find one of God's commands to the Hebrew people regarding food. In Deuteronomy 14:9–10 we read that sea creatures that have both scales and fins may be eaten, but if they have only *one* of those characteristics, they are considered unclean and not fit for eating.

Scholars and Jewish leaders have debated the reasoning behind the rules God lays out in the first five books of the Bible, and there are dozens of plausible theories. What's obvious is that rules like these not only made it easier for God's people to identify good food from possibly dangerous food, but also created ideological boxes that helped people understand the world around them.

So imagine you're an ancient Hebrew fisherman, out casting your nets into the sea one day. When you drag up your net you find a few mackerel, some jellyfish, and a lobster. You take one look at the scales and the fins on the mackerel and think "fish." You know without a doubt that's a fish, and it's good to eat. But what if you've never seen a jellyfish or a lobster before? Are they fish? Well, you can't see any fins or scales, so therefore they are outside the category of "fish," and can't be eaten. Though you may live your whole life without experiencing the wonder of garlic-butter lobster tail, you also miss out on being stung in the mouth by that jellyfish. These categories kept people safe and helped order the world.

Because these categories applied to every part of life—from the grain in the fields to the dinner table to the temple sacrifices—it's not surprising to find the same kinds of separations in the Genesis 1 creation account. Almost all of this first chapter deals in dualities like light and dark, earth and sky, land and water. Then, we get to verse 27:

> So God created humankind in his image,
>   in the image of God he created them;
>   male and female he created them.

Based on the dualities we've seen in this chapter, it's not surprising to find humans broken into two groups here: male and female God created them. But this verse does not discredit other sexes or genders, any more than the verse about the separation of day from night rejects the existence of dawn and dusk.[2] As M Jade Kaiser puts it, "This chapter talks about night and day and land and water, but we have dusk and we have marshes. These verses don't mean 'there's only land and water, and there's nowhere where these two meet.' These binaries aren't meant to speak to all of reality—they invite us into thinking about everything between and beyond." In the same way we call God the Alpha and Omega, implying all things from first to last and in between, the author of Genesis 1 is merely using the same dualistic poetic device to corral the infinite diversity of creation into categories we can easily understand.

The reality is that, for as long as there have been humans, there have been people who fall outside of the male/female binary. In a creation story from Sumer, another Mesopotamian society and neighbor to what would become Israel, we find references from 1600 BCE to humans who are created with reproductive organs that are not immediately identifiable as "female" or "male."[3] In the Mishnah and the Talmud, the Jewish compilations of oral law put together between 200 CE and 500 CE, we see several examples of individuals who don't fit male or female categories within Jewish culture, including those whose sex characteristics are indeterminable, those who have sex characteristics associated with more than one gender, and those whose characteristics change over time.[4] This tells us that even the descendants of the Hebrew people who recorded Genesis 1 did not necessarily assume that the gender categories seen in verse 27 were all-encompassing.

In the ancient Mediterranean world, people born with indeterminate or ambiguous sex characteristics were called hermaphrodites, after a Greek god who was said to have both masculine and feminine sex characteristics. Today people with differences in sex development identify themselves as intersex, and we know that they make up between 0.018 percent and 1.7 percent of the world's population.[5] There are many different kinds of intersex variations, all having to do with the way someone's body develops in response to chromosomal patterns and hormone production and reception. While some intersex people know about their variations from the time they're very young, others may not find out about them until puberty or much later in life.[6] Throughout history, doctors have attempted to "fix" intersex infants through surgical intervention before a child can make any decisions for themselves, and sometimes even without the knowledge or consent of the parents.

Fortunately, intersex advocates all over the world are finally seeing the positive results of their push for self-determination, and groups like interACT and the Intersex Campaign for Equality are helping stop unnecessary surgeries on babies identified as intersex at birth. All this begins to tell us that the interactions between chromosomes, hormone production, and physiology are much more complicated than we once thought. Not all people are born male or female; if we try to enforce that binary, we put ourselves in the position of claiming to know better than God. Indeed, as theologian and specialist on intersex history Megan DeFranza puts it, "The simplistic binary model is no longer sufficient. It is dishonest to the diversity of persons created in the image of God."[7]

Because intersex people are equally God's image-bearers, it's important that endosex people (those of us without intersex variations) be careful of paying attention to our intersex siblings only when it's convenient for us. There's a history, especially in trans communities, of using the existence of intersex people as a talking point, while ignoring our duty to act in solidarity. As a trans person who talks a lot about gender diversity, I know I'm guilty of this myself. I know what it's like to be seen as an "issue," rather than as a person, and yet I notice myself falling into this trap all the time. Hans Lindahl, communications director for interACT, described their experience this way: "I'll never forget my first queer zine fest, when a nonbinary person came up to me to say, 'Oh, you're intersex? That's my favorite argument.' Sure, plenty of us love smashing binaries, but intersex people do not exist to be arguments. We've got enough to do fighting for our own basic human rights. We're not here to validate anyone else's identity. You're valid with or without us!"[8] As we continue to learn more about the beautifully diverse world God created, we must do so hand in hand, and not at the expense of someone else's humanity. For more information on supporting your intersex siblings, please see the Further Reading section at the end of this book.

When we attempt to box God's creation in by looking to Genesis 1:27 and expecting every person on earth to fall into line, we're asking the text the wrong question. If Genesis 1 was meant to describe the world as it is, the biblical authors would have needed a scroll hundreds of feet long! Thank goodness we don't have to slog through verse after verse that reads like a biology textbook on taxonomy, naming creature after creature from the elephant down to the paramecium. Just as we wouldn't expect astronomers to cram things like comets and black holes into the categories for sun or moon, we shouldn't expect all humans to fit into the categories "male" and "female," just because those are the only two listed in Genesis 1. Instead of asking the text to define and label all that is, we can ask God to speak into the space between the words, between biblical times and our time, and between categories we see as opposites.

When I asked M Jade Kaiser if they identified with the concept of in-between places in space and time, their answer surprised me. I had always assumed that all nonbinary people identified somewhere between male and female, and as M explained, that's a fairly common misconception. While the term "nonbinary" has become a simple way to refer to someone who doesn't have a strict male or female gender identity, the term is intrinsically flawed. "To say that you're nonbinary innately suggests there is a binary, and my whole point is that there's no such thing," M clarified. "We've created this formula and forced our understanding of gender into it."

Instead of seeing themselves as halfway between male and female, M and many other nonbinary people experience their gender as something completely different.

"I'm very convicted to speak about my own nonbinary identity not as an 'in-between,' but as a 'more,'" M told me. "So, for instance, as someone who's bisexual, I don't think of myself as half gay and half straight. I'm something else. I know some nonbinary people think of themselves as half man and half woman, but I don't. When we open the [gender binary] boxes, it's much more a scattering of things than a line."

Since noted sexologist Alfred Kinsey began publishing his reports on sexuality in 1948, people in the Western world have become more aware of sexuality as it exists along a spectrum. While some people may identify as strictly gay or strictly straight, rating as either a 1 or a 6 respectively on the Kinsey Scale, more people tend to fit somewhere within the mid-range. In the same way, over the past twenty or thirty years, we've become more comfortable with the idea of gender—especially gender expression—existing along a spectrum with points all along from A to Z—or F to M, as it were.

But charting our identities along a line in two dimensions has its limitations; namely, it doesn't accurately reflect the human diversity we observe. We don't see each other, or ourselves, in only two dimensions, and bisexual and nonbinary advocates are suggesting that it's long past time to update our ideology. Perhaps, instead of insisting that each person can be charted along a line, we should be looking up and seeing the multitude of sexualities and gender identities that exist in 3D, sprinkled through space like the stars.

This expansion in our understanding of the world also opens the door to a new reverence for God's creation. In acknowledging when we've misunderstood something about the world, and changing our theories and behavior in response, we're admitting our humanity and humbling ourselves before the Creator. In the same way, when we recognize that our language doesn't accurately represent what is, we create new words to illustrate those concepts.

"Once I said I was not a cisgender woman, the response was, 'Oh, you must feel really masculine.' But masculinity is not something that I feel represents who I am either," M admitted. "Our language for masculinity and femininity represents our reliance on the idea of a binary. I desperately want a third word, because I don't feel like a masculine person and I don't feel like a feminine person. I desperately wish there were more words for naming our different ways of being in the world."

Genesis 1:27 doesn't give us any new words to help us understand the reality of human gender, but it does provide us with a new theological concept. We are told that humans are made in the image of God—the *imago Dei*, as theologians call it. Because the creation of male and female is mentioned almost in the same breath, many people have wondered if the two are somehow related.[9] Which part of us reflects the image of God? Might it have anything to do with our gender?

In his famous work *Church Dogmatics*, Karl Barth laid out an in-depth study of the way the *imago Dei* has been interpreted over time. A later writer summed up his findings by saying, "Each interpreter has given content to the concept solely from the anthropology and theology of his own age."[10] In other words, each great thinker looked at the world through the lens of their particular time and place, as we all do. For instance, Athanasius of Alexandria, a bishop in the fourth century, believed that the image of God given to humans was our logic. Considering the importance of logic among the Greek Stoics and within the Roman Empire that ruled Alexandria at the time, it would make sense for Athanasius to come to this conclusion. It also makes sense that when we observe the behavior of nonhuman creatures, one thing that seems to set us apart is our ability to reason.

Not all scholars have come to this same conclusion—far from it. It's probably easiest to group theories about the image of God into three categories. One group of thinkers believes, like Athanasius, that we reflect the image of God in some way through a nonphysical characteristic we've been given. A second group believes that God's image is stamped on us in a bodily sense: through our gender, the shape of our bodies, or even the way we walk on two legs. A third group sees the image of God as something relational, which affects the way humans relate to God and to the rest of creation.

The earliest work that suggests the image of God has to do with our physical bodies can be found in an article by German scholar Theodore Nöldeke in 1897. Given that Christians have understood the Creator God we see in Genesis 1 to exist without a body, many people considered this a stretch. Then in 1940 another text study was done regarding the Hebrew words for "image" and "likeness." The same words were used to describe statues and other artwork in the Bible, suggesting that perhaps there was some physical connection.[11] A third study published several years later pointed out that these same two words are used in Genesis 5:3 when Adam fathers his son Seth: "Adam . . . became the father of a son in his likeness, according to his image, and named him Seth." "God created Adam in his image; Adam begot Seth in his image. The second statement is very clear: the son looks like the father; he resembles him in form and appearance. The first statement is to be interpreted accordingly: the first human resembles God in form and appearance."[12]

But there's a crucial difference between these two passages, in the verb that's used to describe producing a new person. For God, that verb is "create," while for Adam it is "beget." While fathering a child is in some ways an act of creation, any parent can tell you that you don't get much of a choice when it comes to that child's looks or personality. On the contrary, when God creates, God has the perfect freedom to make things in whatever way God wants.

Some modern scholars have suggested that the image of God is represented in our bodies, and that this image is most fully realized when a cisgender man and a cisgender woman join together in marriage, essentially putting back together something that had been separated.[13] Others, like theologian James Brownson, disagree: "The fact that male and female are both created in the divine image is intended to convey the value, dominion, and relationality shared by both men and women, but not the idea that the complementarity of the genders is somehow necessary to fully express or embody the divine image."[14]

Near the end of his survey of the *imago Dei*, Barth concludes, "The passage Gen. 1:26–31 does not seem to pay any more attention to the body of man than it does to his soul or intellectual and spiritual nature."[15] Indeed, it would have been strange for the ancient Hebrew people to think of a human as something broken up into mind, body, and soul, as we do today. This sort of thinking is a product of Greek philosophy, and wouldn't have existed at the time Genesis 1 was written. Hebrew Bible scholar Claus Westermann put it this way: "The discussion whether the image and likeness of God referred to the corporeal or the spiritual aspect of the person has brought us to the conclusion that the question has been placed incorrectly." Instead, he says, this verse "is concerned neither with the corporeal nor with the spiritual qualities of people; it is concerned only with the person as a whole."[16]

For M Jade Kaiser, living as a reflection of God's image is possible only when you're living as a whole person—authentically, and without certain sections severed or hidden. When I asked M if they subscribed to any specific theory about the *imago Dei*, they introduced me to the reformer John Wesley's sermons on the subject. "I love John Wesley's approach to the image of God. For him it's about relational capabilities, not about a single innate characteristic." Wesley imagined the *imago Dei* to be made up of three different parts: he preached that people were made in God's natural image ("a spiritual being, endued with understanding, freedom of will, and various affections"); in God's political image ("the governor of this lower world, having dominion over the fishes of the sea, and over all the earth"); and in God's moral image ("in righteousness and true holiness" and "full of love").[17] He believed this was our default way of being before the fall, but that people are still able to live into these characteristics with God's help.

For M, the possibility of living into the moral image of God is most striking. "Wesley uses a breath image and says that we breathe in the compassion, generosity, and the love of God, and we should be exhaling the same thing to others. So it's all about how we orient ourselves toward each other and toward creation."

The thing is, we can't be in right relationship to each other if we can't see each other. We can't be fully present in any relationship if we're walling off part of ourselves or hiding beneath a mask.

M sighed. "It's really hard to be your best self when you're in a cage." They began to tell me about their experiences in seminary before coming out as nonbinary. "I would find myself getting mad at people for using 'she/her/hers' pronouns for me, which wasn't fair at all, because they didn't know! I was inhibiting my relationships in order to stay safe. My relationships with others were inhibited, my relationship to myself was deeply inhibited, my relationship to my community was inhibited. I was limited in my ability to live into the image of God within myself."

After M came out, things started to change. Rather than trying to conform to the current sociological expectations of men and women, M began to express themself in ways that accurately reflected who they were. They began deconstructing the walls they had built and the masks they had put on, and they took a leap of faith. They allowed others to see what God had always seen.

So how is God's image manifested in our bodies? In the same way it's manifested in the rest of our being. The image of God was not given to humankind in bits and pieces, with some living in your left arm and another bit in your soul and another bit in your ability to argue and reason. It is a gift that resonates throughout all that we are, like the deep tones of a bell rung far away. It awakens us and moves us forward toward God and toward each other.

As we talked, M and I agreed that it would be impossible to try to live into the image of God that we bear while we were also trying to deny our gender identity. We had to say yes to who God created us to be before we could begin imaging God in the world. The one had to come before the other, because otherwise our own defenses got in the way. When I asked M how they explained the relationship between this big theological concept and their own gender, they thought for a minute before answering. Finally, M said: "My trans-ness is only related to the image of God in me inasmuch as it allows me to naturally, politically, and morally be in right relationship with myself, with my community, and with creation as a whole. It has nothing to do with it and everything to do with it."

5
Biblical Culture Shock

I remember the first time I ever got stopped for being in the wrong bathroom. I was eleven or twelve years old, walking into the women's bathroom at Disneyland, sporting my favorite blue baseball cap—on backwards, of course. The rest of my family had gone on a ride that I wasn't particularly interested in, and so I was stopping in by myself to wash my hands and do what everyone else does in these situations. I had barely walked through the door when a woman turned around and stared at me.

"Hey, you're not supposed to be in here!" she said, in a voice sharp with alarm. I looked around to see whom she was talking to, but she kept staring right at me. Right at the kid with the baggy T-shirt, the sunburnt arms, and the bowl-cut. "This is the ladies room," she clarified, a bit calmer this time.

"I know!" I said. I wasn't sure how to explain to her that while I'd never felt much like a lady myself, this was the bathroom that the F on my birth certificate suggested that I use, and the one I'd always used alongside my mom and my sisters.

She just kept staring at me like she didn't believe what I was saying, and I could feel my stomach start to churn. I turned around quickly and went back out the door, and for the rest of our trip I never went back into a bathroom by myself. Afterward, I felt a tickle of pride that she had thought I was a boy, and the memory made me smile. In the moment, though, I felt terrified.

All over the world people use clothing as part of their gender expression—from kilts in Scotland, to the huipil in Central America, to the gho in Bhutan, to the hijab worn by many Muslim women. We have expectations about what certain kinds of clothing mean in our own culture, and we use that clothing to signal things about ourselves to other people. This isn't a skill we're born with, though; it's something that other people have to teach us. Most of us get a sense of this when we're young. In the United States, adults tell children that pink is for girls, and short hair is for boys. By the time we're in high school, it's not just our parents and teachers who are policing the way we express our gender; our peers are also in on the game. When I met that woman in the bathroom at Disneyland, she was reacting to the stereotypically masculine clothes I was wearing and jumped to some conclusions based on those observations. That wasn't her fault—our brains are made to categorize things quickly—but it's important to note the way that we respond to our knee-jerk reactions. Our unconscious thoughts don't matter as much as what we do about them. But how much can we really tell about someone by the way they dress?

Gender expression was scrutinized in biblical times too, and we have one specific verse that often gets leveraged against people who dress "outside their gender." That verse is Deuteronomy 22:5: "A woman shall not wear a man's apparel, nor shall a man put on a woman's garment; for whoever does such things is abhorrent to the LORD your God." But what exactly is women's clothing and men's clothing? Is this verse referring to clothing within one particular culture in one place and time, or is it a hard-and-fast rule for everyone?

The answers to those questions depend on whom you ask. Some biblical scholars believe that Deuteronomy 22:5 was written specifically for the Hebrew people in their time and place, because dressing in the clothes of another gender was associated with the cults of other gods.[1] Other theologians believe this verse to be a continuation of the Torah laws we talked about in the last chapter, where all life is classified and separated into different categories that are forbidden from mixing. In the Talmud, Rabbi Eliezer ben Jacob suggests that the "man's apparel" in the verse refers to armor and weapons for war, and that the verse's original purpose was to keep women from going into battle.[2] The Jewish scholar Rashi says in his commentary on Deuteronomy 22:5 that the prohibition is against anyone dressing in the clothes of another gender in order to mix among that other gender for the purposes of adultery or some other kind of heterosexual immorality.[3] Interestingly enough, Rashi states immediately afterward that he believes the verse applies only to clothing that is used in this way, and suggests that it's OK to wear the clothing of another gender as long as you're not using it to sneak off and make out with somebody you shouldn't. The great Catholic theologian Thomas Aquinas also touched on this passage in his section of the *Summa theologica* regarding modesty in apparel. He concluded that Deuteronomy 22:5 was written, first, because dressing in the clothing of another gender might allow for "sensuous pleasure," and, second, because this practice was associated with the worship of other gods. "Nevertheless," he continues, "this may be done sometimes without sin on account of some necessity, either in order to hide oneself from enemies, or through lack of other clothes, or for some similar motive."[4]

Regardless of why this verse was written, we have to ask, is it still relevant for us Christians today? While many of our Jewish siblings still follow the Mosaic law, Christians have historically found ways to pick and choose. We no longer pay much attention to the laws in the verses before 22:5 (which command us to help our neighbor's donkey or ox when we see it fallen in the road) or the verses after it (which command that we may never kill a mother bird when we take her eggs, but must always let her go free). Even if we look at other instances of the use of the word for "abomination" in Deuteronomy, we find rules that hardly seem relevant for us, such as Deuteronomy 25:13–16, which says that people who carry two kinds of weights in order to cheat others economically are an abomination. But if we took that rule seriously, perhaps we would be a little harder on those who give predatory loans, manipulate the housing market, and price gouge people for their insulin!

Let's say we're going to take Deuteronomy 22:5 at face value and hold to it strictly. We have to ask ourselves if that's possible in an era of global Christianity, where different cultures with contrasting ideas about dress and gender gather together to become the church. Will we demand that all Christian women from Seoul to São Paulo wear sun dresses, or that all Christian men from Mogadishu to Memphis wear a kanzu (the white robe worn by many men in eastern Africa)? Will we make space for diversity, or will we try to homogenize everyone into accepting our personal cultural expectations?

We have to ask the same questions about what some Christians call "biblical gender roles." The doctrine that supports biblical gender roles in many evangelical circles today comes from the Council on Biblical Manhood and Womanhood (CBMW), a group formed in 1987 "to set forth the teachings of the Bible about the complementary differences between men and women."[5] According to the CBMW's founding document, biblical manhood looks like "loving, humble headship," and biblical womanhood looks like "intelligent, willing submission."[6] Rachel Held Evans, a scholar who attempted to spend a year living out these principles, describes the model this way: "'Biblical submission,' according to the CBMW, requires that women yield to their husbands as the primary breadwinners, defer to them when making decisions on behalf of the family, look to men as the spiritual leaders in the home and church, and avoid pursuing careers that place them in a position of authority over men."[7] In short, complementarity and biblical gender roles insist that men are created to lead and women are created to follow, and that these two genders are fundamentally different, but must be paired.

The Christians who subscribe to these views cite several biblical passages in support of their argument, one of which can be found in Genesis 2. Here we read another version of the creation story, in which Adam and Eve are created at different times. In Genesis 1, God creates the first two humans simultaneously, but in Genesis 2:7 we read, "Then the LORD God formed man from the dust of the ground, and breathed into his nostrils the breath of life; and the man became a living being." It's much later in the narrative, when God has already created the garden of Eden, that another human comes on the scene. In Genesis 2:18 God says, "'It is not good that the man should be alone; I will make him a helper as his partner.'" God brings every created animal to Adam, hoping to find the right mate, but unfortunately Adam is not keen on any of them. Finally, God puts Adam to sleep and takes a piece of his side— usually translated as "rib"—which God makes into Eve. Adam sees Eve for the first time and says, "'This at last is bone of my bones and flesh of my flesh; this one shall be called Woman, for out of Man this one was taken'" (Gen. 2:23).

When complementarians look at this text, they note that Adam was created first and that Eve is described as a "partner" ("helper" in some translations)—all evidence that women were created to follow.[8] The problem with seeing women as followers in Genesis 2 is that you could just as easily argue, as many women have, that God goofed up the first prototype in Adam but finally crowned creation with the invention of Eve. In these stories it's uncertain whether it is better to be created first or last.

Then there's that word "helper." Does it really mean that Eve was created as a sort of godly secretary? Rachel Held Evans argues no, and that when you look at the Hebrew words *ezer kenegdo* used to describe Eve, you actually get a much more powerful sense of her purpose. *Ezer*, "helper," is used in reference to three people or types of people in the

Old Testament: twice to refer to Eve, three times to refer to nations that help Israel militarily, and sixteen times to refer to God as the helper of the Hebrew people.[9] The other part of the phrase, *kenegdo*, essentially means "of the same type"; so, when Adam first sees Eve, his song that affirms her as "flesh of my flesh" is spot-on—they share a special connection as the only two of their kind.

Additionally, some non-LGBTQI2A-affirming theologians believe that this splitting of one human into two shows us that men and women are created heterosexual and cisgender, and have a biological and theological imperative to come back together again, sexually and in marriage. Theologian James Brownson takes them to task when he points out that "the Genesis text portrays marriage as a solution, not for 'incompleteness,' but for aloneness."[10] It's not Adam's gender or lack of gendered characteristics that causes a problem—it's the fact that he craves relationship and community. Additionally, rather than suggesting that Adam and Eve or men and women are created to be different from each other, Brownson points to Adam's recognition of their sameness. He confirms that "the primary movement in the text is not from unity to differentiation, but from the isolation of an individual to the deep blessing of shared kinship and community."

So now that we have a sense of what Christianity has done with gender expression and gender roles, let's take a look at what these heady theoretical ideas actually mean for transgender Christians going about their daily lives.

Aidan Wang is a Taiwanese transgender man from Taipei who thinks of himself as a "third-culture kid." He's spent most of his life with one foot in the Eastern culture of Taiwan and one foot in Christianity—a Western import. When Aidan was in kindergarten, his parents converted to Christianity and began attending a nondenominational evangelical church, and Aidan himself started school at a missionary academy.

Growing up Christian in Taiwan means being part of a true subculture. Only 3.9 percent of the population identify themselves as Christian, while the majority of Taiwanese citizens are practitioners of either Buddhism (35 percent) or Taoism (33 percent).[11] When Aidan started at the Christian academy at around six years old, he experienced a bit of culture shock without ever leaving the country. Gender expectations were different at church than they were at home, and things that never seemed to be a problem before suddenly became complicated.

He smiled for a second when he told me, "I knew my identity [as male] since I was two years old! But growing up Christian meant, back in the day, no mention of transgender people. I had no idea what transgender meant. I knew I started liking girls when I was in third grade, and I learned in school that being gay was a sin, and since I was in a female body and I like girls, I thought I was gay."

While Aidan felt comfortable wearing the clothes he liked at home and around the city, at church there were different expectations. "Outside of the church, people didn't think it was weird that I wore shorts and pants all the time. I would wear dark colors like blue and black. They didn't think it was weird that I cut my hair short. They just thought, 'Oh, cute!'"

I asked him if that was the norm for girls in Taiwan. He responded,

Yes, people here are more androgynous. More gender-blended. There isn't a big distinction between men and women's clothes. There isn't really a women's section or men's section. Well, there is, but people don't really pay attention to that. Men here have smaller frames and less hair growth than men in the West—nobody really has big beards. It's OK for women to have shorter hair and wear sports clothes, flannel shirts, shorts, and things like that. And it's OK for men to wear tighter pants or tighter shirts. So when you walk down the street it's very common for people to not know what your gender is.

But in church things were different. "In the church women are supposed to be more spiritual. They have to be proper;

the clothing needs to cover you more. It's OK for girls to wear pants, even in church, but they wanted me to wear more pink. . . . I guess just be more feminine. Maybe wear more girlish shirts, more girlish shorts."

The tradition of men's and women's clothing being of similar shapes but varying in color and pattern can actually be found in Taiwanese history, both among the Han people, who migrated to Taiwan from China from the 1600s up to the mid-twentieth century, and among many of the indigenous peoples of the island.[12] Customarily both men and women wore robes or full-length wraps with long sleeves, and it was only the color, textile pattern, or kind of needlework that distinguished the two. These days, clothing remains fairly androgynous, but certain colors and styles are more common among one gender than another.

The differences between expectations at home and at church were even more obvious when it came to gender roles. Aidan's mother was an enthusiastic feminist who had a passion for education. "When she was growing up, women were not allowed to be educated," he explained. "She pushed back really hard on that. She's the only person to graduate from college in her family, because she believes women are capable of doing anything." That go-get-'em personality served her well in the academic world, but when she converted to Christianity, she faced the same pressure from so-called biblical gender roles as evangelical women in the United States.

I asked Aidan if "submitting" to men's leadership was hard for his mother. He laughed and said,

> Oh yeah. She is always pushing back in church. People would ask my dad to lead a small group and she'd be like, "No, he can't, I will lead." Like at first she thought, "Oh my, this is the culture? Oh, I should really listen to this Christian culture, I will submit, I will be quiet." But then, in her nature, she can't. Because my dad can't lead—he's submissive like me. I'm a more passive guy. I don't talk much, but in church I have to be vocal. I have to lead

prayer, I have to be a small group leader. I hated that. I felt a lot of pressure.

This is where the culture clash is most obvious, because while men are expected to lead in church, Taiwanese culture treasures men who are what they call "warm-hearted."

In Taiwanese culture there's a pressure on men to be the provider, or, we say, to be able to feed the wife. So if you can't feed the wife, you can't get married. As a man you should provide everything your wife needs—everything that makes her happy. If you want to be a good boyfriend, it means you have to carry your girlfriend's purse, buy her tampons, serve her in any way, listen to her every word, and girls kind of get to boss you around. Guys aspire to this. We have a term for it—it's called "warm man." Like you're warm-hearted. We want to be the warm man. It goes along with the motto "happy wife, happy life." So then I think a lot of women are uncomfortable in church because of that, because they're called to submit, right? They have to be submissive. I think that's where the pushback is—it's totally different for us.

Examples like the ones Aidan brings up should make us take a critical look at the principles and behaviors that Christianity is imposing on people around the world. While there are certain parts of Christian belief that aren't relative—like the Ten Commandments or Jesus' Sermon on the Mount—cultural components might need to be evaluated differently. Should we be insisting that cultural practices and rules created for one people at one specific place and time be the rule of law for all people, forever?

It's telling that we have some pretty great examples of biblical characters who didn't fit the gender mold, even in their own time. Think about Joseph, for instance—the one with the "Technicolor dream coat." As it turns out, that coat may be more than it appears.

Here's the set-up for Joseph's story:

Joseph, being seventeen years old, was shepherding the flock with his brothers; he was a helper to the sons of Bilhah and Zilpah, his father's wives; and Joseph brought a bad report of them to their father. Now Israel loved Joseph more than any other of his children, because he was the son of his old age; and he had made him a long robe with sleeves. But when his brothers saw that their father loved him more than all his brothers, they hated him, and could not speak peaceably to him.

(Genesis 37:2–4)

You might notice that this Bible translation, the New Revised Standard Version, calls Joseph's coat "a long robe with sleeves," rather than the "coat of many colors" that we find in the King James Version. The truth is that we don't know exactly how to translate the Hebrew words *ketonet passim*, which are used to describe this piece of clothing, because this combination is used only twice in the whole Bible. Most of the time translators can figure out a word's meaning by looking closely at the context, especially if the word is used often. When a word is hardly ever used, though, we lose some of the nuance. If you are reading a collection of children's stories that reference a stuffed bear with a fondness for honey who lives in a forest with an owl, a rabbit, a donkey, and a pig, those words by themselves don't evoke anything—unless you've already read the stories of Winnie the Pooh! We know that the Hebrew word *ketonet* means "garment, robe, or tunic," because we see it used all over the Bible to refer to clothing. But we don't know what the word *passim* means when added to *ketonet*. The only other time we find this combination of words is in the terrible story of Tamar, King David's daughter, who was sexually assaulted by David's son Amnon in 2 Samuel 13. Verse 18 tells us that Tamar "was wearing a long robe with sleeves; for this is how the virgin daughters of the king were clothed in earlier times." Apparently this piece of clothing that Tamar was wearing had both gender and status connotations attached to it.

So what are we to make of the fact that this garment, the *ketonet passim*, is worn by only two people in the Bible: Joseph, and Princess Tamar? Theologians have been chewing this one over for hundreds of years and coming up with all kinds of answers.[13] Some believe that the outfit must really be a gender-neutral children's garment (but how do we understand the gender and status explanation in Tamar's story then?), while others think that maybe men's and women's royal robes were so similar as to be indistinguishable (but then why the fuss over properly gendered clothing in Deut. 22:5?). In the end, all we know for sure is that "this apparently beautiful and luxurious garment that serves as a mark of distinction for the virgin daughters of the king is the same garment with which the patriarch vested his favored son."[14] If this is the case, the alienation and abuse Joseph receives at the hands of his brothers makes even more sense. As a person assigned male at birth but who dresses in clothes associated with women, Joseph fails to measure up to expected gender expressions.

We see another gender rebel in the form of Deborah, the female leader of the Hebrew people during a period in which the Israelites were enslaved by the king of Canaan. Judges 4:4–5 tells us, "At that time Deborah, a prophetess, wife of Lappidoth, was judging Israel. She used to sit under the palm of Deborah between Ramah and Bethel in the hill country of Ephraim; and the Israelites came up to her for judgment." One day Deborah called a man named Barak to visit her. When he came to hear her prophecy, she told him that God had chosen him to lead a band of Israelite warriors against the Canaanite king's most powerful general, Sisera. Barak thought about it for a minute. If he won, he would secure freedom for the Israelites, but if he lost, his people would probably be oppressed further. Eventually he said, "If you will go with me, I will go; but if you will not go with me, I will not go" (Judg. 4:8).

Scholars disagree about whether Barak refused to go without Deborah because he was scared, or because he realized it would be wise to bring along a prophet who is in touch with God, to keep the battle on track. In either case, Deborah

responded by saying, "I will surely go with you; nevertheless, the road on which you are going will not lead to your
glory, for the LORD will sell Sisera into the hand of a woman"
(Judg. 4:9). And so she went with him, along with ten thousand warriors, out onto the battlefield itself. Deborah advised
Barak and told him when the time was right to attack. When
the fight was over, Sisera the Canaanite general was the only
opposing soldier left alive.

Sisera ran from the battlefield, right past the tent of a woman
named Jael. Somehow Jael recognized who he was, and she
invited him into the tent to hide. Sisera asked her for a drink,
and then asked her to keep a lookout and to tell anyone looking for him that he hadn't come that way. Jael agreed, but as
soon as the exhausted Sisera fell asleep, she picked up a sharp
tent peg and drove it right through his temple, killing him
instantly. Barak ran up to the tent, hot on Sisera's trail, and
Jael flagged him down and led him to Sisera's body, thereby
fulfilling Deborah's prophecy that God would give the final
victory to a woman. And not just one victory, but a triumph
that would secure the Israelites' freedom! In Judges 5 Deborah
and Barak together compose a song retelling the whole story
and thanking God for their liberation.

Both Jael and Deborah do some unladylike things in these
chapters, from leading and directing a battle to killing a high-
ranking military officer with just the tools at hand. When looking specifically at Deborah, one scholar notes, "Her gender is
stressed almost disproportionately at the beginning of ch. 4"—
by referring to her as both a female prophet and a wife—"and
she describes herself as a mother in ch. 5. But what other characteristics make her female according to the androcentric society's designation of what is female? She is not the caring mother,
rather a mother who is a military commander. She is a prophet,
judge and a leader, all of which are traditional male traits."[15]

Would Deborah pass the test of biblical womanhood, as
defined by Christian complementarians? If these heroic biblical characters who spoke with God and liberated thousands
don't fit the criteria, who can?

Western Christianity has had a significant effect on Taiwan, despite the small number of practicing Christians who live there. In May 2017, Taiwan became the first Asian territory to recognize same-sex marriage, but this victory for LGBTQI2A Taiwanese didn't come easily. Resistance to same-sex marriage had been coming from Taiwanese Christians since the late 1990s and had grown steadily over time as the issue became more prominent in Western churches. One group, the Alliance of Religious Groups for the Love of Families Taiwan, organized a protest in November 2013 that included thousands of people who opposed any pro-LGBTQI2A legislation.

Chen Chih-hung, the Alliance's spokesperson at the time, believed that it was up to Christians to educate Taiwan's other faith groups on the dangers of homosexuality. Chen explained,

> Christian groups take the lead on this issue since Asian religions haven't traditionally seen homosexuality as a big deal. Churches in the U.S. and Europe have confronted the impact of gay marriage directly. . . . Since only a small percentage of Taiwanese are Christians, we share what we know with other religions so that they understand the seriousness of the situation. . . . Christian churches in Taiwan are informed by churches abroad about what gay activists have been doing here. . . . We lack experience. They have told us how serious the issue is and what strategies [gay rights advocates] deploy.[16]

Perhaps, unsurprisingly, groups like Chen's Alliance are supported by conservative evangelical groups in the United States in terms of both knowledge and resources. Two US-based organizations, Focus on the Family and the World Congress of Families, have branches in Taiwan and Hong Kong that seek to effect church communities and legislation.[17]

Aidan has experienced firsthand this new focus on anti-LGBTQI2A attitudes in churches. After he medically transitioned several years ago, he decided to find a church that he thought might welcome him. "I started going to this church that I liked, and right at the beginning I told my pastor about my identity. I told him I'm transgender and asked if he's OK with that. And at the time he had no idea—he had never met a transgender person before. Never heard of it! The only thing he shared was that he was not gay-affirming, and since I'm a man and I'm heterosexual, he had no problem at the time. He welcomed me, and I stayed at that church for five years."

The problems began when Aidan started seriously dating a woman. The two of them would go to church together on Sundays, and suddenly it seemed as if the pastor wasn't as friendly anymore. "I think he was caught up in the whole marriage-equality fight that was happening at the time. I think that made him stop and think about it, consider it, and decide that he's not OK with me being transgender. He kind of tightened his view on what was OK and what's not, so originally it was OK to be trans but not OK to be gay. Then it became not OK to be either."

"How did you know he wasn't OK with it?" I asked.

"They pressured me to stay celibate, and I didn't think that was a fair expectation on me," Aidan laughed and went on:

It was a very evangelical, charismatic church, so what they did was tell me, "The Lord told me in a dream. I saw a vision in my dream, and I saw the Lord stamping the word 'celibacy' on your forehead, and he specifically told me that I ought to tell you." That kind of thing. No mention of Scripture or anything, no talking through—it's just their vision, their dream.

At the time, being the submissive person I am, I didn't fight back. I panicked, in my heart, but then I thought, oh no, this is just a misunderstanding. I'm sure these people love me, they care for me, and there's a way to talk through this. So I didn't say anything at the time. But then over the next few weeks I sent them articles, you know, like, just things to let them read and consider, but it didn't help. Every Sunday after that I would show up, but I could see very clearly the pastor going to my girlfriend and whispering in her ear. So then afterward I would ask her, "What did they tell you?" And she would tell me they said things like "We're praying for you." "We're worried about you." And, "Remember what the Lord says!" Stuff like that.

This pressure and prospect of losing either his church community, or his girlfriend, or both, caused a lot of mental anguish for Aidan. On top of that, there was always the tiny voice of doubt in the back of his head whispering, "What if they're right about you?"

> I struggled with hell for the longest time while I was at that church, because that's what my girlfriend was concerned about. Hell. She was concerned about going to hell for dating me. So then we started having so many conversations about that that I got scared, and my pastors didn't help, you know. They were seeing all these visions! And I panicked so much about going to hell. That was always in the back of my mind growing up, and it just got worse.

Eventually, Aidan left that church, and he and his girlfriend broke up. He started thinking more critically about some of the things he'd learned in his time at Christian schools, and about the things his nonaffirming pastor had said. He began reading dozens of books and articles about gender identity, faith, and the Bible, trying to find a way to put the pieces back together again. When it came down to it, though, the trauma that he had been living through, while being told over and over again that he was inherently wrong and bound to an eternal punishment, became too much to bear.

"How would you describe your faith now?" I asked him. "Honestly, I think it's amazing that you'd have any left after those experiences."

Aidan smiled again, sadly this time. "What it came down to was that some days I have to believe that hell just doesn't exist. Other days I believe that if Jesus came to save us, he came to save all of us, and even if hell does exist, he loves us too much to let us suffer forever.

"If two-years-ago me saw me right now, he would freak out! He would not believe I'm like this. Because . . . I'm gonna be a bit emotional about this." He gulped and looked down.

I remember what it was like to be me two years ago. God was everything. . . . And for me to be me now, when my relationship with God feels like nothing sometimes? I'm still kind of struggling with that. I'm still trying to make sense of what's going on. But it feels so much better than being terrified all the time. Maybe I'll be able to go back some day. But I was a trans Christian in the church for eight years. And as a trans Christian out of church right now, I just can't believe how I lived through that.

He sighed. "It's kind of a miracle."

6
What's My Name Again?

When I was born, in the late 1980s, my parents decided to gift me with what they thought was an original and beautiful name: Alison.* As it turned out, Alison—or one of the various alternate spellings—made it into the top fifty names for girls that year and for a couple of years afterward. From middle school on, whenever I'd walk into a new class, it seemed as if at least two more Alisons would crop up, and we'd all be forced to either pick nicknames or go by our last names instead. I was never into shortening my name, because I thought Ali sounded even girlier than Alison did. But then one day my uncle Rick dropped by our house. He'd come over to help mow the lawn, and I was out dribbling a basketball in our driveway. He walked across the yard to the house, and as he did, he yelled, "Hey, Al!" I remember looking up and waving and thinking to myself, "Yes! He gets it!" He was the only person to ever call me Al, but every time he did it, he made me feel two inches taller.

*A note for people practicing trans allyship: I'm sharing my birth name with you here because I don't mind sharing my story! Remember, though, that it's never polite or appropriate to ask a trans person what their birth name was. If they feel comfortable enough with you to volunteer that information, they'll do it in their own time and in their own way.

Names are incredibly powerful things. Whether given or chosen, our first name identifies us as an individual, and our last name identifies us as part of a community. For transgender people, names can take on an additional sense of meaning. They become another way in which we express our gender. Some trans folks choose to keep the name they were given at birth, especially if that name is gender-neutral, like Robin, Taylor, or Jamie. But sometimes the name we were given at birth just doesn't fit, and we decide to choose a new name altogether—something that gives other people a better sense of who we are.

Renaming is as old as language, and we have some fascinating cases woven right into our foundational biblical texts. In these scriptural examples, a new name is given in recognition of an identity somebody already has, or the new name is given to recognize a change in identity.

In Numbers 13 we find an example of someone being given a new name to illustrate a new identity. Moses and the wandering Hebrew people find themselves on the doorstep to the Promised Land, but they're not sure what to do next. God tells Moses to send out some spies to do a bit of reconnaissance, to see what kind of people already live here. Moses chooses one leader from each tribe to go out and look around, among them a young man named Hoshea son of Nun. Verse 16 tells us, "And Moses changed the name of Hoshea son of Nun to Joshua." We're not explicitly told why Moses changes his name, but Joshua does become Moses' second in command and eventually takes his place as leader after Moses' death. In the Middle Ages a French rabbi named Samuel ben Meir—better known as Rashbam—suggested that it was customary to give a new name to somebody who had moved up to such a high rank,[1] and so it's very possible that Moses decided to bestow the new name and the new title at the same time, essentially gifting Joshua with a new identity.

While most names in the Hebrew Scriptures are gifted from one human to another, or from God to human, there is a single

WHAT'S MY NAME AGAIN?

case of a person giving God the Creator a new name. This distinction goes to Hagar, the woman enslaved by Abraham and Sarah, who becomes pregnant with Abraham's son and then runs away to escape Sarah's abuse. Hagar meets an angel of God in the wilderness in Genesis 16; the angel assures her that God is with her and her unborn son. Verse 13 says, "So she named the LORD who spoke to her, 'You are El-roi'; for she said, 'Have I really seen God and remained alive after seeing him?'" *El-roi* in Hebrew means "God sees" or "one who sees." In this case, Hagar is not changing God's identity; she's giving a new name to recognize the identity that God already has.

One of the most famous name changes in the New Testament is found in the Gospel of Matthew:

> [Jesus] said to [the disciples], "But who do you say that I am?" Simon Peter answered, "You are the Messiah, the Son of the living God." And Jesus answered him, "Blessed are you, Simon son of Jonah! For flesh and blood has not revealed this to you, but my Father in heaven. And I tell you, you are Peter, and on this rock I will build my church, and the gates of Hades will not prevail against it."
> (Matthew 16:15–18)

Usually, when we read this passage, we pick up right away on what Jesus has done. He has given Simon a new name. What we might miss at first, though, is that Simon has just renamed Jesus as well! In the Gospel accounts of Matthew, Mark, and Luke, the idea that Jesus is the Messiah—the anointed one—is a bit of a secret, and this particular account is the very first time that anyone dares to call Jesus the Messiah out loud. What Simon does, when he's asked about Jesus' identity, is give Jesus the name that recognizes who he already is. Simon's declaration does not make Jesus the Messiah; it just recognizes it formally. In the opposite way, when Jesus tells Simon, "You are Peter, and on this rock I will build my church," Jesus is also giving Peter a whole new identity as the foundation of the community.

When a transgender person changes their name, they often work within these same categories: either taking on a name that highlights something true and established about their personality and their connection to others, or embracing a name that shows the world how they've changed and who they aspire to be.

River Cook Needham's name came to her one day while she was walking along the banks of the Upper Iowa River. "I wanted to keep my initials, so I wanted a name that started with R, and I wanted something that was gender-neutral and could be very ambiguous if I ever needed it to be," she explained when I asked about her name's origin. "When I was in college I lived near the Upper Iowa River, and I would walk the trail multiple times a day and pray and think. I was just known for being associated with the river. And one day I was like, 'River, that's a nice R word. It could be a name. It could totally be a name!' And then it was a name!"

But for River, finding a name was one of the easier parts of coming out as trans. She grew up as the only child of a Southern Baptist missionary father and a mother who was physically and mentally ill. Her early childhood was spent moving from place to place within North America. "We sort of lived a nomadic lifestyle, going from call to call to call," she said, thinking back. "When I was twelve, we went through a period of homelessness, and that was the first time that I knew something was different about me. Like, I knew something was up. I didn't have words—I didn't have anything—but I knew something was different. And that was the first time my mother asked me if I was gay."

The question caught River off guard, and she experienced a moment of recognition and intense fear. "I knew that at a certain level that was language I might use for myself one day, but I knew that I couldn't then, because I wouldn't be safe."

When River was in her senior year of college, though, the hiding became too much. By the time graduation rolled around, River found herself living through a complex personal trauma and trying to deal with coming out at the same time. She sighed heavily when I asked about her family's reaction. "I came out for the first time to my parents as a gay man, and all hell broke loose. It was a hellish nightmare. I was kicked out of my home church, and I was kicked out of my house for about three weeks to a month."

Leaving home was a big deal for River, who had been home-schooled up until college, so that she could continue her education while moving around, and so that she could serve as primary caregiver for her mother. Several years later, when she followed her call to ministry and began attending seminary, River found herself living with a group of men in the seminary's provided housing. Since she had never had siblings and had never lived in shared housing with other men before, this provided another opportunity to think deeply about both sexuality and gender. "And I realized, oh my gosh, I'm not gay! Because there's something very different about these guys that I just do not get!" But if sexuality didn't explain that difference, what could it be? River did some research, and by the end of first semester she was trying out different pronouns and names and attempting to understand how her awareness and experiences differed from the cisgender people around her. In August, at the end of that first summer in seminary, she began to piece together some answers. It was then, too, that River found her name.

Not all transgender people find the right name right away. In fact, lots of trans folks find themselves in the same position their parents once held—scouring baby books, making lists, and saying names out loud to see how they sound. You might end up trying out two or three names before you find one that sticks. Those who want to illustrate an established piece of their personality may make a previous nickname more formal. Other trans folks want to solidify their ties to their family and community and may scan the family tree for names that seem to fit, or if it's possible, they'll ask their parents what other names were considered when they were born. Many people

pick a characteristic—either one that describes them currently
or one that describes who they hope to be—and find names
that hold that meaning in another language, like Asher, which
means "happy," or Valencia, which means "brave." You might
even pick the name of a favorite fictional character with whom
you have identified strongly or some of whose personal attributes you admire!

One of the most common ways of changing a name, both
in the Bible and for trans folks today, is to change the spelling
of the birth name slightly so that it sounds similar but has a
slightly different connotation or meaning. For instance, you
might change your name from Bobbi to Bobby, from Mason
to Madison, or from Emily to Emile. There's a great example
of this kind of slight name tweaking in Genesis when God
renames Abraham and Sarah:

> Then Abram fell on his face; and God said to him, "As for
> me, this is my covenant with you: You shall be the ancestor
> of a multitude of nations. No longer shall your name be
> Abram, but your name shall be Abraham; for I have made
> you the ancestor of a multitude of nations." . . . God said
> to Abraham, "As for Sarai your wife, you shall not call her
> Sarai, but Sarah shall be her name. I will bless her, and
> moreover I will give you a son by her. I will bless her, and
> she shall give rise to nations; kings of peoples shall come
> from her."
>
> (Genesis 17:3–5, 15–16)

Even though Abram did not have any children with his wife
Sarai prior to this point, his birth name meant "exalted father,"
which probably felt like a painful irony. When God changes
his name, though, he becomes Abraham, which means "father
of many." God hands him not only a new name, but a new
identity and a new promise. The change in spelling from Sarai
to Sarah doesn't change the basic meaning of her name—Sarah
means "princess"—but the fact that God gives Sarah a new
name means that God intentionally gives the new identity and
blessing to both Abraham and Sarah equally. As we find out

later in their story, the covenant God makes with Abraham is null and void if Sarah is not included.

When we look at stories of renaming in the Bible, we often find that a character is handed a new name they never asked for. While I'm sure Abraham treasured the new name and promise God gave him, and while Peter probably felt honored in the moment Jesus proclaimed him the bedrock of the church, not everybody comes by their new name so easily. Some people have to fight for it.

Jacob and Esau were Abraham and Sarah's twin grandsons. Even before he was born, Jacob, the younger twin, was a known troublemaker. Genesis 25 tells us that when the first twin was born, he was covered in downy baby hair, and so his parents named him Esau, which means "hairy." The second twin was born immediately afterward, holding on to his brother's heel, so his parents named him Jacob, which can be translated "one who holds the heel," which in turn suggests another meaning, "usurper." Up into his young adulthood Jacob was trying to outdo his older brother. While Esau was strong, Jacob was smart and sly as a fox. Eventually Jacob got his brother to sell him the inheritance that Esau should have inherited as the firstborn son, and tricked their father into giving him the family blessing that went with it. Jacob was driven away from home by the fear that Esau might try to kill him in order to get back the inheritance and the blessing.

Years later, God told an older and more mature Jacob to return to his family. Jacob was incredibly afraid, but he packed up his new household—made up of livestock, servants, two wives, and many children—and headed back home. On the last night before the convoy was set to meet Esau, Jacob decided to split up the caravan, sending gifts ahead to sweeten up Esau, and sending the women and children off in another group to safeguard them against retribution. Jacob decided to spend the night by himself—or so he thought.

> So Jacob was left alone, and a man wrestled with him till daybreak. When the man saw that he could not overpower

him, he touched the socket of Jacob's hip so that his hip was
wrenched as he wrestled with the man. Then the man said,
"Let me go, for it is daybreak." But Jacob replied, "I will not
let you go unless you bless me." The man asked him, "What
is your name?" "Jacob," he answered. Then the man said,
"Your name will no longer be Jacob, but Israel, because
you have struggled with God and with humans and have
overcome." Jacob said, "Please tell me your name." But he
replied, "Why do you ask my name?" Then he blessed him
there. So Jacob called the place Peniel, saying, "It is because
I saw God face to face, and yet my life was spared." The
sun rose above him as he passed Peniel, and he was limping
because of his hip.

(Genesis 32:24–31 NIV)

Jacob's new name—Israel—is a tricky one for translators,
but it's most often interpreted as "one who has striven with
God," or "one who has struggled with God and persevered."
This imagery—this wrestling with God and humans—is
incredibly familiar to transgender Christians who have spent a
portion of their life grappling with their faith and their gender.
Sometimes we have to fight to have our gender recognized, and
sometimes we fight to be seen as Christians, and sometimes it
feels as if we're just holding on to God with both hands and
refusing to let go until God gives us something. That hunger
and thirst for righteousness, for justice, for blessing, and for
grace can leave us ecstatic when we finally receive it, but it can
also leave us limping.

It's been years now since River received her new name, and
many of her family members still won't use it. "My mother
called me River for the first time a couple of months ago. My
father still won't call me River. Because of his religious background he just . . . can't. He won't call me a name—he'll just
point at me."

This isn't unusual for Christian parents who don't know
how to respond when their child comes out as transgender. If
they've been told that being transgender is against God's will,

they may feel torn between their faith and their love for their child. In these cases Christian parents and their trans children are wrestling in almost exactly the same fight. Both are struggling to understand how to honor God and love themselves and each other at the same time. Parents may start to use their child's birth name more often because it reminds them of a time when their kid was younger and things felt less complicated, but this can lead to the transgender person feeling as if their parents either can't really see them or don't care about who their child is as a flesh-and-blood human being. At other times parents may use a trans person's birth name to make a point about their own disapproval, but this just triggers another flight-or-flight response in their child which can end in harsh words, or even the loss of the relationship altogether.

These kinds of reactions from parents make transgender people feel as if they have to make a nuisance of themselves just to be heard, and sometimes it can be almost as bad with friends and siblings. When I asked River about how friends and extended family reacted, she said,

> Well, I'm only in contact with two of the friends I had before transition, so I think that speaks volumes about how hard it was for the people in the Christian circles I was raised in. I had to turn into an unpleasant person for a while to get people to honor my name, so there's a lot of tension there. I had to spend about three months getting really cranky with people about using my name, but at that point they realized it was important, and some people started honoring it, which I really appreciated.

After this initial struggle River was able to gather a group of new, supportive friends who helped her hold a sort of funeral for her birth name. They gathered on the shore of Lake Michigan one weekend, and each person wrote down their memories of River's birth name on scraps of paper. After each memory was read aloud, River burned the pieces of paper. "One of my friends talked about the joy that she felt when she heard my old name," River remembers. "Another friend wrote about when she first met me. Another person wrote about important people in her life who have that same name. I got to hear the memories, and I got to burn them up, and I get to let them be memories that I can choose to take with me if I want to, but I don't have to. It was a very powerful ceremony, for me."

Trans folks can't realistically expect people to turn on a dime and start using a new name or new set of pronouns without any practice, but the best thing friends and family members can do to show support is to make a concerted effort. It takes time for your brain to create new neural pathways with new language, so make sure you're practicing new names and pronouns out loud so your body can make the connection. Practice in the shower, or while driving, or with a friend! You'll slip up occasionally, especially in the beginning, but just apologize quickly, correct yourself, and move on. As the old saying goes, when it comes to the gift of a new name, it's the thought that counts.

Using a transgender person's chosen name rather than their birth name shows basic respect, as well as demonstrating that you believe them to be who they say they are. If a cisgender person came into a business meeting and introduced herself as Evelyn Smith, you wouldn't turn around and say, "Welcome, Evie!" nor would you greet the new person in church with a name tag that says "Ted" with "Good to see you, Edward! Ted is short for Edward, right?" Using a transgender person's birth name—unless you've received special permission beforehand—can feel invalidating at best and malicious or even dangerous at worst, since the use of someone's birth name might out them as transgender and put them in harm's way. Most importantly, using a trans person's chosen name shows them that you care for and support them, and studies have shown that having a chosen name used at home, at school, at work, or with friends reduced suicidal thoughts in trans youth by 29 percent, with a compounding effect if used in multiple contexts.[2]

River is currently working on her PhD in theology. Her focus is on the work of liberation for fat, disabled, and trans people through the lens of process theology, and she's passionate about the intersection of faith, transgender identity, and mental illness. I asked her whether she found labels like "transgender" or "mentally ill" or even specific names to be helpful or hurtful. In response, River told me about a recent experience she'd had when she checked herself into a hospital because of a problem with her medication.

After being diagnosed with a bipolar disorder, River had been prescribed a medication that was supposed to help regulate the mania and depression, but within a week the meds had induced a hypermanic state that left her unable to cope. River laughed a little as she explained, "I completely lost control, and I decided on the spur of the moment that I needed to dye my hair blue, but on the way to the store to buy the hair dye I kept thinking, 'I should drive into that concrete embankment.'" River made it back home safe and was in the middle of dyeing her hair when a friend called. "I picked up, and somehow, thanks be to God, she made me stay on the phone until I found someone who could get me to the hospital."

Once at the hospital, though, River faced other problems. "I was finally admitted around midnight, and when I woke up the next morning I was woken up to a name that was not my own, and referred to with the wrong pronouns. I was told that because that's what it said on my driver's license and birth certificate, that's what they had to use." (Hospitals and clinics do not have to use the name and gender marked on your legal documents, and health-care best practices recommend always having a place on intake forms to note both a person's gender identity and their chosen name.)[3]

"I had to fight for three days, and every time I saw that name, I had to erase it and replace it. It was not a fun, happy encounter. There was one person in the hospital who was good at honoring my name, and that was because she was queer and the spouse of a trans person, so she was helpful in educating the staff and doing the work that I couldn't necessarily do as a patient there." River took a deep breath and added, "If she hadn't been there, I would not have made it."

As a person who is transgender and living with a mental illness, River knows that words have a huge potential for both harm and healing. People can choose to use River's birth name and cause frustration and anxiety, or people can choose to call River the name she prayed over, meditated on, and eventually embraced; and that can lead to a stronger and safer relationship. In the same way, River pointed out that labels like "mentally ill" and even "transgender" can be used both positively and negatively. Both of those labels carry social stigma and can be used to write someone off as a weirdo—as someone not worthy of respect, care, or love. On the other hand, personally claiming a label means that it will be easier to find other people like you, and to find the resources you need to live a healthy, happy life. In some cases, the struggle for a name or a label becomes so emblematic that it creates a community that hadn't existed before. Think of Jacob and the way he embraced his new name, Israel, which would signify his descendants for thousands of years to come.

That same struggle for a name, and for survival, endures today for many trans folks. As River put it,

> There's something very powerful about living with mental illness and having my trans experience, because both of those things make it incredibly difficult to stay alive. And there's something powerful about claiming it and saying, "Yeah, this is part of me, and I get to live with it." There's power in naming that, because it gives you resources to draw upon. It gives you community, it gives you different places to look for and find things, and it gives you the ability to honor your experience in ways that are life-giving.

7

God Breaks the Rules to Get You In

In mid-November 2013 I stumbled across a piece of Scripture that changed my life. I was twenty-five years old at the time, starting my second year of work for a master's degree in biblical studies, and just beginning the process of coming out as transgender. On the one hand, I felt a sense of relief at finally facing something I'd been running from for so long. On the other, now that I had internally admitted this truth about myself, I felt as if I was harboring a dangerous secret. The happiness I felt at making some sense of my own inner workings was quickly overshadowed by the potential for crisis that hovered over every conversation with my parents.

In fact, part of the reason it had taken me so long to admit that I felt decisively male was because I was terrified of telling my family. I knew that telling them I was trans would be hard on my dad's belief system and on my mom's fears for my safety. The idea of putting my parents through the wringer by explaining that I wanted to begin hormone therapy right away seemed mean, somehow. It would push them into a world where friends and family members would train the spotlight on their parenting skills and ask why their firstborn couldn't just fit in the body God had given them.

I knew that, if I told them I was trans, these conversations were going to be part of our new reality. We would be asked to explain how my trans identity fit into our faith, and that was something I didn't have an answer for yet. In my heart, my relationship with God hadn't changed, because I hadn't really changed. In coming out to myself as transgender, all I was doing was acknowledging something that had been part of me for as long as I could remember—a part that had never interfered with my faith before. I had grown up singing "Jesus Loves Me" and internalizing the message that God knew me better than I knew myself. I thought that if these things had been true my whole life and if my experience of gender had been a bit different that whole time, then God's love and my trans identity could not possibly be mutually exclusive.

But I still had this tickle in the back of my mind—an echo of conservative theology I'd internalized growing up—which whispered that it was fine if my gender was a little bit unconventional, as long as I didn't attempt to do anything about it. It sounded and felt very much like the messages I had received as a teenager when I came out as bisexual: God still loves you, but don't act on those feelings—or else. That meant hormone therapy and surgery were out of the question, as were changing my name or my pronouns.

As a student of biblical texts, I had found only one verse that had anything to say about changing one's body in relation to one's physical sex characteristics. Deuteronomy 23:1 commands, "No one whose testicles are crushed or whose penis is cut off shall be admitted to the assembly of the LORD." I had to wonder whether this verse was meant as a prohibition against any kind of bodily modification of sex characteristics, or whether it was meant to be read plainly—as a constraint placed solely on people with those particular reproductive organs. If it was the latter, what did that mean for transgender women who chose to remove penis and testicles during gender-affirming surgery? Regardless, this lone verse seemed to set a troubling precedent.

I had a lot to work through as I tried to imagine the ways in which my faith might intersect with my newly understood transgender identity. Because I had what I believed was a strong relationship with God, and because my gender identity was just a fact, my question was not, "Do I have to choose between my gender identity and my faith?" Instead, I found myself asking, "Is it possible to fully embrace both parts of my identity and still be welcomed into Christian community?"

Over Thanksgiving break that same year, I found myself scrambling to pick a topic for my master's thesis. One evening I grabbed my Bible off the top of a stack of schoolbooks, planning to scan through several of my favorite passages and hoping to find something intriguing. I sat down on the floor next to my bookshelf and plopped the large study Bible, complete with extensive notes and highlighting, down in front of me.

As a kid, I remember treating the Bible like a Magic 8-Ball. Our pastor said all answers could be found in Scripture, so I'd squeeze my eyes shut tight, open it to a random page, stick my finger down, and then open my eyes to see what God had to say about my particular circumstance. The best part was that if I didn't like or understand the answer, I'd just run the whole process over again!

I hadn't tried anything like that in more than a decade, but on this particular night I balanced the cover of the big book between my palms and let it fall open on its own. Thump. Right smack in the middle of the page on the right-hand side, Isaiah 56:3–8 floated slowly off the page and into my heart:

> Do not let the foreigner joined to the LORD say,
>   "The LORD will surely separate me from his people";
> and do not let the eunuch say,
>   "I am just a dry tree."
> For thus says the LORD:

To the eunuchs who keep my sabbaths,
   who choose the things that please me
   and hold fast my covenant,
I will give, in my house and within my walls,
   a monument and a name
   better than sons and daughters;
I will give them an everlasting name
   that shall not be cut off.
And the foreigners who join themselves to the LORD,
   to minister to him, to love the name of the LORD,
   and to be his servants,
all who keep the sabbath, and do not profane it,
   and hold fast my covenant—
these I will bring to my holy mountain,
   and make them joyful in my house of prayer;
their burnt offerings and their sacrifices
   will be accepted on my altar;
for my house shall be called a house of prayer
   for all peoples.
Thus says the Lord GOD,
   who gathers the outcasts of Israel,
I will gather others to them
   besides those already gathered.

I was floored. I could swear I had never heard these verses before in my life, despite having read through the book of Isaiah for a class only the year before. I felt an immediate connection to the eunuch and the foreigner. Their fear of separation, fear of being forgotten, fear of being kept out of God's family—all based on identities as unchosen as the place of their birth and as intrinsic as the shape of their body. Their fears were my fears too. Yet here was God, speaking through the prophet Isaiah, quieting those fears and promising an unequivocal welcome.

The next day I walked into my thesis adviser's office with my Bible and asked him if I could write about Isaiah 56:1–8. I had to know, was there a direct connection between the experiences of eunuchs in the ancient world and transgender people

today? Could this text be interpreted as a call for a full welcome
for gender-expansive people?

Before I could begin to answer these questions, I required a bit
of context. As it turned out, there was a link between Deuteronomy 23:1—the verse about modification of genitalia—and
the text from Isaiah that I was now exploring.

The book of Isaiah itself was created over a period of about
two centuries, beginning during the late eighth century BCE.[1]
Because it was written over such a long period of time, and
because of the stylistic cues and historical references in the text,
we know it was written and compiled by at least three people—
though we refer to all of them as Isaiah. At the time of First
Isaiah, the original united kingdom of Israel that we remember
from the stories of King David had been split up into two separate kingdoms called Israel and Judah. First Isaiah lived in the
kingdom of Judah; in his writings, which span from chapter 1
to chapter 39, we find histories, prophecies, and some incredibly colorful warnings to the leaders of both kingdoms. Isaiah
1:2–3 opens the book this way:

> Hear, O heavens, and listen, O earth;
>   for the LORD has spoken:
> I reared children and brought them up,
>   but they have rebelled against me.
> The ox knows its owner,
>   and the donkey its master's crib;
> but Israel does not know,
>   my people do not understand.

Not a very auspicious beginning. Israel and Judah were, at
the time, very powerful kingdoms with a large wealth dispar-
ity. They also had a tendency to go to war against neighboring
kingdoms, unprovoked, in the hope of gaining more resources.
First Isaiah warned the people of Israel and Judah that God
was not pleased with the way things were going and that, if
they continued to abandon the oppressed, cheat widows, abuse

orphans, and generally pervert justice for the most vulnerable in their society, God would release a terrible vengeance on the two communities and on their land.

Neither Israel nor Judah paid much attention to First Isaiah's warnings, and God's people were attacked and ravaged first by the Assyrian Empire and then by the Babylonian Empire. Family members were intentionally split up and enslaved, rulers were imprisoned or killed, homes were burned, and the temple—God's holy resting place, built by King Solomon, and home of the ark of the covenant—was demolished.

This is where the next Isaiah figure came in. Second Isaiah wrote from chapter 40 to chapter 55 and spoke tenderly to the people who were then enslaved in Babylon. You may recognize the opening words to the Israelites in Isaiah 40:1–2:

> Comfort, O comfort my people,
>   says your God.
> Speak tenderly to Jerusalem,
>   and cry to her
> that she has served her term,
>   that her penalty is paid,
> that she has received from the LORD's hand
>   double for all her sins.

Second Isaiah was the one to announce the light at the end of the tunnel. He related God's promise to take care of the people, to make a way for them to return home and to rebuild. Second Isaiah foretold that the Persian king Cyrus would overthrow Babylon and allow the Israelites to return home, and this is exactly what happened beginning in the year 538 BCE.

Finally, in the last thirty years of the sixth century, the people of Israel and Judah began coming out of Babylon and returning to their homeland. It's during this time that Third Isaiah started writing. The final section of the book of Isaiah, beginning in chapter 56, contains his work, which tends to bounce frantically from comfort and encouragement to frustration and disapproval, like a babysitter saddled with the care of too many toddlers. This was not far from the truth, since in many ways the people of Israel had to start life all over again upon their return. Third Isaiah was the prophet sent to guide the people through the process of rebirth and rebuilding.

Back home, the Israelites were immediately stumped by the lack of a temple. Where were sacrifices supposed to take place? How and when and where should the temple be rebuilt? Who should take on the priestly duties for the people, now that many of the families who had passed the task from generation to generation had been wiped out? With the number of Israelites drastically reduced, were laws against intermarriage with other cultures still binding? Furthermore, no one knew what to do with the Israelites who had been castrated in the courts of the Babylonians and the Persians. Wasn't there a verse somewhere in the Torah that forbade them from being part of the community?

Hebrew Bible scholar Joseph Blenkinsopp tells us that "castration was not practiced in Israel, either for court and harem officials, or as a judicial punishment."[2] In contrast, Israel's neighbors—who became Assyria, Babylon, and Persia—all used castration for various purposes. Eunuchs were commonly created in order to form a group of people considered neither male nor female—people who could move easily between gendered spaces. Once Israelite and Judean captives were enslaved, many were castrated and put into service in the Babylonian courts, which provided a new problem for the Israelite community upon return. If Deuteronomy 23:1 did indeed prohibit eunuchs from entering into the assembly of the Lord, how could these marginalized people be reintegrated into the new society?

But Deuteronomy 23 didn't stop at prohibitions against eunuchs. It went on to describe each of the ethnic groups that were off-limits to Israelites when it came to marriage. Realistically, during these decades of exile many of God's people had found love and created families wherever possible. What should be done about these families now? Rebuilding a nation would hardly be feasible with the small number of "pure"

Israelite descendants left. The way to renewal appeared to be blocked at every turn by God's own law. The people needed a way forward.

Into this impossible situation, God spoke an unprecedented word of inclusion:

> Do not let the foreigner joined to the LORD say,
>   "The LORD will surely separate me from his people";
> and do not let the eunuch say,
>   "I am just a dry tree."
>
> (Isaiah 56:3)

It was hard for me to explain initially why I felt such an immediate connection to the eunuch in Isaiah's passage. In terms of cultural experience, our lives could not have been more different. I had no idea what it felt like to be taken away from your family and your home; to be enslaved; then to have your body modified against your will. But there were elements of the story of the eunuch's return to Israel that I did recognize: becoming unwelcome in your community of faith, for example.

Historically, eunuchs were keepers of the king's harem, charged with looking after the many wives that any given king might have banded together. They were trusted with this duty specifically because there was no chance that a eunuch would impregnate anyone and cause trouble with the legitimacy of the royal line. They were allowed into female-only spaces because they posed no threat to men or to their paternity. Eunuchs also acted as court advisers and were allowed into spaces specifically reserved for men, though they weren't considered men themselves. Most eunuchs were castrated prior to puberty, and so they wouldn't develop sex characteristics like facial hair or a deeper voice, meaning that they were visibly different from the people around them.

In the Babylonian and Persian Empires having groups of people outside the male/female binary was not considered a problem, but back home among the Israelites, anything that couldn't be categorized was suspect. Boundaries were the backbone of Israelite law—encoded in Exodus, Leviticus, and

Deuteronomy—and prohibitions were placed on things like clothing made of mixed fibers and fields planted with two kinds of crops. Eunuchs did not have a place in Israelite society. They were neither fish nor fowl.

In Leviticus 21:16–21, Moses is told that descendants of Aaron—those of the priestly family—must not have any physical blemish and must not have crushed testicles, if they are to be admitted to serve in the temple. This strikes all eunuchs from the list of possible clergy. Then in Deuteronomy 23:1 we see the eunuchs forbidden from "the assembly of the LORD" as well, which may have been interpreted as expulsion from places of worship, or may have been a broad stroke that ousted them from Israelite society in general. Whatever the case, eunuchs returning from exile would have found themselves in the midst of institutions that attempted to legislate them out of existence.

For transgender folks in Christian communities today, this description may be all too familiar. We still find ourselves standing on the steps of many churches wondering if we'll be allowed in. We're still denied ordination in the majority of Christian denominations, alongside our lesbian, gay, and bisexual siblings. We still face laws drafted by Christian organizations that keep us from accessing health care, employment, housing, bathrooms, and more.

The other major connection between the eunuchs of ancient times and transgender people living today is the complexity of our reproductive relationships. Though being transgender doesn't make biological children an impossibility, the process becomes far more complicated. Trans folks who choose to have specific kinds of gender-affirming surgery may have reproductive organs removed, and at that point—unless sperm or eggs have been preserved—we do find ourselves squarely in the eunuch's shoes when it comes to family planning.

In ancient Israelite society, children were not only a blessing from God; they were also your legacy. Offspring assured that you would be remembered and guaranteed a future for the community. In Genesis 15, God promised a barren Abraham and Sarah both land and children—tangible evidence of a blessing and a covenant. So it's not surprising that those who were unable to have children were in some ways considered exempt from this covenant. To live outside the covenant was to be outside the community.

The ability to produce offspring was such an intrinsic part of Israelite identity that it seemed nonnegotiable. When eunuchs experienced the physical cutting off that changed their identity, they also experienced a cutting off from the future and from their culture. Still, throughout the Bible, many women who were thought to be barren were blessed with a family and subsequently brought in from the margins of their society. Could something similar be done for the eunuch?

I was considering this problem one spring day about four months later as I walked out of the morning service at the seminary chapel. I thought about the students who had been leading the liturgy I'd just taken part in, and how many of our candidates for ordination didn't look the way the writers of the Bible might have expected them to. For one thing, the authors of the codes in Exodus, Leviticus, and Deuteronomy would have been shocked to see Gentiles reading their sacred texts— and not in the original Hebrew! Jesus' disciples might have been a bit scandalized to see women preaching. Depending on what part of his ministry you caught him in, the apostle Paul would probably have been surprised to see openly LGBTQI2A folks leading prayers and people who had been divorced distributing the elements of the Eucharist. Yet here we were, all of us, the body of Christ, commemorating Jesus' life and death and resurrection, together.

Several of the texts I'd read on Isaiah 56:1–8 were careful to point out that although verse 5 promises the eunuch a place in God's house, that doesn't necessarily point to any eunuch being allowed to become a priest. Benjamin Sommer reminds us that the passage "does not attribute priestly roles to the eunuchs or the foreigners (since they are not said to approach the altar). It merely stresses that their presence and their offerings are welcome on the holy mountain."³ Since only priests would have had permission to approach the altar, it seems that the prohibition against those that Leviticus 21 deemed "damaged" still applied in Isaiah's restoration community.

But does that mean we should observe the same tradition in our Christian communities today? After all, no seminary worth its salt would declare someone unfit for ministry based on a physical characteristic like an amputated limb, or a visual impairment, or a growth disorder—all of which would have been unacceptable to the ancient Israelite community, based on those same verses in Leviticus. (And to further underline the point, many Jewish rabbinical schools today also ordain disabled people. Leviticus 21 says that no one who's blind may hold a priestly role, and yet in 2018 Rabbi Lauren Tuchman was ordained by the Jewish Theological Seminary as the first blind female rabbi.⁴)

I began walking across campus, heading in the direction of the thick wooden doors of the library building. It dawned on me that, whether or not eunuchs and foreigners were accepted into the priesthood, Isaiah did speak an incredible word of welcome to two groups who probably never expected to be included in the new Israel. With just eight verses God had given them both an assurance of a part in Israel's future and a place within the community in their own lifetime. I had been reading an article the day before that suggested Isaiah was attempting to address the stigma against Israelites who couldn't have children. C. E. Hammock, the author of the article, explains that Israelites who did not have children were considered disloyal to the community and to God's covenant. He suggests that this may also have been the motive behind the verses that appear to criminalize sexual acts between people of the same gender. The perception of childlessness as disloyalty was almost certainly heightened during Israel's attempt to rebuild and repopulate their homeland after the huge loss of life they experienced during their captivity.

God remedied this situation by presenting the eunuch with a gift that embraced their identity as a eunuch while also providing them with a key back into Israelite society. In direct opposition to the physical and social cutting off that the eunuch had experienced, God bestowed a name that could never be cut off, a name that Hammock says would "function in the same way as children. For the eunuch, a life without offspring is a life without blessing, [which was] the same issue for Abraham in Genesis 15:2."[5]

Suddenly, as I thought about the word "blessing," and the story of Abraham and Sarah, something clicked for me. I stopped walking for a minute and stared up at the clouds moving slowly across a blue sky. What God was giving the eunuchs, through Isaiah's proclamation, was not just a place in society, and not just hope for a future. By giving the eunuchs the same kinds of gifts given to Abraham and Sarah—a name, legacy, family, acceptance, and blessing—God was consciously associating the two stories in the minds of the people. God was giving the eunuchs a story to connect to—a story that set a precedent, grounded in divine grace.

That was the story I needed to hear. As I walked into the library that day, I felt as if the pieces were finally coming together, but I wasn't sure whether the completed picture would make any difference. As it turned out, the new Israel of Isaiah's time wasn't ready to fully welcome eunuchs, despite God's words. Would the Christian communities I was a part of be any different?

I began hormone therapy in November 2014, a year after I discovered Isaiah 56. By this time I had finished my thesis, graduated from seminary, and come out to my friends and family. Some were taking it better than others.

One night when I was talking with my dad over the phone, he began to ask me about how I understood my gender identity. When we'd had conversations about these issues in the past, it always felt as if we were speaking two different languages. In some ways, I guess we were. The way I talked about gender didn't make sense to him, and the things that seemed obvious to him felt undeveloped to me. He paused at one point, and I could hear him gathering his thoughts in the silence. Finally, he said, "How do you understand being transgender, theologically?"

Nobody had ever asked me that question so blatantly before. I attempted to distill my thoughts on eunuchs in the ancient world into a couple of sentences, but I could tell by the time we hung up that things hadn't come out quite right. That night I went to bed turning his question over and over in my mind. There were so many things I wanted to say!

I wanted to tell him that through Isaiah God gave me a sense of belonging that I couldn't shake. I believed that by declaring those outside the gender binary to be acceptable, God declared me acceptable. I wanted to tell him that when I read that eunuchs would be made joyful in God's house of prayer, I found myself convinced that transgender people are meant not only to survive in Christian community, but to thrive in it.

There were several biblical texts that helped me to understand the confluence of my gender identity and my faith, but it was Isaiah 56:1–8 that helped me understand the power of a shared story. Though the eunuchs did not find themselves in exactly the same circumstances as their ancestors Abraham and Sarah, the blessing they received was similar enough to invoke that ancient memory. In the same way, my life did not mirror the Israelite eunuchs' life perfectly, but the major obstacle to community that we faced was analogous and required a similar resolution that stitched our experiences together.

It is that combination of affirmation and shared narrative that can give transgender Christians the courage to carve out a space for themselves in a global church that often ignores or actively persecutes them. To know that you belong to a God who gathers the outcasts and who commands doors to open before those sitting outside the gates: this is the kind of love that leads to liberation. God did not ask the eunuchs to pour themselves into the mold of Israel's previous societal norms, nor to bend themselves to fit by taking on specifically gendered roles in the current system. Instead, God called for a transformed community that looked like nothing the people had ever seen.

In the extraordinary months to follow, I was given several opportunities to worship with other queer Christians in communities that exemplified diversity in gender, race, class, and nationality. Each time I would look around me at the sea of faces—all different, all hopeful, all so grateful to be together—and think, "This must be something like the vision Isaiah saw. This is what it looks like to become a house of prayer for all people."

8

All the Best Disciples Are Eunuchs

During my last couple of months in seminary I started trying to find a church to join after I graduated. It would have
been weird to keep going to chapel with the other students
every day, and I really wanted to find a community that would
be openly affirming of my identity as a transgender person. I
wasn't sure how to start my search, but luckily I had a lot of
friends who were pastors! I asked around and found out about
this little Lutheran church nearby that met in different places
during different parts of the year. They'd worship outside in a
public park during the summer, and in an extra room of the
Jewish retirement home during the winter, and every month
they'd get together in a local bar and sing hymns. As a bonus,
I heard that most of the people in this little community were
artists, writers, musicians, and generally lovable weirdos—my
kind of people exactly.

After a couple of weeks of showing up, sitting in the back,
and listening quietly to some darn good preaching, I started
getting to know everyone. At the end of each service people
would take turns standing up and telling everyone else about
important things happening in their lives—good and bad.

One person would share something about their job search; a six-year-old would tell us about their recent birthday party; a shy teenager would report about a test they'd gotten an A on that week. These people cared about each other's lives, and it made me feel safe enough to share a bit of mine with them. The week before I started hormone replacement, I went up and told everyone about how excited I was for my voice to drop, and to start recognizing myself in the mirror. Everyone congratulated me, and a couple of people even found me afterward to tell me they were excited to be a part of my journey. It felt amazing.

I kept them up to date during the rest of my transition, and eventually even led an LGBTQI2A ally training session to help everyone get a handle on all those tricky bits of terminology. One day, about two years later, one of these wonderful folks came up to me and said, "Hey, remember that training you did a while ago? Well, I just wanted to say thank you because my child just came out to me this week, and I never would have known what to say if I hadn't been there for that training, and if I hadn't seen you go through your transition. It's helped our family a lot."

Of course I didn't show up to this church the first Sunday looking for a way to change anything or help anyone. I was looking for help myself! But as it turns out, when trans people are accepted into church communities, and especially when they're put into positions of leadership, they can untangle knots and understand things that cisgender folks may not be as quick to perceive.

Similarly, in the Gospel of Matthew Jesus singles out eunuchs, one of the groups of gender-expansive people of the ancient world, as an example of people uniquely gifted for discipleship in the kingdom of heaven.

> [Jesus] said to them, "Not everyone can accept this teaching, but only those to whom it is given. For there are eunuchs who have been so from birth, and there are eunuchs who have been made eunuchs by others, and there are eunuchs

who have made themselves eunuchs for the sake of the
kingdom of heaven. Let anyone accept this who can."
                                         (Matthew 19:11–12)

Lawrence Richardson is a Black trans man and a pastor who has
personally seen what happens when people with marginalized
identities are lifted up as leaders. He grew up part of the Southern Baptist Church, in a family filled with missionaries and ministers, which meant that for the first part of his life his church
community was everything. "Church was something that we just
did because it was in us to do; so it was never a decision for me
to not go to church," he laughed. When Lawrence came out
as queer in high school, though, that changed. "I didn't know
the word 'transgender,' but I knew that I was something other
than what other people thought that I was. I just wasn't able to
articulate it, so I used the label 'queer.' I came out as queer, and
that's when my family told me that I was not allowed to go back
to church because it was not consistent or compatible with the
theology of our church. So I fell outside of the religious community for the first time in my life."

Even though this was incredibly difficult for Lawrence,
it also pushed him to explore religion and faith on his own,
which allowed him to consider things that he might not have if
he'd stayed in his home church. He says,

> I started to really explore religion and spirituality, and to
> start to untangle my own identity. I started going to differ-
> ent churches and visiting different religious communities
> to see how I could connect, because I knew that there was
> God, and I knew that God was separate from the church—
> I just also longed to be part of a church community. So it
> was in college that I got connected with progressive Chris-
> tians and mainline Christian churches that were affirming
> of LGBT people.

It was a huge relief for Lawrence to realize that there were
Christian churches out there that fully welcomed and included

queer folks like him, but there was another important part of his identity that he couldn't leave out. "I grew up in Minnesota, and at the time it was very segregated, so I've always been aware of my racial identity—that was the thing that gave me community first, even before the church. When I came out as queer, I didn't receive a lot of support at first from the Black community, so that was devastating, because not only did I lose my religious community, but I lost the Black community."

But Lawrence didn't give up. He kept reaching out, sure that there must be other people like him.

It can be really difficult to find Black LGBT Christians in some spaces. When I was younger, it felt like you're lucky if you find Black people, and then to say Black gay people, and then to say Black trans people is like, wow, you're asking a lot here. It was really important for me to be able to be in spaces where I could be my whole self and not have to just be, you know, the token Black person, or just be the token trans person, or the only Christian. Because it's difficult to be who you are if there's a part of you that isn't completely accepted in a certain space. As I got older, though, and as I traveled and was able to get out of my little bubble, I started meeting people from all over the place, and I realized that my experience wasn't that rare—that there were Black Christians that also happened to be LGBT everywhere.

Lawrence experienced a call to ministry when he was twenty-one—right in the middle of this search for a new church home. He connected with a Black woman who was also a lesbian and a minister of a church, and she helped guide him through his discernment period, which in turn led him to seminary. Lawrence found the community he was longing for first in the Unity Fellowship Church Movement—a church collective where leadership and members are predominantly African American and LGBTQI2A. His time in seminary required that he take an internship. An internship with a Unity Fellowship church wasn't available, so again Lawrence cast out his net, fishing for community.

"I was looking for work in a church, and I stumbled upon the United Church of Christ in a very serendipitous way. There was a lot about the UCC that I connected with, in terms of affirming a wide range of people and having our theology be wide enough to accept us, and also wide enough to accept God. I was hired as a youth minister in a UCC church, and it became home very quickly." The UCC gave Lawrence the new community he'd been looking for, and also gave him the support he needed when he came out as transgender a couple of years later. There's no doubt in his mind now about where he belongs and where he's called to work. There was a pause in our conversation while he did a little mental math, and then he said, happily, "I've been serving at different churches in the UCC now for ten years!"

Lawrence's quest for a new community isn't unusual among transgender Christians; many find themselves kicked out of their home church after coming out. The search for a new faith community can be exhausting, and too often it feels as if you have to sell the church on the idea of keeping you around. It might seem daunting to a congregation to have to learn about pronouns, or to designate a bathroom gender-neutral, or to have difficult conversations about what it means to affirm LGBTQI2A identities. But transgender people are not a burden for Christianity, or for the church. They come bearing gifts!

Jesus' affirmation of eunuchs' value to the kingdom in Matthew 19:11–12 comes immediately after his teaching on divorce, in which he says no two people should be divorced except in cases of unchastity. The disciples respond, "Well, then it's better not to get married, so you don't take the chance that you might divorce!" Because Jesus' words about eunuchs come directly after this, many biblical scholars have argued that Jesus is referring here not to literal eunuchs, but to some people choosing to be abstinent or celibate.[1] Another group of theologians suggest that Jesus reclaims the eunuch as a positive metaphor for celibacy because Jesus and his disciples had been called eunuchs in a derogatory sense, since some weren't married.[2]

But how and when did we decide that Jesus wasn't speaking literally? He may have been speaking about people who were born with differences of sex development, in the case of intersex folks; about people who had been castrated against their will, as many eunuchs were in biblical times; and about people who had chosen to live their lives as the gender they were, rather than as their assigned sex.

As it turns out, some early Christians did take these verses at face value, either in their own lives or in their teachings, and did choose either to castrate themselves or to live outside the boundaries of their assigned sex, or both. Famous people who took these verses literally include Valentinus, Julius Cassianus, Basilides, Leontios of Antiochia, Melito the Eunuch, Hilarión, Marcarius the Egyptian, and, of course, Origen.[3] If those names don't ring any bells for you, though, don't worry. The long and the short of it is that some early Christians did exactly what Jesus hinted at here, and the practice of castration as a form of religious devotion became common enough that when the Council of Nicaea was called in 325 CE, the very first rule they made barred anyone who had willingly been castrated from becoming a clergyperson.[4]

After the council, leaders in the church also decided that the literal reading wasn't very convert-friendly. As Jesus discovered when he confronted the rich young ruler in this same chapter of Matthew, it's pretty hard to win people over to a new system of beliefs by beginning, "Hey, you know all that money and power you have? Give it all up, and you can join us!" In the same way, early bishops realized they weren't likely to convince any of the nobility to become Christians if castration was included anywhere in the recommended practices. In order to make things a little less scary for people with a lot to lose, "they drew from Middle Platonic and Stoic moral sources and contemporary medical theories that advocated abstinence as a means of preserving and assuring masculinity," and "by turning to an allegorical reading of the text, could offer their male converts the comfort of a less threatening but nevertheless rigorous practice of masculinity."[5] This is when people started tying the Matthew 19:11–12 text to the concept of celibacy, rather than to the lives of eunuchs in Jesus' time.

Theologically and theoretically, the concept of ritual castration for the sake of the kingdom of heaven made a kind of sense for the men of the ancient world. We know that men living in the Roman Empire around the time of Jesus held more power than any other citizens, and indeed that free men were the only citizens, since men could own property and engage in politics, while women, children, and enslaved people were all considered inferior. The problem with always being at the top of the food chain, though, is that you run the risk of falling off. As New Testament scholar J. David Hester put it,

> Men were constantly threatened with the potential of becoming weak through a variety of activities: whether by bathing too much, or by eating the wrong foods, or by engaging in too much sex, by wearing the wrong clothing, even by taking too much enjoyment in unmanly tasks. . . . In this setting eunuchs were the nightmare embodiment of men's worst fears. Eunuchs were a monstrous identity formation, a source of sex-gender confusion.[6]

By making themselves eunuchs, Christian men in the early church were intentionally giving up the power they held as men in their culture. They were taking an action with the direct consequences of placing themselves lower in the social hierarchy. But what are Jesus' final words in Matthew 19? He promises that "many who are first will be last, and the last will be first."

Norwegian theologian Halvor Moxnes sums up this reverse when he asks,

> Is the Kingdom of Heaven in Jesus' preaching a confirmation of the existing ontological fields of sex and gender? Is it not rather a reversal, an opening up of fields? Matthew's gospel itself appears to suggest as much, when it combines the eunuch saying with the story of how Jesus reverses the position of children (19:13–15): "Let the children come to me, and do not hinder them, for to such belongs the kingdom of heaven."[7]

Here Jesus says that it's not the adult males who are the keepers of the kingdom. It's the children, the ones with no social
power at all. In the upside-down world of the kingdom, giving
up riches and power, humbling yourself, and taking a seat at
the foot of the table is just good sense.

While all Christians are indeed called to become a part of the
topsy-turvy kingdom, Jesus says this teaching about eunuchs is
not for everyone. Not every Christian is born intersex, has their
body changed without their consent, or feels the call to a life
outside the gender norms of their time. But some people do
experience this call to a life in which they can open themselves
to God and to others, fully; a life in which they give up the
social power they would have had as a cisgender person; a life
in which they leave stability and power behind to follow Jesus
exactly as they are.

When I asked Lawrence what he'd learned about discipleship as a trans person, he looked serious for a moment. Then
he said, "When I think about the sexual minorities or gender
minorities who Jesus was speaking about here, yes, I believe
they have something to teach society about courage, because
they have to overcome so much to just live from day to day."

Whether you were a eunuch in New Testament times or a
transgender person living today, you're living in a culture that
would prefer that you hide yourself and keep your head down,
rather than choose to live a radically honest life. For trans
Christians like Lawrence who are called to ministry, the call to
recognize your own identity can feel eerily similar. "Some of us
choose to be authentic and choose to be real, and choose to follow our call, either as it relates to the church or to our gender
identity," he explained. "And for some of us . . . well, it's like
Moses. Even if we didn't want to follow, we have no choice.
The call in our souls is just that loud. I'm listening to the call
of God in my life, and I'm going to follow that call wherever it
leads me, even if that leads me to death, and that's not a message that mainstream society can take."

Justin Sabia-Tanis, another pastor and hugely influential trans theologian, has felt this same connection between the calling to ministry and the calling to exploration of his gender identity. He explains it this way: "I believe that God called me out on this journey of gender to learn particular things and to experience the world in a broader way. I was called to trust God and step out into uncharted territory to learn about myself and about who and what God has called me to be. Calling is about what we are to do and about who we are to be, as well as who we will become."[8]

Transgender Christians also give the church a model for authenticity and a new vision of unconditional love. "When you come out as trans, you are basically saying, 'Whether my family, my job, my friends accept me or not, I'm going to live my life as truly as I possibly can,'" Lawrence said. "And the message of the church usually is: you must change and conform and convert before the church will embrace you, love you, and accept you." But while he agreed that churches should hold to their theological assertions, he suggested that there's a difference between statements of belief as a community, and the practice of requiring individuals to agree with a dogma or creed first, before they can be welcomed, loved, or respected. "I feel like church has become a place where those requirements either preclude love from happening, or limit how love is shown. What would the church be like if we just accepted people for who and how they were, and loved them there first, before anything else?"

When a church is trans-affirming, transgender Christians can show up as themselves, unapologetically. By doing that, they show everyone else in the congregation that it's all right to bring their whole selves into the community, that nobody has to "fake it 'til you make it" as a perfect Christian. This kind of authenticity is especially important to younger people, who often see the church as hypocritical and believe that being a churchgoing Christian means that you put on your fake smile alongside your Sunday suit. But once we tell our stories and let ourselves be seen—flaws and all, sins and all, full of beauty and sadness and fear and courage and joy—then we can be Christians who ask for forgiveness, who walk humbly with God, and who love our neighbors as ourselves.

Throughout the Gospels Jesus never once heals a eunuch or uses eunuchs as a negative example. As J. David Hester points out,

> There is absolutely no suggestion that to be a eunuch is to be someone who is in any way in need of "fixing," "healing" or "reintegrating" into society. Jesus heals the blind, the paralyzed, the possessed, the fevered, the leprous, the hemorrhaging, even the dead, in every case restoring them to full societal membership. In the case of the eunuch, however, there is no implication whatsoever of "illness" or social "deformity" in need of restoration. Instead, the eunuch is held up as the model to follow.[9]

Whether you believe Jesus was advocating for castration, for celibacy, or for something else entirely in Matthew 19, the fact that he uses eunuchs as a positive example is huge. As we saw in chapter 4, the rabbis who wrote and collected Israelite law near the time of Jesus recognized the existence of intersex people, and so it makes sense to believe Jesus would have known of people who fell outside the gender binaries as well. Furthermore, his statement in Matthew 19 suggests that he did not see them as broken or as morally corrupt. He saw them as people with a variety of experiences and as people with something important to teach the world about God's kingdom.

More than that, when Jesus lifts up the eunuch as an example for the disciples and for Christians everywhere, he doesn't just say that people who are already eunuchs can be part of the kingdom of heaven. He says that the desire for God's kingdom can sometimes lead to an identity that falls outside the binary.[10] This complicates some Christians' belief that God wants all of us to be cisgender and endosex, and that the binary itself is required or natural.

The fact is that when God calls us to something, it's always a call to move out of bounds. When ministers are called, they're called out of the secular life they knew and into a new relationship with God and others. When transgender Christians are called, they're called to move outside of the gender binary our society values and into a more challenging and yet stronger and more compassionate relationship with God and others. Alongside our spiritual ancestors the eunuchs, transgender Christians are both transforming others and transformed themselves.

As Lawrence so succinctly put it, "I really feel strongly about the fact that the kingdom of heaven is not some far-off place, but it's something that is begun here and now. I believe the only way it can be achieved is if we go against the grain that says we must be just like everybody else, and instead seek God and ask God for direction to be whatever God is calling us to be. Sometimes God calls us to be something unexpected."

9

Nothing Can Prevent Me

Between 2015 and 2018 I made more than one hundred videos on being transgender and Christian and posted them on YouTube. In the beginning it was just a project to make sure I was putting my seminary degree to good use while I worked an unrelated day job, and I expected some pushback. As a general rule, people are more willing to be cruel online, where they can choose to hide behind an anonymous avatar, and I assumed I'd get some rude comments. What I didn't expect was the number of people who would leave extensive diatribes accusing me of not being a "real Christian." For many people, this "real Christian" metric seems to be based on whether or not you agree with their particular interpretations of Scripture or church dogma. We Christians like to do this to each other a lot; we love to point at the person on the other side of the street who looks at the Bible through a different lens, or comes to a different conclusion about its meaning, and declare them heretics.

This kind of behavior is written in our history. In 1520 CE Martin Luther, the founder of the Protestant Reformation, was labeled a heretic for questioning the Catholic Church's

practices regarding the remission of sins. Before that, the
emperor Constantine had to convene a council of around
three hundred bishops in the year 325 CE to decide the official
church position on the Trinity, because there were just too
many gosh-darn heretics running around confusing people!
We find people excommunicating each other and disagree-
ing about the validity of other people's faith in Scripture too,
especially in Paul's Letter to the Galatians and in the Acts of
the Apostles. From what we understand about these texts, the
apostle Paul, Simon Peter, and Jesus' brother James disagreed
about which people should be allowed to be baptized and
become Christians. Some thought that only Jews who wanted
to follow Jesus should be able to convert, while others thought
that Gentiles (non-Jews) should be able to be baptized as well.
These questions were pressing, because, even as the debates
raged in Jerusalem and through letters back and forth across
the Roman world, followers of Jesus were out spreading the
gospel without any official guidelines!

In Acts 8 we find the story of one of these traveling apostles,
a man named Philip, who was teaching in Samaria before he
heard a call from God: "Then an angel of the Lord said to
Philip, 'Get up and go toward the south to the road that goes
down from Jerusalem to Gaza.' (This is a wilderness road.)
So he got up and went. Now there was an Ethiopian eunuch,
a court official of the Candace, queen of the Ethiopians, in
charge of her entire treasury. He had come to Jerusalem to
worship" (Acts 8:26–27).

We've talked about eunuchs already, and how they existed
outside of the accepted gender roles and expectations of their
time, but the eunuch we meet in Acts 8 held several other identities that might have been unfamiliar to Philip. For instance,
the eunuch was from Ethiopia—a place that was considered
"the ends of the earth" in that day and was a military threat
to the Roman Empire.[1] Although their concepts of race and
ethnicity were different from ours today, what's certain is that
the eunuch was an African person who therefore probably had
slightly darker skin and different features from Philip, who was

from the Israelite people of the southeastern Mediterranean. This may have been Philip's first time meeting someone so different from himself, especially while in his position as an evangelist authorized by the fledgling church.

Another thing that marked the Ethiopian eunuch as an outsider was his status as not-quite-Jewish and not-quite-Gentile. It's made clear in the text that he was not born Jewish, but the story never calls him a Gentile either. Additionally, it's the baptism of the clearly categorized Gentile Cornelius in Acts 10 that begins the conversation about Gentile inclusion in the early church. The eunuch may have been what the Bible calls "a God-fearer," which essentially means a person who subscribed to the beliefs of the Jewish people despite not having been born among them. This placed him in between or outside of the established categories when it came to the Jew/Gentile binary of the times. If the eunuch hadn't already been excluded from temple worship because of his status as a eunuch (since the welcome in Isaiah 56 was never implemented), he would have been kept out of the inner sanctums because he was neither a Jew by birth nor a full convert.

Lastly, despite being put in a place of authority, the eunuch may have been an enslaved or formerly enslaved person, since it would have been unusual (though not unheard of) for a free person to be castrated. In either case, the eunuch's position as servant to the queen of Ethiopia would have meant that he didn't have total autonomy. And yet, he had the resources to travel to Jerusalem and to afford what would have been a fairly costly scroll of Isaiah. This means that the eunuch of Acts 8, whose name we never learn, was both impossible to categorize and outside the boundaries of gender, race, class, and religion—a quadruple threat.[2]

The author of Acts 8 obviously doesn't want us to miss out on these middle-ground positions in the story, because he goes out of his way to highlight the fact that it all took place on a wilderness road, calling us to remember that the wilderness has been the no-man's-land for the Israelite people for hundreds of years. Trans biblical scholar Justin Sabia-Tanis believes that "the fact that the eunuch encounters Philip in the midst of all of these 'between' spaces affirms the workings of God outside of human boundaries and conventions." Furthermore, it may be that this whole meeting "is made possible in part by the unusualness of the space and time in which they encounter one another."[3] Had Philip and the eunuch met in another place—such as near the temple in Jerusalem—would the religious gatekeepers of the day have allowed them to have the deep conversation we're about to explore? How do religious gatekeepers affect the lives of outsiders today?

The wilderness is often a familiar space for transgender Christians. It's a space that holds our doubts and our questions, and a place where we can pitch our tents when all other doors have been closed to us. It's a place in between certainties—where we go when we realize we can't stay in the past anymore, but we're also not sure how to walk into the future.

Rev. Nicole Garcia spent a lot of her life in the wilderness. "Growing up, I knew I didn't quite fit the role that everyone else wanted me to fit," she told me. "I was the oldest son and the oldest grandson on my mother's side, so I was given kind of a special place in the family, and there were certain expectations." As the oldest son in a Catholic Latine* family, Nicole experienced pressure to play sports, to date girls, and to radiate a machismo that just didn't come naturally to her. "I didn't have a girlfriend until college—not until my junior year. I had never really been interested in dating at all because I had feelings towards men, but it was not permissible."

Instead of chasing girls and playing football, Nicole spent her time at church. "I was a very good Catholic boy. I always went to mass two or three times a week. I was very involved in the church. At one point I sat on the congregational council! And so when I was eighteen I discerned a call: I wanted to be a priest! I went to my parents and told them of my desire, and

---

* "Latine" is a gender-neutral version of "Latino" or "Latina" and is increasingly being used in Spanish-speaking communities to make language more inclusive! Of course the -o and -a word endings are still used in places where words refer to only one gender, but the -e endings can be used for mixed-gender and non-gendered contexts. Learn more at www.callmelatine.com.

my mom and my grandmother just said no. 'You cannot do that. You have to get married, and you have to have kids.'"

This was a blow that sent Nicole back to the drawing board. She tried to imagine herself doing something else—having some other career outside the church. She decided to apply to graduate school, but after getting in and studying for a couple of years, she realized she was lost. "I would go clubbing, stay out all night, and I started drinking a lot. And in the middle of all that, as I was trying to discern what I was going to do with my life and deciding to leave graduate school, I also had a crisis of faith. I had prayed so hard to God to try and fix me. I knew I didn't fit into the roles that I was supposed to fit into." Nicole felt as if God had abandoned her and ignored her prayer requests to stop being attracted to men, and to stop secretly wearing feminine clothing, which she'd done since she was a kid.

But it wasn't just God's silence that damaged Nicole's faith. She was also coming to understand more about the history of the Catholic Church.

> Being Hispanic, I recognized that the Catholic Church had come and colonized the New World. I'm of mixed race— my mother's family is traced back to the *conquistadores*, and on my maternal grandmother's side we are also Pueblo Indians, so we're a mixture of the Southwest. When I was in college, I took a lot of Chicano studies classes, and it really emphasized the fact that we are a colonized people—that my people are from New Mexico, and that the border moved over us. My ancestors became citizens of the United States because of the Treaty of [Guadalupe] Hidalgo in 1848. So because of what I knew the church did to my people, I could believe in God, but I couldn't believe in the church.

With her faith damaged and her life feeling directionless, it wasn't long until Nicole came to a breaking point.

"By 1989 I ended up living in the back of one of my cousin's trailers and praying to God in detox. I realized my life had gone terribly, terribly wrong. That's when I first went to AA," she explained. Alcoholics Anonymous helped Nicole stop drinking, and it also provided her with a community in which she

could talk about God and faith without the cultural baggage
that accompanied Catholicism or a formal church structure.
"In AA you have to recognize that there's a higher power; that's
part of the program. So when I entered AA, I realized I could
believe in God—as long as we kept our distance. He didn't
mess with me, I didn't mess with him." Nicole found a way to
survive, but she was still wandering in the wilderness.

There are many ways to find a path home when you're lost.
If you're good with directions, you can pick up a map or use
a compass; if you're not, you can always pull out your smart
phone. But what if those items aren't available? In that case you
might ask somebody for directions or find a person who can
guide you home personally. This is exactly what the Ethiopian
eunuch chose to do when he met Philip.

> [The eunuch] was returning home; seated in his chariot,
> he was reading the prophet Isaiah. Then the Spirit said
> to Philip, "Go over to this chariot and join it." So Philip
> ran up to it and heard him reading the prophet Isaiah. He
> asked, "Do you understand what you are reading?" He
> replied, "How can I, unless someone guides me?" And he
> invited Philip to get in and sit beside him.
>
> (Acts 8:28–31)

When I first started exploring this passage, this question—
"How can I understand unless someone guides me?"—seemed
strange, and even unnecessary. In my spiritual upbringing I'd
always been taught that every person can read the Bible and
learn something from it all by themselves. So why should the
eunuch have to ask for help? It was only later that I recognized the desperation in his words. This person had just traveled all the way from Ethiopia to Jerusalem to worship at the
temple, only to find gates and laws barring his way. He'd had
to turn around and head home, and it doesn't take much
imagination to feel the way he probably felt—frustrated, dis-
appointed, confused, rejected, and alone. He'd already tried
reading Scripture for himself, and things hadn't panned out.

It's easy to imagine him wondering what he'd done wrong, or what part of Scripture he'd misunderstood. So when Philip showed up on the road and asked if the eunuch knew what this passage is all about, of course he jumped at the chance to get some answers!

After Nicole came out of her downward spiral, she was also in need of some help, but she had no idea how to ask for it. Because transgender people didn't exist much in popular media in the 1990s (and when they did, they were depicted as mentally ill, or as tragic figures facing inevitable death from violence or HIV/AIDS), Nicole couldn't imagine what life as a transgender woman would look like. In fact, the word "transgender" hadn't even made it into her lexicon, and at the time the closest word she had for her identity was "crossdresser."*

While she didn't want the life her family expected her to have, there just didn't seem to be any alternative. She ended up meeting a woman she cared about, and they got married the next year. She also took up a job in law enforcement and corrections, which helped give her some "macho cred." While she was working as a correctional officer in a men's prison, she found people who she thought could teach her a thing or two:

> There was a former marine gunnery sergeant who took me under his wing and taught me how to be an officer—how to walk, how to talk, how to get the cooperation of individuals who didn't want to cooperate with me. I learned how to beat people up. I learned how to be a man. I was relatively good at it! I got a lot of respect, and I was promoted within a couple of years. The problem was that putting on the uniform was putting on a facade. I was so angry all the time. When I took off that uniform it was just so hard to relax and be who I was, so I started drinking again.

*The difference between these two terms has to do with gender identity versus gender expression. A transgender person has a gender identity that conflicts with their sex assigned at birth, and this conflict is persistent. Someone who identifies as a crossdresser, on the other hand, still identifies as their sex assigned at birth. They just enjoy playing with clothing, accessories, and hair styles that are associated with another gender.

Nicole was able to keep up this act for five years as a correctional officer before it became too much, and she decided to become a parole officer instead, which allowed her to set down some of the anger she'd had to arm herself with. The foundation of her marriage also began to crumble during this time, and after eight years Nicole and her wife decided to divorce. After spending so long trying to be who everyone else wanted her to be, life was starting to come apart at the seams again.

One night, two weeks after she moved out of the house she'd shared with her wife, Nicole was sitting in her new living room with a pint of whisky and a loaded gun. She had tried to do everything that was expected of her, and nothing had worked. She felt as if she was out of options. "I couldn't figure out why I walked away from everything that I was supposed to have," she sighed. "But I decided I couldn't take my own life, and that's when I came back to Jesus."

"How did it happen?" I asked. "What did 'coming back to Jesus' look like for you?"

Nicole laughed. "Well, it wasn't one of those 'oh please, Jesus! Jesus, help me!' moments. It was more like 'OK, you big SOB, if I'm going to come back to you, you gotta ante up this time. Something's got to change.'"

I laughed with her for a minute. I'd never heard of somebody coming back to God with a demand! But of course there's quite a bit of precedent in Scripture for a request like Nicole's. Psalm 44 is a great example. The psalmist presents their case to God, pointing out that the people had done everything God had asked, but terrible things had still happened. The psalmist cries out to God, saying, "Awake, Lord! Why do you sleep? Rouse yourself! Do not reject us forever. Why do you hide your face and forget our misery and oppression?" (Ps. 44:23–24 NIV). Nicole was, in effect, saying the same thing—that she had done everything she had been asked to do, and now it was God's turn. She was asking God to awake and breathe some life into the situation.

Somehow, that breath showed up. "A couple of days later I'm sitting at my computer and a message comes in from the

Colorado State Employee Assistance Program, saying that if you're depressed or suicidal or abusing substances, give us a call and you get six free sessions with a psychologist. And I thought, 'Wow, God, you work quick!'"

Nicole was in therapy later that very same week, and her psychologist was able to help her deal with the depression she had been experiencing. Over time she also opened up about the fact that she often dressed in feminine clothes at home. The therapist referred her to the Gender Identity Center of Colorado and to a support group for crossdressers. That group in turn referred her to a conference on gender diversity, and there she finally found the guidance she'd been looking for all along. "I walked into this conference and I found a couple of hundred people who were just like me! I was amazed. It was incredible," Nicole gushed.

Almost by accident, Nicole decided to go to a workshop on transgender people and medical transition. She was up early on the second morning of the conference, and she couldn't find any of her new acquaintances. "I thought, 'OK, this workshop doesn't have anything to do with me, but I don't want to sit in the lobby by myself.' So I went to the workshop and I heard my story. Everything they said was so familiar! And as I'm sitting there in that workshop, I finally realized that I was Nicole. I was a woman. It just became crystal clear, and a huge weight was lifted off my shoulders."

The educators and other trans folks at the conference gave Nicole language and clarification for something she'd always felt to be true, but beyond that they gave her a community. Nicole made a friend there whom she would keep in touch with for years to come.

One of the trans women I met at that first conference was also a police officer, and so there were a couple of things we had in common. We would talk almost daily for a while. I told her about my faith being reawakened and how God had dragged me to this conference, and that I wanted to find a church, but I knew I couldn't go back to the Catholic

Church. She told me about this wonderful open and welcoming Lutheran church. I initially said no, because being
a good former Roman Catholic, I couldn't go to the church
of a heretical, excommunicated priest! But after the third
time she invited me, I thought, "Maybe God is trying to
tell me something." So I ended up walking into St. Paul's
Lutheran Church in downtown Denver, and the people
were incredible. They were warm, they were welcoming,
and they asked me if I liked the service. The thing about St.
Paul's is they celebrate high church, so it was very Catholic,
and I knew all the words. The only thing they didn't do was
kneel, and I could live without kneeling!

So Nicole was able to find the people who could guide her
home and help her understand what God was doing in her life.
In October 2003, after going through a new members' class
that dove deep into Luther's catechism and kickstarted her love
of Lutheran theology, she officially became a member of St.
Paul's Church. When I asked her how she knew that she was
really and truly accepted as a member of the church, she joked,
"You know you're a part of a church when you're asked to be
part of a committee. I was asked to be part of the Reconciling
in Christ committee soon after I joined!"

Seeing ourselves in Scripture can be a tricky business. While
we want the text to speak to us and our lives, we shouldn't put
our own biases and modern ideas into the writers' mouths, or
assume that the biblical authors lived and thought just as we
do. People have been toeing this line as long as sacred texts
have existed, and it's heartening to see the eunuch in Acts 8
struggling with the very same problem. Fortunately God
placed Philip right in the eunuch's path so that they could try
to work it out together.

Now the passage of the scripture that [the eunuch] was
reading was this:

"Like a sheep he was led to the slaughter,
    and like a lamb silent before its shearer,

so he does not open his mouth.
In his humiliation justice was denied him.
Who can describe his generation?
For his life is taken away from the earth."

The eunuch asked Philip, "About whom, may I ask you,
does the prophet say this, about himself or about someone
else?" Then Philip began to speak, and starting with this
scripture, he proclaimed to him the good news about Jesus.
(Acts 8:32–35)

The passage that Philip and the eunuch read together is
from Isaiah 53:7–8, from what has commonly been called a
Suffering Servant song. In Christian circles this text has historically been understood as a prophecy about Jesus, and how
Jesus would be crucified and suffer for the sake of humanity,
even though he himself was sinless. When the eunuch read the
passage, though, he didn't read it through that lens, because
he had never heard of Jesus, and so he asked Philip whom the
passage was referring to.

The question was important to the eunuch, possibly because
he identified so strongly with the character Isaiah was describing. The eunuch too had experienced humiliation, specifically
in the form of castration if it was done without his consent,
and possibly also in the form of slavery. He had been denied
justice as someone whom God invited to worship in the temple, but who was nevertheless barred by human gatekeepers.
He must have been asking himself if somehow this passage was
about people like him. If it was, that meant that he held a place
in the community he so desperately wanted to be accepted
into! As Rev. Broderick Greer pointed out in his sermon on
this text, given to the 2016 conference of the Gay Christian
Network (now Q Christian Fellowship), the eunuch was not
asking these questions because he had a vague interest. No,
the eunuch was poring over Scripture and teasing out answers
because he had to in order to survive as a gender-expansive,
racially marginalized, royally subjugated person outside the
bounds of the faith he sought to join.

Theology as a form of survival is exactly why transgender people, and particularly trans people of color, find themselves drawn into the story of the Ethiopian eunuch. Nicole saw herself in the eunuch in the same way the eunuch saw himself in the Suffering Servant. Trans people experience humiliation when we're outed without our permission, when we're kicked out of our homes, when we're accused of being dangerous to children and cisgender women, and when we're dismissed as mentally ill. We are denied justice when we're fired from our jobs because of our gender identity, when laws are made to keep us out of public bathroom facilities, when trans women are profiled as sex workers, and when religious gatekeepers deny trans Christians the ability to join with other people of faith in praising God. Worst of all, we find ourselves like those sheep led to slaughter, as the lives of Black transgender women and other trans people of color are violently taken from this earth.

When I asked Nicole about connecting with the story of the Suffering Servant, she made a point I hadn't thought of before. "I consider Acts 8:26–40 crucial to my identity as a transgender woman of color," she explained,

> but I can't say I've suffered as much as many of my sisters. I'm extremely well educated. I have a roof over my head and food in front of me. But the way our society has developed, there are people who are marginalized. People who aren't given the opportunities that I had. I think they may feel like they're suffering, but really, they're being oppressed. There's a difference between suffering willingly, like Jesus did, and suffering at the hands of other people without any choice in the matter. Christ accepted our sins. He took them on himself and he suffered because he chose to suffer, whereas so many people now who are dying and being murdered aren't choosing that. It is thrust upon them.

When we see ourselves in the story of the Ethiopian eunuch— and by extension, the story of the Suffering Servant—we have to remember that we are not told to suffer for suffering's sake, or to let ourselves be crushed by injustice because suffering somehow gets us closer to God. Instead, God decides to move in our direction by choosing to experience suffering alongside us. All the while we're experiencing oppression, God is there, and it's Jesus who's seeing himself in our story.

Finally, after the eunuch hears the gospel and dives deep into Scripture with Philip, the hopeful outsider asks the most important question yet:

> As they were going along the road, they came to some water; and the eunuch said, "Look, here is water! What is to prevent me from being baptized?" He commanded the chariot to stop, and both of them, Philip and the eunuch, went down into the water, and Philip baptized him. When they came up out of the water, the Spirit of the Lord snatched Philip away; the eunuch saw him no more, and went on his way rejoicing.
>
> (Acts 8:36–39)

This is Nicole's favorite part of the story. "This is the whole point!" she said enthusiastically. "Inclusion is not up to us. It's up to Christ. When the eunuch saw the water and heard the Word about Jesus Christ, and he said, 'What's to keep me from being baptized?' Philip didn't say, 'Wait a second, let's look at the law.' Philip said, 'Stop the chariot, you have heard the Good News, you have been called to be a disciple of Christ. You shall be baptized.'"

Justin Sabia-Tanis agrees in his reading of the text, pointing out that the eunuch "brings the particularity of his gender to his encounter with Philip and ultimately to his relationship with God. . . . He is not baptized in spite of being a eunuch or after a lengthy session of apologetics explaining his gender to Philip, but simply at the point at which they passed a body of water."[4] So how did Philip decide that nothing—not race or nationality or gender or status or his physical anatomy or previous beliefs—could prevent the eunuch from becoming part of the body of Christ? Well, probably because God gave him some pretty clear signs. First, in verse 26 he was told by an angel to go out to this road, and then in verse 29 the Holy Spirit told him to get into the chariot with the eunuch. This must have meant that God wanted Philip to meet with the eunuch for a particular purpose, and Philip must have come to the conclusion that his commission in this situation was the same one Jesus had given all the disciples in Matthew 28:19: "Go therefore and make disciples of all nations, baptizing them in the name of the Father and of the Son and of the Holy Spirit." This was confirmed when, right after the eunuch's baptism, Philip was snatched away by the Spirit, as if to say, "All right, that's what we needed! All finished here!"

For the eunuch this encounter ends in incredible, nearly unbelievable joy. But despite the inner transformation that baptism brings, some things stay the same. For instance, the eunuch is still a eunuch; baptism did not change his physical body or anything about his gender. None of the things that made him an outsider in the first place have been changed or "fixed." The author of Acts 8 may be giving us a little hint to that effect when he writes that the eunuch "went on his way," continuing on the same path he'd been on when Philip first found him.

We don't know what happened to the Ethiopian eunuch after his encounter with the Holy Spirit and with Philip, but we do know something about the way this story has affected others. Today, the Ethiopian Orthodox Church traces their legacy as one of the oldest Christian churches on the continent to his testimony. For Nicole, the encouragement found in the eunuch's story gave her the strength to claim the calling she had had since she was a child:

> In 2007 I got up in front of the Rocky Mountain Synod Assembly for the Evangelical Lutheran Church in America and made a bold statement about being a transgender Latina of faith, and I cited Acts 8 as part of why I belong in the church. I was noticed by the regional coordinator of Lutherans Concerned—the LGBT affirming organization for the ELCA—and we had a wonderful talk for about an hour.

Two weeks later I got a phone call from the coordinator, and they asked me to share my story with other churches.

Nicole continued to work with Lutherans Concerned, now called ReconcilingWorks, and to visit and speak with churches who wanted to know more about how to support LGBTQI2A people in their community. "In 2008 I was elected to the board of directors as the transgender representative. I was flown around the country over the next couple of years to give speeches and give talks and do a lot of workshops. Sharing my story—and getting to hear the stories of others—really helped to solidify who I was as a child of God."

But Nicole didn't stop there. After spending so much time talking about theology and the Bible with other people, she decided that she wanted some more formal training, but she wasn't sure how to go about getting it. Then, during a regular midweek service at her home church, the Holy Spirit struck again. "One Thursday morning I went to services at St. Paul's. During communion I watched Pastor Kevin raising the host above his head and saying the words of institution, and I was just like, 'That's where I need to be! I have to be a pastor! I have to be ordained!' So I told Kevin right afterward that I needed to be a pastor, and he said, 'Yes! Yes, you do!'"

Rev. Nicole Garcia was ordained in 2018 as the first queer, transgender Latina pastor in the Evangelical Lutheran Church in America. Today she's working as a counselor, as an activist, and as the clergywoman she's always been called to be. When we talked about how Acts 8:26–40 affects her ministry, she pointed out that this story contains a biblical imperative for Christians:

An angel sends Philip down the road and the Spirit commanded him to get into the chariot. God isn't just suggesting these things; God is saying, "Go do it." That's what we must do. We must spread the Word and minister to people without our human biases getting in the way. We must meet people where they are. We have to recognize that the Gospel is not just for one type of person—this tremendous gift of grace has been given to all the world.

In a way, the story of Philip and the Ethiopian eunuch is a story about two conversions. The eunuch may be the one who gets baptized, but Philip is the person who has to change his metric for who's in and who's out. Even though this story is two thousand years old, a third conversion is still taking place: will the church eventually realize that when God's love overpowers all human distinctions, nothing can prevent us from full inclusion?

10

Even Jesus Had a Body

During my early college years I remember at one point coming across a quote that was credited to C. S. Lewis, though I now know it was misattributed.[1] "You don't have a soul. You are a soul. You have a body." I loved this idea when I first heard it, and because I wasn't yet familiar with any theology concerning my body, I grabbed onto it like a life raft. Of course! This must be why I feel so uncomfortable in this meatsack I'm forced to wear! My body is just a crummy old shell for the real me: the soul. As someone experiencing gender dysphoria, I found that this explanation gave me a reason for the discomfort I was experiencing.

But, as it turns out, there are quite a few problems with this idea. First and foremost, there's no biblical backing for it. As we saw in Genesis 1, the Hebrew people didn't think about humans as divided beings. We are made in the image of God, and that image is woven throughout our entire existence. There are the hundreds of verses that tell us that our bodies are important to God—from the Levitical codes that talk about what we should and shouldn't do with our bodies, to the concern Jesus has for the bodies of people he meets, feeds, and heals throughout his ministry.

In the letters of the New Testament we do see some conflict between our bodies and other parts of us, especially in Romans, Galatians, and Ephesians, where Paul sets up a flesh vs. spirit dichotomy, but this way of thinking came from Greek philosophy, not from Scripture.[2] Take Romans 8:5, for instance: "For those who live according to the flesh set their minds on the things of the flesh, but those who live according to the Spirit set their minds on the things of the Spirit." Paul is clearly getting at something true here by saying that what we want to do is not always what we should do, and that we should set our minds on what God wants. But by using "flesh" as a catchall for bad things and "spirit" as a category for good, he sets us up to think that our physical bodies are intrinsically sinful and bad—which just doesn't hold up when we look at the rest of the Bible.

Many trans Christians find themselves asking questions about the connections between their body and their faith; so let's take a look at some of these other body passages in Scripture through the lens of one person's story.

Asher O'Callaghan grew up in Littleton, Colorado, as part of the Church of Christ—not to be confused with the United Church of Christ, a progressive and LGBTQI2A-affirming denomination. Asher described his home church as conservative and fundamentalist: "I grew up with a good dose of fire and brimstone and hell. And I was just a sensitive kid, so the hellfire thing didn't go over well for me. I always had a feeling that I was going to hell, and that resulted in a lot of sleep issues, and just a lot of fear and guilt and shame. So religion sort of became this guilt-ridden, duty-driven thing for me."

Even though Asher didn't come out as bisexual until high school, and then as transgender after college, he still felt the internal sense of difference that so many LGBTQI2A people experience during their youth. That scared him, because he knew his church's position on homosexuality, and his fear grew even deeper. "I didn't love God. I was just terrified and wanted to appease God. I actually remember thinking that in middle school, coming to realize, the first commandment Jesus gives is to love God, . . . so I'm screwed! Because I can do all of this stuff for God, or at least I can try, but loving God? I'm too scared. I don't know how to do that."

When he reached middle school, Asher decided to get baptized. "Churches of Christ have believer baptism, and most folks get baptized around middle school, because that's kind of the time when you go off of your parents' fire insurance policy," he laughed. "That's when you're considered to be culpable and accountable for your choices." But it wasn't just Asher's age that had him thinking about baptism as a safeguard against hell. It was also a sermon he heard the Sunday after the shooting at Columbine High School just a few miles away. "Right after the shooting our preacher gave a sermon that was like, 'even in places where you think that you're safe, you're not.' The whole theme was, 'You never know when you're gonna die, so figure it out.'"

The next week Asher volunteered to be baptized. For a while it seemed to help, but before long the fear was back. When he got to high school, he joined Young Life, an evangelical youth ministry group. To Asher, coming from a Church of Christ background, the Young Life theology seemed too good to be true:

> It was the first time that I was introduced to this God that loved me. Like, actually loved me. Love that meant more than just, "I love you and I've done all I can do, but you didn't hold up your end of the bargain, so you're going to burn in hell forever." It was a love that could actually be transformative for me. But it was also kind of terrible to think about, because I was taught that most Christians just believed what they wanted to believe, rather than actually taking the Bible seriously, as we did in the Church of Christ. So I was kind of stuck, because I wanted to believe in this wonderful God that my Young Life leaders had taught me about, but I just couldn't. It felt like a fairy tale.

By college Asher had sunk into a deep depression. His anxiety about hell was still around, he was having doubts about his faith, and when he came out as bisexual, his college youth group refused to support him. He found a therapist and began taking medication that helped his anxiety and depression, but the therapist wasn't LGBTQI2A-affirming and suggested techniques common to conversion therapy.

"She suggested at one point that my sexuality was the result of having 'a wounded gender identity,' and that if only I understood that God sees me as a beautiful daughter, then I would be able to fully live into my permanently straight sexuality. But that didn't work! She then suggested at one point that I put a rubber band around my wrist and snap myself when I had 'gay thoughts.'"

Unsurprisingly, this didn't work either. Instead, it was a painful reminder of Asher's battle with self-harm. "If cutting myself badly enough that I needed to go to the emergency room and get staples wasn't sufficient to change me, I don't know how a rubber band would do it," he sighed.

For Asher, having a body was a liability. Being made of flesh and blood meant that you were predisposed to sin, and that you were a finite being who was going to die. Even worse than that, having a soul alongside your unruly body meant that death wasn't the end—that something worse was coming. The fear that this instilled led to an urge to punish or purify the body as much as possible, in order to escape greater punishment later.

After college Asher decided to pursue another degree. "I thought I wanted to get a PhD in religion. I wanted to study the religious people and poke them around a bit, like an amoeba in a petri dish," he laughed. "It felt empowering!" Rather than being on the receiving end of doctrine and discipline, academia allowed Asher to observe from a safer distance. But that distance didn't last, because when he took a class on queer theology, it became obvious that faith was going to become a personal matter again.

He met a couple of new friends in this class, and one Sunday they invited him to come to church with them. Asher agreed, and the group ended up at a local Lutheran church.

> It was the first time I'd ever experienced liturgy, and it was weird and wonderful. What really got me was the communion table. They said, "Everyone without exception is welcome to the table." And I went, not thinking much of it, but then, every single week I found myself thinking, "I need to go back." Not because I felt a sense of duty or obligation, but because I felt it sustaining me. I felt hungry for going through the line and getting the Eucharist again. I felt like it was holding my life together.

Suddenly the body that had caused so many problems— the body that threatened rebellion and sin and death—was the thing leading him toward a physical manifestation of grace. Asher felt a spiritual hunger that fueled his curiosity, but also a physical hunger that propelled his legs back into that church week after week.

> "I started going there regularly, and the preaching was fabulous, and the Lutheran theology fit me. I didn't even know that congregations like that existed! I felt like I could finally be myself in a religious community. I felt like I was at home with my faith identity. And I think that gave me the guts to start facing up to the gender stuff."

Not long after Asher joined this welcoming church, he came out as transgender and decided to begin transitioning. He talked with his pastor about commemorating his transition in some way, and they worked together to create a liturgy to remember his birth name and bless his new one:

> On Baptism of Our Lord Sunday our whole community had a renaming rite for me. It was the first time that I remembered my baptism in a positive way, because my baptism had been such an awful, fearful thing. And I was anointed, and everyone greeted me by my new name for the

first time. It was amazing—finding a home where I could be my full self, where my gender identity and my sexuality and my faith all went together, and weren't seen as mutually exclusive. It meant that I didn't have to disembody myself to be a part of the community. I didn't have to dismember myself. That experience set me free. It just unleashed something inside of me that was like, "Well I have to do more of this!" I couldn't help myself! I had to figure out a way to go and do this thing for others, so that other people can have this experience. Because this is such good news! This could change the world!

Asher's experience of being put back together—of being "re-membered"—is something intrinsic to the theology of the church. First Corinthians 12 is all about the way in which different members of the church bring their particularities, their gifts, and their perspectives together to create a whole that is more than the sum of its parts. Paul uses a body metaphor to describe this action and says in verse 12, "For just as the body is one and has many members, and all the members of the body, though many, are one body, so it is with Christ." Essentially, Paul is saying that by joining with Christ in our baptism, we are also joined to every other person who has ever been baptized. He goes on to say:

Indeed, the body does not consist of one member but of many. If the foot would say, "Because I am not a hand, I do not belong to the body," that would not make it any less a part of the body. And if the ear would say, "Because I am not an eye, I do not belong to the body," that would not make it any less a part of the body. If the whole body were an eye, where would the hearing be? If the whole body were hearing, where would the sense of smell be? But as it is, God arranged the members in the body, each one of them, as he chose. If all were a single member, where would the body be? As it is, there are many members, yet one body. The eye cannot say to the hand, "I have no need of you," nor again the head to the feet, "I have no need of you." On the contrary, the members of the body that seem to

be weaker are indispensable. . . . If one member suffers, all
suffer together with it; if one member is honored, all rejoice
together with it.

(1 Corinthians 12:14–22, 26)

This text is absolutely essential to understanding why the
church is called to affirm transgender Christians. Here we are
told that no member of the body is dispensable, no member can
deem any other person unnecessary, and just because someone
does decide to say someone else is dispensable or unnecessary
does not make it true. Through his baptism Asher is just as
much a part of the body of Christ as any other Christian in the
world, and his gifts and needs and suffering and joy affect all
other members.

Of course there are limits to all metaphors, and so while
it's true that no human being can remove another from the
body of Christ, we do sometimes have to remove parts of
our individual bodies. I don't think Paul was saying that
you couldn't have your appendix removed if you needed to,
for instance. But what remains true is that our bodies are
important. In fact, biblical scholar Christina M. Fetherolf
believes that Paul intentionally chose to use this metaphor
in his letter to the Corinthian Christians because they had
such a negative view of physical bodies. She writes, "At
least some of the assembly believe that the physical body is
irrelevant, a notion which Paul negates when he weds the
physical and material to the divine and spiritual through
his use of these bodily metaphors. It is the collective, physical community, not any building, which houses the Spirit
of God."[3]

Of course, the most undeniable confirmation of the importance of bodies comes in the form of a baby born in a man-
ger in Bethlehem. As Asher puts it, "God coming as a child
and then growing up and going through puberty, and having
a human life with a human body—I think that declares once
and for all unequivocally, undoubtedly, that flesh is hallowed.
That our bodies are holy."

Theologian James B. Nelson echoed this in a joyful way
when he said about the opening to the Gospel of John:

> We claim an incarnational tradition. "In the beginning was
> the Word, and the Word was with God, and the Word
> was God." And when the Word came to dwell with us, it
> became—what? A book? A creed? A theological system?
> A code of morality? No! To the everlasting embarrass-
> ment of all dualistic piety, it became flesh. Note well how
> counter-cultural this conviction is. The opening words of
> the Fourth Gospel were undoubtedly shocking to its first
> readers, steeped as they were in the belief that the world was
> impure and that "flesh" was the root cause of that impurity.
> Now they are told that God was living and loving in this
> fleshly and fully human life of a carpenter, turned itinerant
> rabbi. It was a jarring claim.[4]

So if Jesus himself had a body, and it was through life and
death in that body that the whole world was redeemed, why do
we subscribe to the idea that bodies are awful things we must
overcome, or that they're a secondary and disposable thing
separate from our true identity?

Even after Jesus' resurrection from the dead, he goes on
doing very bodily things. In Luke's account we see Jesus meeting his disciples after resurrection and attempting to reassure
them by asking for breakfast:

> He said to them, "Why are you frightened, and why do
> doubts arise in your hearts? Look at my hands and my feet;
> see that it is I myself. Touch me and see; for a ghost does
> not have flesh and bones as you see that I have." And when
> he had said this, he showed them his hands and his feet.
> While in their joy they were disbelieving and still wonder-
> ing, he said to them, "Have you anything here to eat?" They
> gave him a piece of broiled fish, and he took it and ate in
> their presence.
>
> (Luke 24:38–43)

The disciples have a very similar reaction in John's account
of another postresurrection meeting, and it's here that we

meet the famous doubting Thomas. All the disciples are gathered together in a room with the doors locked because they are afraid of meeting Jesus' same fate at the hands of the Roman government, when Jesus appears to them suddenly. The only disciple not present at the time is Thomas; when the other disciples tell Thomas what happened, he replies, "Unless I see the mark of the nails in his hands, and put my finger in the mark of the nails and my hand in his side, I will not believe." The very next week the disciples gather again, hoping for another sighting, and this time Thomas is with them.

> Although the doors were shut, Jesus came and stood among them and said, "Peace be with you." Then he said to Thomas, "Put your finger here and see my hands. Reach out your hand and put it in my side. Do not doubt but believe." Thomas answered him, "My Lord and my God!" Jesus said to him, "Have you believed because you have seen me? Blessed are those who have not seen and yet have come to believe."
>
> (John 20:26–29)

Jesus' physicality after his resurrection can be powerful for transgender Christians, especially those who often field questions about their own bodies either in heaven or after Jesus' second coming. As a Lutheran, Asher confesses a belief in the resurrection of the body at the end of time; so I asked him what he thought his body might look like. He responded,

> I have no idea, to be honest. But I do know that it will be a body—I do think that the resurrection is going to be material. It's not just going to be spirits floating around in the sky. I don't know what my body will look like, but I think it's going to have to be pretty similar to my body now. I take great comfort in the fact that when Jesus is resurrected, it's clear that he still has wounds. I mean, I would hope that they weren't painful anymore, but they're still there. It gives me great comfort, that he still had scars, because as someone who's dealt with a lot of self-harm I still have a lot

of scars, and they're part of who I am now. I wouldn't want them to go away, because they're part of my story.

That recognition resonated with me too, as a transgender man who has had top surgery—a reconstruction of my chest that left me with two horizontal scars below my pectoral muscles. I wouldn't want to lose those scars either. They're a sign of the journey I've undertaken, and they're one of the many things I love about my body for that very reason. If Jesus' body retains the features that make him recognizable to the disciples in the upper room and during their beach breakfast, then I hope I too will keep my defining physical characteristics in some fashion.

Body theology and the belief in God's incarnation in Jesus are important for all Christians, but even more so for those whose bodies have been marginalized, ignored, or oppressed. Nancy Eiesland, the author of the groundbreaking book *The Disabled God: Toward a Liberatory Theology of Disability*, wrote that she had a similar connection with the recognition of Jesus' postresurrection wounds. After feeling defeated by the lack of accessibility for disabled people in Christian spaces, she read the story of Jesus' appearance to the disciples and concluded, "Here was the resurrected Christ making good on the promise that God would be with us, embodied, as we are—disabled and divine. In this passage, I recognized a part of my hidden history as a Christian. The foundation of Christian theology is the resurrection of Jesus Christ. Yet seldom is the resurrected Christ recognized as a deity whose hands, feet, and side bear the marks of profound physical impairment."[5]

Eiesland goes on to say that Christians must not only develop theology that includes disabled bodies, but that they must let that theology be created by disabled people themselves. "Such a theology must not be construed as a 'special-interest' perspective, but rather an integral part of reflection on Christian life. We must come to see disability neither as a symptom of sin nor an opportunity for virtuous suffering or charitable action. The

Christian community as a whole must open itself to the gifts of persons with disabilities, who, like other minority groups, call the church to repentance and transformation."[6]

Black theologians also have an incredible amount to teach the church about embodied theology—especially in the United States, where Black bodies have been considered inferior and disposable. In a country built on the backs of enslaved Africans, and in our modern world where Black people are gunned down by police and "mysteriously" found dead in prison cells, calling Black bodies holy is another necessary and revolutionary act. While some Black theologians do find a touchstone in Jesus' body after resurrection, many see themselves most clearly in the crucifixion itself. As famed theologian James Cone asserts,

> When we encounter the crucified Christ today, he is a humiliated Black Christ, a lynched Black body. Christ is Black not because Black theology said it. Christ is made Black through God's loving solidarity with lynched Black bodies and divine judgment against the demonic forces of white supremacy. Like a Black naked body swinging on a lynching tree, the cross of Christ was "an utterly offensive affair," "obscene in the original sense of the word," "subjecting the victim to the utmost indignity."[7]

In fact, while much of white, European theology tended toward centering the importance of the soul above the importance of the body, it was Black Christians who held on to the physicality of Jesus in their theology and in their spirituals and reminded the world that Jesus walked, talked, ate, cried, and slept. Black womanist theologian Kelly Brown Douglas has said that enslaved Black Christians actually helped clarify theology and make it more accessible to everyday people, because they had to use language from their own experiences to explain God's work in their lives, since they were blocked from studying theology formally. Yet, despite the fact that for a large portion of American history Black people were barred from seminaries and institutions of higher learning, they managed to communicate a truth that the ancient Christian councils had a hard time describing. Said Douglas, "Their testimony of Jesus as one who understood their tears and pain, as one who walked with them, talked with them, and understood their grief affirmed that Jesus was a real historical presence who brought God to earth. The enslaved testimony clarified what the Nicaea/Chalcedon councils attempted to declare: that in Jesus, God was actually [in the flesh], incarnate, an embodied reality in human history."[8]

Theology done from the perspective of marginalized groups creates a richer, more comprehensible, more compassionate Christianity. To ignore the contributions from people with bodies different from our own is equivalent to saying some bodies are not as holy as others—that some members don't belong in the body of Christ—despite scriptural witness to the contrary.

Once transgender Christians have gotten to the point where they understand their bodies to be both whole and holy, the next question is often, "Is it all right to change my body?" Answers to this question usually dovetail into conversations about whether or not God made a mistake during someone's creation and conception. Some Christians will cite Psalm 139 as proof that God foreordained certain things about a person, and so those particular characteristics shouldn't be changed. But is that an accurate reading of this passage?

> For it was you who formed my inward parts;
>   you knit me together in my mother's womb.
> I praise you, for I am fearfully and wonderfully made.
>   Wonderful are your works;
> that I know very well.
>   My frame was not hidden from you,
> when I was being made in secret,
>   intricately woven in the depths of the earth.
> Your eyes beheld my unformed substance.
> In your book were written
>   all the days that were formed for me,
>   when none of them as yet existed.

How weighty to me are your thoughts, O God!
How vast is the sum of them!
I try to count them—they are more than the sand;
I come to the end—I am still with you.
(Psalm 139:13–18)

When I asked Asher about his thoughts on this psalm, he was quick to point out that these verses don't refer only to God's creation of our bodies, that the reference to our "inward parts" or "inmost parts" encompasses us as whole beings. "I think God knit together my body and my identity," Asher explained. "I think God gave me this body and this identity, and that's exactly what God intended from the start."

Even though we're made in a certain way before we're born, we don't stay exactly as we were originally made. "I think that God knit us together in our mother's wombs, but I also think that God is active in our lives, knitting us together in every moment," Asher said. "God's been knitting me together every day since. I don't think that as soon as we were born God was like, OK, all done! I think that creation continues."

Asher and I notice the wonder the psalmist feels toward the end of the passage when he tries to comprehend God's infinite thoughts, the incredible variety and wide expanse of God's creative abilities. It's too much for the psalmist to take in, and surely too much for human beings to understand. So why is it that we seem determined to put limits on what God can and can't do, and when that work is finished?

Indeed, the continuing nature of creation is something that's observable even in the first chapters of Genesis. Asher pointed to Genesis 1:28, where God gives Adam and Eve dominion over creation, and Genesis 2:19, where God brings every animal to Adam to receive a name, making Adam a partner in the creative effort:

I think that God intends for us to make choices and to actively have an impact on creation, for better or for worse. That's part of our having free will. For example, God gives Adam the right to name things. All of creation wasn't already shaped; God gave out jobs to continue the process. And part of our job as humans is to interact with God, and not to create our own identities, but to become more fully who we are. Based on what we see in Genesis, I think that God is fine with us making choices in that process.

Scholar and theologian Terence Fretheim also believes humans have a role in creation as evaluators and problem solvers. He believes that "if God not only evaluates the world as good but reevaluates an aspect of the world as 'not good' (2:18), and if the only creatures capable of evaluating are human beings made in the image of God, then God here sets a key human task within ongoing creation."[9]

He also lifts up the blessing that God gives to the first human beings as the moment in which God actively shares creative power. "To bless others is an act of giving power and potentiality to them; it is another dimension of the divine power-sharing activity. . . . Blessing is understood to be integral to the creative process itself; it enables creatures to participate in the ongoingness of creation. . . . Creation has to do, not just with beginnings of things, but with a continuing process of becoming."[10]

Human beings exist somewhere in the middle of that becoming process—somewhere between the moment God begins to knit us together in the womb and the moment we experience resurrection alongside Jesus in God's new heaven and new earth. In the meantime, we do our best to honor our bodies and to use our creative abilities to bring forth life—and maybe even more than life. While we talked about choice and free will, Asher smiled. He said, "You know, I think God delights in the fact that humans are interactive. We're not mindless—we create things and we fix things and we argue and we find new ways to solve problems. I think God likes to see us being creative. I think we bring God joy."

11

Life beyond Apologetics

The year before I came out as transgender, I visited a lot of churches. One week I'd go to an Episcopal church that I'd heard had a wonderful organist. The next Sunday I'd go to an evening service at a new church plant filled with twenty-somethings and acoustic guitars. Then the next week I'd head over to a Methodist church because I wanted to hear a particular pastor's sermon. I hardly ever visited the same church twice. That wasn't because I didn't like them; it was because I was afraid. I was feeling more self-conscious about my body than ever before, and while everyone was friendly enough, I could also tell that people were having a hard time pinpointing my gender, which for me felt awkward. I was so nervous about my voice—which was about two octaves higher than it is now and never failed to make people go, "Oh, I'm sorry, I mean ma'am"—that I never spoke to anyone when I could avoid it.

My solution to this problem was to try my hardest to be invisible. I would come in after the service had already started, take a seat in the back, and make a dash for the door as soon as the last hymn was through. Leaving on my own terms was preferable to having people kick me out, which I was afraid they'd do if they found out I was trans.

Of course, this also meant that I wasn't giving anyone the chance to tell me that I was welcome! I was hungry for a community in which I could pray and read Scripture and sing and share my life, but I was so scared that I allowed myself only to nibble on the crumbs from the communion table. Sometimes, when you're starving, any bite of food at all seems like the best you can hope for, and it's hard to dream of a full meal, let alone the kind of kingdom feast Jesus talks about in the Gospels. You start to trick yourself into thinking the scraps are enough.

When I started studying the theology of LGBTQI2A people, one of the things that became obvious is that we've had to spend a lot of time doing something called apologetics—the scriptural or theological defense of an idea. Almost every book on the faith of queer folks deals with apologetics (this book included!) and has a chapter that explains why the story of Sodom and Gomorrah is not actually about same-gender relationships or why God's creation of Adam and Eve doesn't mandate the existence of only two sexes.

Because Christians have spent so long vilifying LGBTQI2A people and using Scripture to make their point, queer Christians have had to engage with these very same passages in order to defend themselves. This is all well and good as far as it goes, because even when two people disagree about what a particular piece of text means, at least they're meeting on common ground. The problem comes when LGBTQI2A Christians begin to feel as if their faith is made up of only apologetics and defense mechanisms. In a way, it's the same problem that transgender people have when they find themselves focusing entirely on their gender dysphoria and scrambling away from all the things that cause them pain and anxiety, rather than intentionally moving forward toward what some like to call "gender euphoria"—the contentment, authenticity, and joy that you experience when you get to be yourself.

But if we spend all our time focusing on what's wrong, how do we do what's right? If we spend all our time trying to use

Scripture to defend ourselves, when do we get to see the Bible as a life-giving fount of grace for all people? When do we get to hear God speaking into our lives, if we're focused on proof-texting our arguments? In short, it's a good and healthy thing to recognize that the theological crumbs that we once cherished are no longer enough. We need a full, whole-grain loaf of the bread of life.

Taj Smith also experienced some hesitation about visiting a new church when he stepped through the doors of the United Church of Christ community down the road from his college campus. He hadn't grown up religious, but his mom had always encouraged him to explore different faith traditions. Taj had a real interest in religion and could often be found reading about Buddhism, Islam, and other world faiths. He'd also tag along to church with friends, and they introduced him to evangelical Christianity. As a teenager he joined the youth group at a huge church in town, partly because it was a place to hang out with classmates and partly because he was genuinely interested in the subject matter.

When Taj told people that he was queer, though, things went south. "I stopped going there after a number of folks told me that it wouldn't work with me being queer and that I needed to pray harder," he sighed. Because Taj had been assigned female at birth and hadn't yet come out as trans, some people took issue with his attraction to women. "That hurt. I left, and I thought of myself as an atheist for a while after that."

By the time he got to college, he had begun to feel an internal tension between the LGBTQI2A advocacy he was so passionate about and the faith that he'd held on to when he was younger. "I was involved in a lot of queer organizing, but I felt like I didn't really fit because I had this faith background thing, and people weren't super into that in college. So trying to figure out my place was always a bit of a struggle." He finally found a group of progressive Christians at his school who were feeling similar tensions, and Taj began to believe that it might be possible to regain some faith and hold his two worlds together.

It was his experience with the United Church of Christ congregation that finally made that connection possible. Taj smiled when he remembered the avalanche of change during that year:

> I tend to say that my transition and my experience of religion in that church are inseparable. I came out as trans in that church, and I came out the same year I decided I wasn't going to go to law school, and I was going to go to seminary instead; so it was kind of this whole big shift in schema. It was like God was saying, "Everything you're doing right now? You need to stop that. You need to do all of these other things that you want to do, but think you can't."

In fact, when I asked Taj if he could remember a time in his life when he felt totally loved and affirmed as his authentic self, he told me about an experience he'd had in this UCC congregation:

> The first Sunday I went back to my church after I came out as trans, I just remember standing in front of the table full of name tags, and staring at my name tag and thinking, "I can't put that on." I remember looking blank. And one of the greeters comes up to me and she says, "You need help finding your name tag?" And she laughed, and I laughed, and I said, "No, I think I need a new one." And she just kind of looked at me, and so I said, "Yeah, I need a new one, like, forever." And she went, "OK!" And she got me a new tag and she said, "Why don't you write your name on this one and we'll have a new permanent one for you next week!" And she handed me an order of service and I went inside and thought, "That was the easiest thing ever!" That church became a safe haven for me. Being in that church throughout my entire transition, and growing with that church through that time, was so necessary for me. They were probably the most supportive people in my life, other than the handful of friends I had. Faith and my gender identity are so linked for me that I don't know how to talk about one without talking about the other.

For Taj, this experience solidified his understanding of himself as a loved child of God and gave him the healthy foundation from which he could respond to his calling. He had finally found a group of people who could accompany him on his journey toward wholeness while nourishing his faith and relationship with God at the same time. These kinds of experiences—where trans people are fully affirmed by their church community—show more than tolerance and go beyond defense and apologetics. These experiences are life-giving in the most literal sense.

In John 10:1–18 Jesus describes himself as the Good Shepherd—one of the most familiar and beloved metaphors in Christian tradition. Rather than acting like a bandit, who climbs over the fence and scares the sheep away, the Good Shepherd enters through the gate and calls the sheep by name, and the sheep follow him because they know his voice. Jesus explains, "The thief comes only to steal and kill and destroy. I came that they may have life, and have it abundantly."[1]

While some theologians believe the abundant life Jesus mentions here is in reference to life after death, others point to the numerous instances where Jesus works to improve the lives of people in the present. For example, think about the story of Jesus feeding the five thousand, which is the only miracle story that is told in all four Gospels. On that occasion Jesus asked the disciples to find food for the more than five thousand people who had gathered to hear him preach. Jesus felt a concern for the people because it was evening and nobody had eaten for most of the day. The disciples reported back to Jesus that there wasn't any place nearby to get food and that the only meal among the masses consisted of five loaves of bread and two fish. Jesus didn't give another sermon about the importance of spiritual food. He just went ahead and provided what people actually needed in that moment. Jesus blessed the food and told the disciples to pass it out among all the people. In the end there was enough for everyone, with twelve baskets of food left over—another lesson in abundance.

The respected theologian Justo González points out two important things about that story: first, that Jesus' blessing and breaking of the bread to feed the five thousand is very similar to the blessing and breaking of the bread at the Last Supper and, second, that Jesus' concern with physical human needs is a model for Christian communities. He says, "This is a story about feeding, not just about rituals or religious practices. . . . If the feeding of the multitude is a sign of the feeding that takes place at Communion and in the final banquet of the kingdom, then the feeding that takes place at Communion must be a sign of a faith community that actually feeds the hungry and responds to human need."[2]

So if Jesus says he comes so that his flock might have abundant life, what does that mean for transgender Christians? And if that abundant life includes caring for human needs like food, shelter, clothing, and medical care as well as spiritual care, what does that mean for churches?

Let's take those questions one at a time. First, if Jesus came to bring abundant life to all who follow him, that means that transgender Christians should be able to stop spending every single bit of their energy defending themselves against those "clobber passages," in order to concentrate instead on becoming better disciples. We should be able to move from survival practices to thriving faith. Jesus didn't come to make things marginally more bearable. He came to give us abundant and eternal life or, as scholar Robert Kysar puts it, "the peculiar quality of life resulting from a proper self-understanding in Christ that cannot be annihilated by death."[3] If transgender Christians could move beyond apologetics, we would have more time and resources to devote to spreading the gospel, to providing help to the needy, to confronting injustices, to dismantling racism, to serving our neighbor, to praying, to practicing kindness, and to loving God.

When I asked Taj what moving past a focus on apologetics and toward abundant life would look like for him, he suggested that the next move might be what he calls "liberating the text." "Apologetics has to exist because the Bible is gendered uniquely in favor of male bodies," he explained. "So dismantling that [hierarchical] structure in the text so that it can't be recreated in the church is important."

So, for instance, when we read a translation of the Bible that always refers to God as "he," that subconsciously suggests that we ascribe male attributes to God, which in turn equates maleness with godliness. Taj suggested that by liberating the text from references to God as male we remind ourselves that God is beyond human constructions of gender, while also keeping ourselves from instituting sexism in our churches and using the Bible as an excuse.

But as wonderful as it might be to move beyond apologetics, Taj makes a good point when he says that there's a good reason for apologetics to exist. Trans people still do the work of defending themselves theologically, because not all Christians have had the opportunity to educate themselves about trans experiences, and with these Christians apologetics are warranted. These Christians may have questions and doubts and misunderstandings that are worth the time and energy spent in good conversation and relationship-building. In other cases, though, trans folks are forced into defending themselves because a church or an individual Christian absolutely won't consider affirming them or helping them in any way. This is when Jesus' response to human need gives us a command to act.

So how can Christians—both individually and as church communities—help transgender people access abundant life? First, we have to remember that "abundant life" does not mean "a life of abundance." Jesus is not saying that Christians should want or expect hundred-dollar bills and membership in the yacht club. What Jesus says is that he brings us life in abundance—more life than you can shake a stick at! So much life that you can't take it all in! Beyond just more life, Jesus is promising a better life. As scholar Brendan Byrne explains it, abundance "is not merely quantitative. The mission of the Son is to communicate to the world a qualitatively enhanced life: life that, beyond mere mortal existence, is a participation as 'children of God.'"[4]

So what do transgender people need in order to experience life abundant in both quantity and quality? Anneliese Singh, a researcher and professor of counseling and human development at the University of Georgia, has spent years studying resilience among transgender populations. Resilience—the patterns of learned behavior and the access to resources that allow a person to cope with difficult circumstances—is especially important among groups that face discrimination and violence. She determined that there were five things that predicted high resilience for trans folks across the board: the ability to create and define your own sense of self; the recognition of your own self-worth; awareness of oppression, so that you can protect yourself; connection with a supportive community; and the cultivation of hope for the future.[5] In light of this, we can assume that Christians can help instill resilience by making sure trans folks can take the time to figure out and define their own gender identity; by reminding them that they are worthy of love and belonging as human beings and children of God; by actively dismantling the transphobia that undergirds their oppression; by inviting trans folks into our communities and making them feel welcome; and by walking with them and supporting them in their spiritual journey.

Faith is an important component of resilience, and Dr. Singh found that this is especially true for trans people of color. She found that

> participants described their spirituality and having a sense of hope for the future as being integral aspects of their resilience. For most, being raised in religious homes was closely connected to how they understood their gender identity. . . . However, some participants also experienced their families and/or religious institutions using religion to judge or "punish" them for their gender identity and expression. . . . Participants reported they "returned" to their spiritual beliefs and spirituality to cope with traumatic life events. They noted that this connection helped them cultivate a sense of hope for the future despite the traumatic life events they experienced.[6]

As a Black trans man who has lived these connections, Taj Smith confirms the way trans folks often yearn for a relationship with God. "There's so much hunger for spiritual development throughout the different trans communities I've been in. People are really seeking something that's bigger than them, whatever that is. They know that there's something that propelled them into transition and into embracing who they truly are, but a lot of times they can't encounter that in a church because of the dogma that gets in the way."

Too often the church is a stumbling block that catches the feet of trans people on the road to God, rather than the sanctuary that houses the fountain of living water.

When I asked Taj what he imagined when he thought about the concept of abundant life, he pointed directly to the importance of a spiritual family:

> Abundant life looks like community. It looks like the celebration of people as people, and not as numbers to fill pews. I find that there are churches I go to where I know people are talking to me because (a) I'm a young adult, or (b) because I'm Black, or (c) because I'm part of some other diversity initiative. But when people are just genuinely welcoming, and when people do their best to welcome you and situate you in the community as you are, that's really what it looks like—to have a community to come home to, and to be able to say, "Yes, I'm a part of that." Isolation, to me, is what death is.

Part of becoming truly integrated into a community is figuring out what your role might be—what part of the body of Christ you represent. Each person in a community has a unique perspective and distinct gifts, and it can be hard to toe the line between accidentally tokenizing people and instead appreciating the things that make them different. Taj nodded when I tried to articulate this tricky situation. He agreed that he didn't want to be seen as just the Black person, or just the trans person:

My role and my perspective is going to be different than the person sitting next to me because of the way I'm perceived in the world. I feel like I'm looking at the world from a really unique vantage point, especially at this moment in history. I see the world as a Black man, but I've also seen the world as a Black woman. I think about what it looks like to have the privilege to pass, and to be able to fly under the radar, and how I bring these perspectives to whatever community that I'm in.

In the beginning Taj wasn't sure if his new UCC church home would be able to appreciate the different perspectives he brought to the table, and if they couldn't accept those, he wasn't sure whether he'd be able to find a role in the community. As it turned out, though, the church was ready and willing to find ways to support him, even if they weren't instinctively sure what to do.

I felt so affirmed when I was approached by someone from my church and invited to join the men's group. I didn't end up going because I wasn't sure if I would feel comfortable in that space at that time, but knowing that that was an option for me, and feeling like the community was really figuring out how to embrace me and love me—that meant so much. They loved me before I came out, and I knew that, but I didn't love myself before, so I was hard to hold on to. But after coming out and starting the transition process I could say, "Hey, this is me coming into myself," and then to feel really seen by people in the church, who were much older than I am and who were predominantly white—it felt so good! Those people were showing up!

This is when trans Christians experience life in abundance—when they are welcomed into community; when they are loved for all of who they are; when their differences are respected; when they know they can count on their community to help with their daily human needs; and when they feel safe enough to drop their defenses in order to take on Jesus' gentle yoke of discipleship. That may sound like a lot to ask of a church, but in reality these are commitments we try to make to the cisgender members of our communities. So why not include trans folks? After all, if the life Jesus promises is abundant, surely there's enough to go around!

12
Does Gender Matter Anymore?

When it comes to baptism, I was kind of a late bloomer. When I was born, my parents were attending a nondenominational church that didn't practice infant baptism, and by the time I was old enough to make the choice myself, I wasn't sure I believed in Christianity anymore. In high school I spent a lot of time shadowing the other kids in my youth group as they went through the Lutheran practice of confirmation, and I watched them struggle with their questions and their doubts. I had a lot of doubts myself, but they all revolved around two central points.

The first question I had was, "Can I be baptized if I don't believe every single piece of Christian doctrine?" After quite a few long conversations with my pastor, he finally gave me an answer that I could live with. He told me that Christians hold the church's beliefs and creeds like one of those colorful parachutes you play with in kindergarten. Everybody takes a hold of a piece of the edge, and together we can carry and lift heavy things placed in the middle. Sometimes the people around you take up some of the slack for you, and at other times you carry a little more weight for them, but together we can keep the whole thing balanced. In short, he told me that I didn't have to believe every single piece of Christian doctrine myself; I had a community to help me hold the faith.

The second question I wrestled with in high school was, "Would the church still want me if they knew I was . . . different?" At the time I knew I was bisexual, and I knew something was up with my gender, but that was about all I had to go on. It felt like if the people in my church found out that I didn't fit a heterosexual, cisgender mold, they wouldn't want me anymore, and they'd either rescind the baptism offer or require that I straighten myself out. That fear stuck with me for a long time. I decided not to be baptized or confirmed during high school, but kept studying as I went away to college, determined to understand why I felt such a call to Scripture and to theology. Finally, when I was twenty years old, I came across a passage that provided an answer to my second question about belonging: "For in Christ Jesus you are all children of God through faith. As many of you as were baptized into Christ have clothed yourselves with Christ. There is no longer Jew or Greek, there is no longer slave or free, there is no longer male and female; for all of you are one in Christ Jesus" (Gal. 3:26–28).

When I read these verses for the first time, I felt something click into place. The connection to baptism, negating gender as a barrier to acceptance, the metaphor of adoption into a faith family: this all spoke directly to my heart. I decided that this would be my baptismal memory verse, and I headed back home from college to ask my old pastor about setting a date. On June 22, 2008, I was baptized in front of the people who had walked with me throughout my faith journey.

In 2016, eight years later, I was invited to come back to my home church to tell the story of my transition. As I stood in front of the congregation reliving the time I spent in youth group, in choir, in the pastor's office, on service trips, and over tea with amazing friends, I realized none of my fears had come true. I had been able to hold on to my edge of the big faith parachute. I had been able to find Christian communities that knew who I was as a transgender man, and who accepted me. I had been able to bring my whole self to God and to the church. Or rather, I hadn't done all these things. I had just followed the breadcrumbs from the communion table that God kept dropping along the way. I just kept knocking on the door of the kingdom, and God kept opening up.

Galatians 3:28 isn't the only verse in the Bible that seems to downgrade the importance of gender in Christian identity. In fact, this same "neither X nor Y" formula shows up several times in the letters attributed to the apostle Paul, and it's always paired with a reference to baptism. New Testament scholar Wayne Meeks believes that Galatians 3:28 is actually a core part of a pre-Pauline baptismal formula—like a prayer that was said over every new Christian as they were baptized—and points out that the same "unification of opposites" is found in 1 Corinthians 12:13 and Colossians 3:11.[1] It was apparently pretty important to early Christians that things like gender, ethnicity, and social status not be recognized as barriers to inclusion or to a relationship with God. But why was it so important to the Galatians?

To understand why Paul included these words in this particular letter, we have to zoom out a bit to what was happening in the new Christian church in Galatia. Essentially, Paul had come to Galatia and ministered to the Gentile people there, eventually baptizing them and helping them to get a community going, before he left to start churches elsewhere. While he was with them, he stressed that it wasn't necessary to become Jewish before becoming Christian—an idea that may seem silly to us today, but was a serious issue in the first century. Jesus himself had been a Jew, his twelve disciples were all Jewish, and Jesus' tendency to eat with Gentiles was scandalous at the time. It wasn't until the Holy Spirit started showing up to all kinds of people all over the place in the book of Acts that the disciples eventually decided that it was OK for Gentiles to become Christians. Still, a few of Jesus' original followers thought that Gentiles should have to keep the same laws and cultural customs that the Jewish people did. They argued that Christian Gentile men should at least have to be circumcised, as all Jewish men were, and as Jesus himself was.

Paul pushed back on that, and said that being circumcised was not necessary for inclusion in Christ's church, that the only thing necessary for inclusion was belief. Soon after he'd left the church in Galatia, the Galatians started writing to him, telling him that other Christians had come and said they must all be circumcised. You can imagine the panic and confusion they felt about this news. It seemed as if they must either fix themselves by being circumcised and leaving behind many of the customs that made them Galatians, or leave Christianity. It was a tough choice.

So that's where we are when Paul shows up on the scene with his words in Galatians 3. He points the people of Galatia to Abraham as an example, because God blessed and chose Abraham when Abraham wasn't circumcised. Therefore, nobody had the right to deny that God had also blessed the Galatians, even though *they* weren't circumcised. In the end, Paul says, circumcision isn't good or bad. It's just a social custom, not one that's going to get in the way of your relationship with God or your inclusion in the kingdom. In the end, there is no longer Jew or Greek (circumcised or uncircumcised), no longer slave or free, no longer male and female, for we are all one once we're joined with Christ in baptism.

But Paul's assertion here raises another question: if we're all one in Christ, then do these distinctions between genders, races, ethnicities, and classes matter at all?

For Rev. Lynn Young, Paul's words in Galatians 3:26–28 regarding social customs are pure gospel. Paul insists that belief and response to God's call—not conforming to cultural mores—are the hallmarks of inclusion. That means a lot to someone who is not only Christian but also Native American—someone who's not just male or female, but is Two Spirit.

Lynn, who uses the pronouns ze, zir, and zirs, has been walking a blended path that encompasses Christian belief and

Native practices for many years. Ze explained, "Spiritually, I identify as a Native American Traditionalist Christian. These identities exist side by side. Neither is subservient to the other. They work synergistically together, and I really believe that I couldn't be the person of faith that I am or the Christian that I am without this integration."

But Lynn didn't always know about zir Native heritage, and didn't always have the connection with Christianity that ze has today. "I was born and raised in a family that was casually United Methodist, and so it was those kinds of liturgies and things that I was familiar with. I knew when to stand and when to say the Apostles' Creed and knew all those things by heart, but none of it felt like it had anything to do with me. It didn't really impact who I was. As a young child and into my mid-teens I was a victim of sexual abuse, and so the idea that there was this all-knowing, all-loving God character didn't make sense to me. I didn't deny the existence of God, but the idea that God was an entity that gave a crap about the day-to-day doings of people in general, and me specifically, wasn't anything that I understood."

It wasn't until a family trip up to the north shore of Lake Superior that Lynn had any meaningful connection with God. Ze remembers it vividly:

I was about six or seven, and I was sitting on this giant slab of rock in northern Minnesota with my feet in this icy stream, and I remember feeling so energized and so plugged in to something so much bigger than myself that I could not articulate, but that I could not deny. It was something that deserved and received my awe and reverence and curiosity and devotion. It was something that was a saving force for me. I was grounded into a bigger system into which I belonged. It didn't reach out a mystical hand and snatch me out of a bad situation, but it embraced me and comforted me and it said, "You belong." So that presence has been part of my life up until this moment. That is who I am. And so as I became aware of my Native heritage about twenty years ago, that made total sense to me. I started to understand why I felt the way I do, because I really do believe that our bodies carry generational memories.

Lynn's mother was Native American, but she had been adopted as a baby and didn't have any connection to her culture, which meant that Lynn didn't know anything about zir Native roots until ze did some digging zirself as an adult.

My mom's people are the Oglala Lakota, who are from the plains in North and South Dakota. Since I live in Indiana, I'm not connected so much with the Oglala Lakota who are currently living on their homeland in the plains, but I'm very connected to the intertribal Native community here in Indiana. Our group here is made up of a bunch of Native folks from different tribal affiliations who find themselves in community because of location. We're Cherokee, Potawatomi, Miami, Lakota, and Huron.

Lynn was blessed to find a group of people who had similar experiences and histories, and even in seminary, Lynn found kindred souls. "I've met several people in my Christian journey that are also connected in the same way. For instance, in my field placement in seminary, my supervising pastor was of Cherokee descent, but studied for six years with a Lakota elder."

As one might guess, the intersection of Christian and Native identities can be a tricky thing to navigate because of the colonization and genocide that Native people have faced and continue to experience at the hands of white Christians. Richard Twiss, another Native Christian, has spoken about the way he was taught to understand Galatians 3:28:

One afternoon I asked one of the pastoral leaders how I was supposed to relate to my Native culture as a Christian. I distinctly remember him opening the Bible he was carrying. He read from Galatians 3:28 where Paul said, "There is neither Jew nor Greek, slave nor free, male nor female, for you are all one in Christ Jesus" (NIV). After reading it he commented on how cultures should all blend together for us as Christians, and then concluded by saying, "So, Richard, don't worry about being Indian anymore—just be like us." . . . I believed that church leader. I really had no choice, being a new Christian, and he, being in a position of spiritual power/authority, gave an answer from the Bible about cultures. So for the next twelve years I lived the Christian life as it was culturally modeled for me by non-Native friends and Christian brethren—something I later found to be less than I am, and much less than the Lord Jesus wants me to be![2]

This was the same bind that the church in Galatia found themselves in back in the first century—right in the tension between diverse ethnicities and a collective identity in Christ. There are two ways to interpret what Paul says in Galatians 3:28 about our being one in Christ: either it means that we're all whitewashed and homogenized and our differences are erased, as Richard's pastor declared, or it means that we're called to find a way to make our different identities fit together, like the bright shards in assorted colors that make up the stained glass windows of a cathedral. Are we called to sameness, or are we called to oneness?[3]

Randy Woodley, another Native theologian, argues for the latter option. He says, "Paul's argument in the book of Galatians for freedom in Christ applies to cultural divisions, too. The purpose of worshipping God in our own culture is so that we may be free in the expression of our devotion. How often I have seen Native American elders attending a worship service and been brought to tears as they expressed deep appreciation for seeing Jesus 'finally worshipped in our own Indian ways.'"[4]

Some people Lynn meets don't understand the way ze holds together these pieces of Native spirituality and Christian faith. "Some of my Native Traditionalist friends who are dear, beloved people to me, don't get how in the world I could ever identify as Christian, because that is the religion of our oppressors, the religion of the people who tried to kill us, and did kill our ancestors, and that's all true. But that's not Christ's fault." Of course, there are always the Christians who believe Lynn should get rid of zir Native heritage, the same way Richard's pastor suggested he forget his. I told Lynn, "You know, it seems hard enough to hold two things together like that when people don't understand. How on earth do you also find the heart to openly identify as Two Spirit—something else that most people don't get?"

Lynn laughed and said,

> One of the many ways I've tried to explain my gender journey to people who don't get it is to say that, as I began to really dig into it and explore it and find the meaningful points for me, I felt like I was given this dirty floor and a toothbrush. As I started to scrub this floor I started seeing things, and as things were revealed, it turned out that this floor was an amazing mosaic, even though each piece by itself didn't seem to be anything in particular. None of those pieces are unimportant because they all have to exist together to create the whole picture. So I've arrived at this place of knowing myself as a Two Spirit person, and that Two Spirit is my gender. There's a feminine part of me, and a masculine part of me, and there are also parts of me that are so intertwined that are both of those and then some, and they don't have a name that fits within European gender constructs.

The term "Two Spirit" (also written "two-spirit") was first coined by Native Americans and members of the First Nations tribes of Canada back in 1990 to create a cohesive English term for Native sexualities and gender identities that have existed in multiple tribes for centuries.[5] It also replaced the term "berdache," which had been used by white anthropologists to refer to any Native person of any tribe who seemed to diverge from heterosexual and cisgender expectations.[6] These days Two Spirit people are speaking for themselves, forming organizations all over North America, and carving out their own niche in modern Native life.

Lynn first recognized zir Two Spirit identity when ze accompanied a friend to the Philadelphia Transgender Health Conference. As soon as ze stepped through the door,

> it was like I had been looking at the world through a straw and somebody said, "Oh honey, put that down." And I thought, "Wow! Look at all these wonderful people living their authentic lives in ways that I would never have dreamt of." It was like this domino effect started in me that made me question everything and not take anything for granted. And I was asking all these questions, and I met several Two Spirit people there that first year. I realized that I didn't have to be male or female. I realized I could be a mosaic of things. And as I explored that culturally with some folks and as I read more, I finally got it.
>
> We have all these shards of identity in us, whether it's our sexuality, our gender, our faith, our age, our cultural identity, our personal trauma histories—all of those things that are part of who we are combine to create our whole identity. I'm not just one piece—I'm not just the Christian, or just the Native person, or just Two Spirit, or just the survivor, or just the grandma—that small piece isn't me; only the whole reflects who I am. I am all of this.

So what was Paul thinking about these different pieces of our identity when he penned Galatians 3:28? And what does this verse mean for our understanding of gender? Was Paul saying that gender was no longer important—that through our baptism in Christ our gender identities were all erased or irrelevant? I very much doubt it. What Paul said about gender in this verse was revolutionary in that it confirmed that there was no patriarchy or misogyny in God's new kingdom; it broke down the barriers between genders and between people of different genders and God. But Paul still upheld the gender binary in the rest of his letters.

Wayne Meeks directs our attention to Paul's beliefs about gender expression and gender roles in other parts of the New Testament: "Paul insists on the preservation of the symbols of the present, differentiated order. Women remain women and men remain men and dress accordingly, even though 'the end of the ages has come upon them.' Yet these symbols have lost their ultimate significance, for 'the form of this world is passing away.'"[7] So essentially, Meeks believes that when Paul talks about gender in his letters, he's telling people to keep their gender presentation as culturally traditional as possible, because the kingdom revolution that God promised hasn't happened yet. At the same time, he's telling Christians that in certain ways they should act as if that kingdom is already here.

Confused yet? I wouldn't blame you! This is one of the mysteries of life as a Christian: we are citizens of two worlds at once. We're human beings who live in a time when things like gender, class, and race are all important to our understandings of ourselves and each other; yet we're also called to be part of a new kingdom where things like sexism, poverty, slavery, and racism no longer exist. Geerhardus Vos, the father of Reformed biblical theology, once called this mystery "the already but not yet." God's new vision for the world is already being enacted and is already transforming us, but it hasn't fully arrived, and it's nowhere near done turning things upside down.

In the meantime, what Galatians 3:28 calls us to remember is that even though our gender identities matter, they don't get between us and God. As Lynn explained,

> This isn't about not using labels. I feel like there are ways in which labels are really important, because if they're freeing for you—if they're tools of liberation for you—use them. But which label you use? That doesn't matter to God, in terms of whether or not God loves you or accepts you. Free or slave, Greek, Jew, male and female—none of that gets in the way. And if the Scripture enumerates all of those things, then I have to believe sexuality and gender identity have got to be part of that same paradigm. A whole paradigm is being named, not just the few categories named here.

In Wayne Meeks's history of the Galatians 3:28 formula, he ends by admitting that maybe Paul's vision of unity through diversity in Christ was too revolutionary—and maybe even too dangerous—for his time. You can imagine a sparkle in Meeks's eye, though, when he finishes by saying, "The declaration that in Christ there is no more male and female faded into innocuous metaphor, perhaps to await the coming of its proper moment."[8]

What better moment than this to begin reminding Christians of the oneness we inherit through our baptism? What better teachers of strength in diversity could we have than people like Lynn, whose very lives are made up of many different identities sewn together with the threads of the Holy Spirit? Perhaps it is time to edge the "not yet" closer to the "now."

Conclusion

The Trans-Affirming Toolbox

In Luke 15 we find Jesus doing what he did best: talking and eating with sinners. The religious authorities of Jesus' time are criticizing him for this lax behavior and judging him by the company he keeps. In response to their concerns, Jesus tells this story:

> "Which one of you, having a hundred sheep and losing one of them, does not leave the ninety-nine in the wilderness and go after the one that is lost until he finds it? When he has found it, he lays it on his shoulders and rejoices. And when he comes home, he calls together his friends and neighbors, saying to them, 'Rejoice with me, for I have found my sheep that was lost.' Just so, I tell you, there will be more joy in heaven over one sinner who repents than over ninety-nine righteous persons who need no repentance."
>
> (Luke 15:4–7)

Many of us probably heard this story for the first time as children—it's a Sunday school favorite, and for good reason! It's incredibly comforting to imagine yourself as the lost sheep, riding back home on Jesus' shoulders after an exciting but ill-advised adventure. There are times when this story is exactly the gospel message we need—when we need to hear that we are worthy of God's love, and that God will risk anything to have us back home again.

But what if we imagined this story a different way? What if the lost sheep didn't wander away from the safety and goodness of the shepherd? What if it was just trying to escape the cruelty of the flock? Sheep will occasionally pick out a flock member who doesn't fit in—maybe because of an injury or a strange marking—and they'll chase that individual away. There are times when I think Christians need to see ourselves more in the ninety-nine sheep who stayed put, and ask ourselves if we may have been part of the reason that the lost sheep got lost in the first place.

I don't mean to lay on the guilt too heavily here—in reality, we all have lost-sheep days and flock-sheep days—but I think this metaphor holds up. Christians have been driving LGBTQI2A people away from the church for decades—and then asking us why we won't come back and repent. Take a look at what Jesus does with this situation, though. He leaves the ninety-nine sheep behind to go in search of the one who needs help. This is such a powerful metaphor because it goes against everything we've been taught about the greater good. Any economist will tell you the shepherd should cut his losses and move on!

But what's at stake for Jesus in this situation isn't just that one single lost sheep, and it's not just the ninety-nine back home. It's the integrity of the flock as a whole. Saving just the main group or just the individual wouldn't do any good, because the flock is more than just the sum of its parts. When Jesus goes after that lost sheep, what he's telling the flock—what he's telling us—is that, as a community, *we need each other to be complete.*

In this book, transgender Christians have shared their stories and the ways that Scripture, faith, and gender identity interact in their lives. I hope you've been able to read these stories and come to the same conclusion the shepherd did: that our faith communities and churches aren't complete without trans folks and their experiences.

At the messy, lovable, chaotic potluck that is life in the church, transgender Christians have a lot to bring to the table. We can help the church see Scripture through different lenses. We can help other Christians understand their own gender identities. We can help to break down barriers created by sexism and misogyny. We can remind people of the diversity of God's creation, and of God's unlimited nature. We can stand in the gaps and bridge middle spaces where others may be uncomfortable or uninformed. We can help make connections between the sacred and the secular, making the church more relevant for the world. We can provoke people into asking questions about themselves and about God that they may never have thought to ask before.[1] And that's all while most churches still don't affirm our existence as Christians! Imagine what we could do if we worked together, instead of against each other.

If we want to bring the flock back together, we'll need to be able to imagine the future differently, and it can help to have some examples to follow. Let's take a look at a few churches and individuals who are already doing great things.

— We can learn so much from allies like Sister Luisa Derouen, who spent twenty years providing spiritual care with and to transgender people, but was forbidden by her supervisors to talk about it.[2] In 2014 she was finally given permission to come forward and share the work that she had done to support trans Christians, and she now writes frequently in support of full inclusion for trans and gender-expansive Catholics, both in public and in letters to church leaders.[3] Her insistence on God's love for trans people is pushing Catholic leaders to reconsider exclusionary policies.

— Pastors like Jeffrey Dirrim are starting church ministries that reach out to homeless transgender youth, providing community, food and supplies, love, and affirmation.[4]

— Churches like the Unitarian Universalist Fellowship of Fairbanks, Alaska, have started programs to help transgender people get their legal documents changed and raised money for the numerous fees inherent in the process.[5]

— Many faith communities like First Congregational Church of Santa Barbara, California, have opened their doors and begun sharing space with transgender community centers and support groups.[6]

— When Gov. Greg Abbott of Texas put forward a letter pushing state services to designate gender-affirming care as child abuse, there was a risk that supportive parents, teachers, counselors, and other mandatory reporters would face criminal charges for supporting trans youth. Despite the risk, clergy members like Rev. Natalie Webb took a stand. They decided to risk noncompliance in order to protect the people in their care, because, Rev. Webb stated, "My commitment to the body of Christ and to the children who are created in God's image is definitely more important than what the governor thinks."[7]

These individuals, churches, and communities are acting as Jesus' hands and feet in the world to a population that needs them. Even more than that, through their actions they're recognizing that transgender people are children of God, and part of this flock and family.

If you're wondering what your church can do to support the trans people in your community, why not begin by asking a few questions and taking stock of where your community is right now:

— *Education.* What steps has your community taken to become more knowledgeable about gender identity and trans experiences?

— *Conversation.* What kind of spaces has your community made for internal conversations about gender identities and welcoming transgender members?

— *Consensus.* Has your community written any kind of statement of welcome or affirmation that explicitly includes trans and gender-expansive people?

— *Connection.* Is your community part of a nationwide LGBTQI2A affirmation program, such as Reconciling-Works Lutherans, More Light Presbyterians, Reconciling Ministries Network United Methodists, Association of Welcoming and Affirming Baptists, or Call to Action Catholics?

— *Follow through.* What concrete steps is your community taking each week, each month, or each year to support transgender and gender-expansive people?

These questions can help you begin conversations with other community members and leaders in your church, but what about some concrete examples of those action steps? Here are a few suggestions to get you started:

— Create an advocacy group in your church that will commit to dialogue with your denominational governing body regarding trans inclusion.

— Hold a liturgy for Transgender Day of Remembrance (November 20),[8] and celebrate Trans Day of Visibility (March 31).

— Offer continuing education classes on topics related to gender and gender identity.

— Have a presence at your nearest LGBTQI2A Pride celebration.

— Encourage participation and leadership of transgender people in the life of your church.

— Keep trans faith resources in the church library.

— Have prayers and/or liturgy available for name changes, preparation for surgery, preparation for hormone therapy, and coming out/inviting in.

— Create a gender-neutral restroom in your church building. This can be especially simple if you have a

single-occupant restroom in the building—all you have
to do is change the sign.

—Include gender identity and gender expression in your
nondiscrimination hiring policy.

—Use inclusive language for the congregation (gender-
neutral pronouns like the singular "they" for people
whose gender identity you don't know; "siblings in
Christ" rather than "brothers and sisters," etc.) in your
sermons, liturgies, bulletins, and fliers.

—Use gender-expansive language for God (including
other pronouns like "she" and "they" alongside "he";
including nongendered titles like "Creator, Redeemer,
and Sustainer" alongside "Father, Son, and Holy
Spirit").

—Create a community outreach plan that helps explain
what your church is doing to welcome and affirm transgender people.

—If there is a piece of trans-exclusionary legislation on the
table in your state or local government,[9] start an after-
church letter-writing campaign and get involved in
transgender-affirming political advocacy as a group. Let
your elected leaders know that your faith prompts you to
support your trans siblings!

—Make sure all church leaders—youth leaders especially—have had some training on gender diversity
so they can respond compassionately and knowledge-
ably when a transgender person visits your church, or
when an existing member comes out. (See the list of
resources for people in ministry in the Further Reading section.)

—Include theological texts from transgender Christians in
your teaching, preaching, and Bible studies.

—Include stories of gender minorities like the ones found
in this book in your youth curricula to help trans youth
connect to their faith.

—Include LGBTQI2A-ally training in your new member
classes.

"All right, all right," I hear you say. "Those are a lot of good ideas. But what if I'm not connected to an affirming church community right now? Is there something I can do as an individual?"

Absolutely! Whether you're part of another kind of community that's working toward trans inclusion, or whether you're someone with a transgender coworker or a transgender family member, there are dozens of ways that you can support the trans people in your life. Here are just a couple of ideas:

— Educate yourself on the basics, and then keep going! You're reading this book, so you've already made a great start. Scholarship regarding trans issues is growing all the time, and there's always more to learn.
— Always use someone's correct name and pronouns. If you're not sure what pronouns someone uses, just ask. If you make a mistake, apologize, correct yourself, and move on—no need to make a big deal about it. Don't forget to practice pronouns that are new to you!
— Read the work of transgender educators, theologians, and justice workers. (You can find many good examples in the Further Reading section below.)
— Think about how you use gendered language in your everyday life, and about the times when you assume something about someone's gender. Consider moving from greetings like "Good morning, ladies!" to "Good morning, folks!" when you're meeting a new group of people.
— Practice interrupting negative conversation. If you hear someone speaking badly of a transgender person because of their gender identity, consider stepping in and explaining why that behavior isn't OK.
— Be vocal about your support so that the people around you know it's all right to express their own support, or even to come out to you if they need a friend.
— Don't ask invasive questions about a person's body or about their birth name.

— Don't "out" someone by talking about their trans identity with others.
— Watch out for backhanded compliments! Phrases like "You're so pretty for a trans woman!" are actually much more harmful than they are kind. If you want to compliment someone, compliment a talent they have or something they're wearing—something unrelated to what their body looks like, or how well they're "passing."
— Get involved in policy change, and stay aware of possible trans-exclusionary laws in your state and local government. We're currently at a moment in history where trans people are being especially targeted, and we need all the help we can get. Writing letters to your elected officials and attending demonstrations or protests can be great ways of standing alongside your trans siblings.
— Offer to help transgender people navigate possibly unsafe spaces like bathrooms and locker rooms. Sometimes having a buddy with you is the difference between a fun night out and a trip to the hospital.
— Donate to organizations that help transgender people get access to affordable medical care, housing, safe jobs, and legal advice. Bonus points if the organization is led by trans people themselves!

Now, for my transgender siblings. If you're a trans or gender-expansive person yourself, the resources you'll require will be different from the ones churches and cisgender allies need. The most important thing you can do for yourself as a trans Christian, especially in difficult times, is to give yourself permission to give and receive love—love from God, love from others, love from yourself. No matter what happens, no matter what others say, no matter whether you're surrounded by supportive people or feeling all alone, the Good Shepherd is with you. The Creator of the whole universe is proud of you. You bring God joy. There will be times when you'll need help, and it's brave to reach out and ask for the support you need. There will also be times when you'll be gifted to support others, and as Francis of Assisi said, in giving you will receive.

That's why the second most important thing is to get connected to a community, either in person or online. In the Further Reading section of this book, you'll find recommendations for online organizations that can get you started. Rest assured that more resources are being created every day, and every Sunday there's a new church opening its doors to people just like you. If you don't have access to a physical or online community of trans people of faith yet, know that there are organizations and individuals who are working every single day to bring those resources closer. You're not forgotten, and you're not alone.

Don't forget to practice some spiritual self-care. Most of us have experienced some form of rejection, and building spiritual resilience is a difficult thing to do, even under the best circumstances. Let me tell you about three kinds of spiritual self-care that have helped me:

— *Reading the Psalms.* If you've ever felt like yelling at God or staying in bed all day crying, Psalms is the book for you. Alternately, if you've ever felt like dancing because you're just so happy to be alive, or singing about how beautiful the sunrise was this morning, Psalms is also the book for you! This collection of 150 songs and poems is a great way to get into reading the Bible if you're not too sure where to start, and it's a collection that reminds you that you're not alone. No matter what emotion you're feeling right now, there's probably a psalm for it, and knowing that someone more than two thousand years ago understands something about how you feel can remind you of the ways that we're all connected.

— *Practicing Sabbath.* As a transgender Christian, it's pretty likely that you spend a good amount of time defending yourself, educating people, and just trying to muddle through your own life. Being trans can be exhausting, and Scripture tells us that rest is not only good for us;

it's good for our relationship with God. Taking time
each day to journal your way into prayer, or taking a day
each week to unplug from all the bad news and outrage
on social media, can help you recharge and reconnect
with who you are and how you experience God in the
everyday.

— *Finding a dialogue partner*. It's way too easy to get stuck in
our own heads when we're spending a lot of time thinking about faith and gender. There's an ancient practice
of finding a dialogue partner to help you think things
through and offer some outside views. That partner
can come in the form of a friend, a therapist, a spiritual
adviser, a pastor, or even a journal that you keep yourself.
Allowing ourselves to ask scary questions about what we
believe is actually a profound opportunity for growth,
and getting those words outside of ourselves in some way
can help us lay down our worries in preparation for that
Sabbath rest.

Finally, don't be afraid to ask for help. If you're noticing a
decline in your mental health, or even if you just need somebody to talk to, you can always reach out to others via Trans
Lifeline, the crisis line made for trans people, by trans people.
You can reach them at (877) 565-8860 in the United States
and (877) 330-6366 in Canada. If you're outside North America, you can connect with the Befrienders, who have support
hotlines worldwide in dozens of different languages, by going
to www.befrienders.org. You can also talk with people via text
or online chat through the other organizations you'll find listed
in the Further Reading section under Helplines.

We face difficult obstacles as trans people, but that doesn't
mean that joy and happiness aren't possible! There are so many
transgender Christians out thriving in the world, and you've
met just a few of them here. I hope that their stories have given
you a sense of what our future in communities of faith can
look like. Together—and alongside those who fight to end racism, sexism, xenophobia, and discrimination based on physical

and mental ability—transgender Christians will continue to work for justice for all people. We will hold in our hearts the truth that civil rights activist Fannie Lou Hamer proclaimed: Nobody's free until everybody's free.

So what happens when transgender Christians are able to flourish and find community, and when churches are able to see the gifts that those trans Christians bring? First, the rates of violence against transgender people fall, because Christian groups are no longer advocating trans-exclusionary viewpoints and legislation. Then, the minority stress that transgender people experience weakens, because they live amid a community that supports them spiritually, physically, and emotionally. People who once walked away from Christianity because of the church's negative treatment of LGBTQI2A individuals begin to come back, curious about the way grace is showing up in the midst of resurrected relationships.

The time and resources that once went into fighting this particular battle in the culture wars now go to summer lunches for school kids, building low-income housing, and welcome packages for refugee families. Transgender leaders, many of whom have experience in community organizing, begin to create outreach programs that take worship into local parks and retirement homes, rather than waiting for people to stumble into the sanctuary. The church grows, the gospel spreads, kids get to grow up in love and in safety, and justice begins to roll down like water.

Most importantly, when transgender Christians are accepted and celebrated in Christian communities, the Good Shepherd's flock is put back together, and we once again become more than the sum of our parts. We get a preview of God's kingdom here on earth, and Luke 15 tells us there is rejoicing in heaven. We say yes, individually and communally, to the love of God that seeks to bind us together, and we are transformed.

Afterword

Spiritual Care for Gender-Expansive Christians: A Conversation with Professor Susannah Cornwall

When I was first imaging what a second edition of *Transforming* might look like, I knew right away that I wanted to include a chapter on spiritual care. After years of work with Transmission Ministry Collective, the online organization I founded to support trans and gender-expansive Christians, I know a lot more about what spiritual care looks like in practice. I have also found that there is a desperate need for more educational resources for cisgender ministry professionals who want to support their trans congregants. I'm deeply thankful for books like Chris Dowd and Christina Beardsley's *Transfaith: A Transgender Pastoral Resource*, Bernard Schlager and David Kundtz's *Ministry among God's Queer Folk*, and Ross Murray's *Made, Known, Loved: Developing LGBTQ-Inclusive Youth Ministry*, all of which you'll find in the Further Reading portion of this book, but there's so much more to be said! Countless trans Christians are looking for church homes, and as you'll soon read, there are many places in our world where spiritual care can be practiced outside the sanctuary or pastor's office.

I first learned about Professor Susannah Cornwall because of her work on the Controversies in Contextual Theology Series, and I was pleased to see her name again when I found out about the Modeling Transgender Spiritual Care Project. This project—which you'll hear more about below—was undertaken at the University of Exeter, where she serves as a Professor of Constructive Theologies and Director of the Exeter Centre for Ethics and Practical Theology. When I reached out to her about this conversation, I joked that I wanted her to be the "one token cisgender person" interviewed in this book centered on trans experiences, and I'm thrilled she agreed.

She's demonstrated a great ability to work alongside intersex and trans communities and translate experiences into data and conclusions that broaden the way for everyone. I hope that the dialogue in this chapter will be galvanizing for people in ministry and thought provoking for anyone in Christian community with their gender-expansive neighbors. (Note that this interview has been edited for length and clarity.)

Austen: Can you tell us a bit about your academic background? How did you become interested in researching the experiences of intersex and transgender people of faith?

Susannah: I studied theology as an undergraduate, and I'd done some work around body theology and feminist theology both then and in my master's. I was interested in questions around embodiment in quite a broad way, especially from the lens of eschatology and resurrection bodies, so that was all there in the background.

And then it was one of these really serendipitous things; I came across an article one day, in a magazine called *New Internationalist*, which looks at social issues. The theme of the special issue was equality, and there was a short column written by a woman called Esther Morris Leidolf, who is a well-known intersex activist.[1] She was writing in this column about the fact that she'd been born with a condition that meant she had no vaginal opening, and that when she was about twelve or thirteen, she'd been taken into hospital, put under anesthetic, and they'd created a vagina for her, but with no conversation beforehand about the fact that that was going to happen, which must have been so distressing.

It was the first time that I'd ever come across any discussion of intersex where it wasn't called "hermaphroditism." It was my first introduction to the intersex activism movement, which was really gathering momentum in the 2000s. I was really interested in what had been done about this theologically, because it wasn't something that I remembered having come across, and when I started to do some poking around, I found there was very little. There was an article I came across at the time by Sally Gross called "Intersexuality and Scripture."[2] But other than that, there was hardly anything.

So, for me, this article sparked all kinds of questions. Given that there are conservative theologies around things like same-sex relationships, which often assume that God created people male and female, and complementarity, and all the rest of it, I thought, "Well, if things are a bit more complicated than that at a biological level, what does that do to those sorts of theologies?" Theologies of disability, for example. That's not necessarily a comfortable comparison, because some people will say, "Well, are you saying intersex is a sort of disability?" and that's not where I'm coming from. But lots of the questions about what constitutes a healthy body or a good body or a problematic body, about what happens to diverse bodies in the resurrection—will differences be healed or disappeared?—have been talked about for years and years in really helpful ways in disability theology, so I was bringing intersex into conversation with that.

Then I looked at writing that had been done already in trans theologies, in particular, by trans Christians.[3] It can be really problematic to lump intersex and trans together because inter-sex is more explicitly to do with biological differences, often. Trans identities sometimes involve that, but not always. So again, it was a case not of flattening out those differences, but asking, "What have been some of the responses to trans theo-logians?" What have trans theologians been doing in terms of being able to say, "Clearly, things are just a bit more compli-cated than some conservative theologians will have us believe."

Austen: Your research on that question, and on intersex and trans theology more generally, has become a big part of your academic career. It's important to note, though, that you don't share these identities. How do you engage in this work as someone who's practicing allyship?

Susannah: Something that I was aware of then—and have become even more aware of, the longer I've worked in these areas—is that I'm an ally, but I'm an outsider to these com-munities. I'm not an intersex person. I'm not a trans person.

And I don't want my work to displace the work of people from those communities. At the same time, I'm aware that I have certain privileges, which have included things like access to research funding, a salaried post, and academic networks. As well as the fact that there's nothing inherently about my identity that tends to cause people to say, "You can't be trusted or you shouldn't be taken seriously," whereas, sadly, that's often been the case for LGBTQIA+ people. I've wanted to try and use those privileges responsibly. For example, creating paid opportunities for people from those communities to come and do guest teaching for me or paid consultancy, trying to create networking opportunities for activists and practitioners and academics to meet and work together, writing collaboratively with trans or intersex people.

When I receive speaking invitations now, as much as is within my power, I'm trying to say, "Will you invite a trans theologian as well? Can we share the platform? Can that person be a respondent, or can we share what you're asking us to do?"

I also have a group of—I guess I'd call them critical friends—trans and intersex people who will do things like comment on draft work for me. Clearly, there will still be things in what I say that they probably don't agree with; there will still be mistakes that are my mistakes rather than their mistakes. But I found that so helpful in highlighting for me where I'm going wrong and where I need to do better.

Austen: I think those are really good, solid examples of what allyship can look like. We want to encourage people to have communities of accountability, so that if they're not from that community, they can be accountable to others. How can we create a community of accountability so that there are people around who can point at a piece of our work and say, "Oh, watch out for this, because it's going to be actively harmful," or "Maybe you shouldn't use this particular word."

Susannah: Well-meaning people can perpetuate harm by speaking on behalf of others, because they think they need to protect them or something. We all have our friends and our default networks that we go to, but I'm really aware that asking people to do that labor *is* labor and it's tiring. Trying to diversify networks is also really good, so that it's not always the same few people who are being approached all the time by everyone to do this kind of work.

And also, obviously, because intersex experience and trans experience are so different and people approach them differently. Those are not monolithic communities. So it's important to have multiple voices in the conversation and understand that probably at various times some people will need to tag out and just take a step back and take a rest from it. That's important.

Austen: Tell us about the Modeling Transgender Spiritual Care Project. Why is spiritual care important or beneficial for trans people who are medically transitioning? And what do we know about how spiritual care for trans people can reduce negative outcomes for individuals and communities?

Susannah: This was a project that I was involved with from 2017 to 2019. In England, where I live, the model for trans and gender-affirming health care is in a transitional period at the moment. For the last decade or so, it has been provided by specialist gender clinics, which are part of the National Health Service. There are not that many of them; there are about seven, housed within mental health-care trusts. That's quite interesting in itself, because of the assumption that this is essentially a mental health-care thing, though that clinic becomes the primary channel for referrals onward for things like hormone therapy and also for surgery where that's appropriate.

There are really long waiting lists for all NHS services, but particularly for gender services. That was the case before the pandemic, it's obviously got much worse as a result of the pandemic. The waiting list is now into multiple years. One particular clinic approached me and said, "We know that these long wait times are a problem. We know that people's mental health is suffering as a result of having to wait for so long. What can

we be doing about it?" And one of the things we were exploring was where spiritual care might fit in, and whether some of
that could be put in place while people were in the very early
stages of being in the system, while they were waiting for other
treatment.

The National Health Service says within its own Contract
of Care that spiritual care is part of its remit,[4] so it's designed to
care for people's mental and physical, but also spiritual health,
and to take account of things like cultural identity as well. And
within the NHS, spiritual care is not solely the purview of specialist chaplains. The idea is that spiritual care is really embed-
ded within all care that somebody receives. But in talking to
people who were providing gender care, by and large we found
they just didn't feel confident doing that. They didn't ask the
question about patients' spiritual care needs, possibly because
faith was not on their radar, or because they said, "I wouldn't
know where to refer somebody if they did want to talk about
that sort of stuff. I don't feel equipped to do it."

So one of the things that we did within the Modeling Transgender Spiritual Care Project was to talk to people who were
on the waiting list and who hadn't yet begun treatment. We
also talked to people who had been through treatment at some
point in the past, either with this clinic or with other clinics.
We asked, "This is part of what the NHS says it does, offering
spiritual care, but were you actually offered any? Would you
have wanted it? What did spiritual care look like for you? If
you were offered it and you thought it was good, what worked
well? What do you think would work well? What would you
have wanted?"

The people we spoke to were people of no religion, Christians, Buddhists, people of various traditions. They were able
to tell us quite a lot about what they thought was and wasn't
good. Interestingly, some of the people who took part were
themselves also providing spiritual care to other trans people,
in either a formal or a less formal way. We found that where
people did have a particular faith affiliation, they said that they
would have welcomed opportunities to reflect on what their

transition or their exploration of their gender identity meant for their faith, but they hadn't been offered those opportunities.[5] And they didn't necessarily feel it was something that they felt safe talking about with a faith leader that they already knew.

Some of the trans people we spoke to said that they did have a religious faith, that it was a really important source of identity and community and support for them. Other people said they would like that, but they didn't necessarily know how to go about finding a safe faith community. They felt that it would be quite risky to disclose that they had already socially transitioned, or perhaps they had questions about gender identity and so on.

Often people didn't feel for themselves that there was a tension between their gender identity and their faith, but they knew that perhaps other people would think there was. There was one person that we spoke to who is a Christian and has actually gone on to provide pastoral care to other trans Christians, but who said that when they were in hospital, they weren't even asked by their medical team whether they wanted a chaplain to come and visit them, because the perception was, "Why would somebody like you want a religious person to come and talk to you? Because aren't all religious people against this sort of thing?" There was just an assumption that these things wouldn't chime together.

Austen: In the US, a lot of times, spiritual care is not taken into account at all in the medical process, because there's no requirement that it should be. But also, because the chaplains that we do have in hospital systems are there just for the days you're in the hospital itself—which is maybe twelve hours maximum for a lot of things—and a lot of the spiritual care burden falls on pastors of the congregation that that person might be connected with. That's not ideal for lots of reasons, one being that there are many people who might want and benefit from spiritual care, but aren't connected to a church congregation, and therefore won't receive any at all.

As I read the report you wrote on this project, I noticed that there was this repeated concern voiced by trans participants—the belief that bad spiritual care would be worse than none at all. It shows religious leaders that this can't be a slapdash effort, but has to be done thoughtfully and in consultation with people in the community.

Susannah: One of the things that I'm quite encouraged by is that in the last five years there seems to be a really rapid increase in the number of churches, and also networks and umbrella religious structures like dioceses and so on, that are investing in training and resourcing on things like gender identity and transition, for clergy and also for lay ministers. And often it involves actual resources. It involves putting money into it as well as time.

I'm heartened that, increasingly, people seem to be taking that really seriously and saying we do need to give some proper time to this, we do need to give some proper thoughts to it, because it takes investment of time and resources to equip people to minister well to people who might, in some cases, have had quite negative experiences in the past. People whose autonomy and self-image might possibly be quite bruised by encounters they've had before, who might be traumatized by their previous interactions with religious communities.

I think part of doing spiritual care well is that investment of money and time, but also just asking what the support groups and networks are in your geographic area. How visible are you as a church or as a community to those charities or to those support groups? You're trying to be aware of them, but are they aware of you as well?

Austen: The other difficult thing is that there's some pushback from ministers and pastors who say, "Well, I can't be prepared for everything. How am I going to be prepared for what I don't know about yet?" That's where making connections in your community for resourcing is the most important thing. You can have a note on your desk that says, "Here's a helpline.

Here's the local community center. Here's a helpful book." Just knowing where you can send people and whom you can loop into the conversation can help you mitigate that stress you feel about being prepared.

Susannah: When I did my research with intersex people of faith, one of the things I found was that in pretty much every circumstance with the people I spoke to, where they had spoken to a priest or a minister or someone about their gender and their faith, that was the first time that that priest or other minister had ever heard anything about intersex. They didn't really know what it was. I think that's less likely to happen now with trans identity, partly because it's a bit later and partly just because trans stuff is being talked about so much more in society generally.

However, one of the things that I've come to believe is that good pastoral care shouldn't be a matter of good luck. It shouldn't be a matter of rolling the dice on whom you meet first, and whether they have been well resourced and have thought about it. Because if a trans person does approach a minister asking for some spiritual support, ideally they wouldn't be the first trans person that that minister has ever met. They shouldn't have to feel that they have to do all the work of educating them. The minister needs to be resourced and up to date, but it's not like you can train everyone once and then that's it, that's done. Resourcing and education need to be a regular thing.

Austen: Some of your research is related to intersex folks, and some is related to trans folks and their experience. One of the things that comes up in both places is this experience of medicalization. For some trans people, viewing transness through a medical lens is helpful. They can say, "Hey, I have a thing that I deal with," rather than "Here's this thing that I am," and it provides a bit of separation. For other trans people, medicalization—and especially the way that we're made to jump through medical hoops just to get things that we need to be healthy—is really troublesome and problematic in a lot of ways. I was thinking of how theology can offer a counterpoint to medicalization; maybe affirming theology and spiritual care can strengthen people so that they can deal with that medicalization, which is what the Modeling Transgender Spiritual Care Project was about in some ways.

Susannah: Yes, different people relate to that medicalizing lens in really different ways. One of the people that we spoke to as part of the project, who was a Buddhist, said that they belonged to a fairly conservative Buddhist community that had quite strong ideas about gender roles. They'd faced quite a bit of suspicion as somebody who had transitioned as a member of that community. For them, a medical lens was really helpful, and one of the things that they wanted was for a doctor or somebody within the medical system to be able to go to educate their Buddhist community and say, "Here's where the science is with this. This is a thing. This is not something that this person has just made up."

Similarly, in my intersex research, I remember talking to a mother of two intersex children in Northern Ireland. They were members of a really conservative evangelical Christian community, and for them it was really important to be able to say to the girls' school, "My daughters have a medical condition, and that means that they need to be able to have private changing rooms for PE, rather than getting changed with the others." There was a real reluctance to say that this could be anything around sexuality or gender identity, because within their own religious tradition, that was too scary a place to go. So I can understand why some people are attracted to that medical lens.

But by and large, one of the things that theology does in terms of offering a kind of alternative is to say it's not just about pathology versus nonpathology. It's not about healthy versus unhealthy, normal versus abnormal. It's about saying, "Look what a diverse species we are! Look how diverse creaturehood is in general." I'm a Christian theologian and I think Christian theological anthropology has the potential to say there are many, many ways to image God. Humans are made in the image of God. Very clearly, humans are very different from one another in terms of gender, in terms of race and ethnicity, in terms of all sorts of things. So if reflecting the image of God looks like many different things, it leads—or it should lead—to a certain circumspection about being certain that we know what good embodiment looks like.

You will come across some (I think) well-meaning conservative theological accounts that say something like, "Well, of course, we're all fallen. Of course, we all sin. Of course, we all live in this world where things have gone wrong. However, trans people and/or intersex people, they're special evidence of the fact that things have gone wrong, because things have gone more wrong for them than they have for the rest of us who are normal. And that's not their fault, but we should feel sorry for them. We should feel compassion for them."

That's problematic because it takes for granted that things like cisgender identity, things like heterosexuality, things like being endosex rather than intersex, are just obviously normal and natural and healthy and part of God's plan. Whereas I think one of the things I'm interested in is asking, Why have we taken that for granted? What's been behind that ideologically? What's been behind that politically? Why is it that, within theology and within society more broadly, we're in this moment where we're so interested in trans people and we're so interested in gay people, but there's so little attention given to analyzing cis people, there's so little attention given to analyzing heterosexual people? Because that stuff is just taken for granted as being normal and healthy.

Austen: I think part of the reason some nonaffirming theologies lean into medicalization is because they can say, "Let's begin with the premise that there's something wrong with you and then explain what's wrong with you with theology," rather than going at it the opposite way around. If you're coming in with the assumption that something is wrong, you can end up begging the question.

Susannah: Definitely. One of the things that I was thinking about was Alex Clare-Young's book *Transgender. Christian. Human.* Alex says there's often this assumption that being trans equals gender dysphoria, always, for everyone, which isn't the case. Alex says, for them it's not like that, and it's not like that for lots of people. Alex says:

> There is a common assumption that all trans people hate their bodies. This is simply not true. Our relationships with our bodies . . . are complicated. . . . For a time, parts of my body caused me significant discomfort. But I also loved parts of it. . . . Just because my body hurt, just because I hurt my body, did not mean that I hated it. I love my body, but I also love being who God has called me to be, and that is an inside out being, not solely defined by embodiment.[6]

There's something really powerful about that. But I think also that coming to have fuller knowledge about one's own identity is of a piece with coming to have fuller knowledge about all kinds of aspects of oneself. One of the things I really love in Justin Sabia-Tanis's work is his image of gender as a vocation.[7] I talk about it a lot when I'm talking to groups of cis people, cis ministers in particular. I say, "You understand the concept of vocation. You understand the concept of having been called to a particular path. What if all of us were more comfortable thinking about gender in that way? Not just for trans people, but for everyone. What would that do?"

As Justin Sabia-Tanis points out, sometimes a vocation is something that's always been with you and you've always been aware of, but very often it comes upon you gradually. Sometimes a vocation is very clearly being called out of something to a different path in one direction forever, but it's not always like that. Sometimes a vocation is for a particular time or a particular season. It can happen violently and dramatically. It can happen gradually and slowly. But there's space for all of that.

I'm reminded, too, of Rachel Mann's book *Dazzling Darkness*,[8] where she is writing about her gender identity, her vocation to priesthood, and her chronic illness. The experience of living with chronic pain, which is not directly related to her gender identity, is very much related to her experience of being in her body. All of those things are interconnected and have an impact.

The diversity of bodily experiences that trans people have are not so different from the diversity of experiences that all people have. However, it's likely that trans people, for various reasons, have had to do a lot of self-interrogation and have had to become better at developing language for that sort of thing than others, who haven't been forced to think about it in the same way. So when thinking about how people might reconnect with their bodies, let's ask where alienation from bodies comes from. Often, it's because society is not particularly hospitable to allowing people to work through that stuff in public.

Austen: Coming into the conversation through the lens of calling or vocation is different from coming into the conversation through the lens of dysphoria, which tends to say, "You must have X amount of distress in order to be real." Coming into the conversation with the focus on calling can reduce the stigma, can reduce a bunch of the issues with medicalization, and can connect people to the experiences of other folks in a way that we can all relate to.

What do you see as the future of pastoral care for gender-expansive people? What changes need to be made on a systems level? What can be done by individual leaders and churches? And then how do you think an expanding understanding of and care for trans people can transform Christianity?

Susannah: In terms of how a better understanding of sex and gender diversity can transform Christianity, let's look at the beauty of diversity that's already present. Let's recapture that sense of mystery and that sense that there is stuff beyond our current understanding, and that that's OK. It can be difficult and painful to be in that sort of place where things are not yet clear, but it's part of the human condition.

In terms of the future of pastoral care, there are lots of really good intentions that accidentally end up wounding people, perpetuating damage when people don't mean to. There's a book chapter that I've just cowritten with Sara Gillingham, who's an intersex Christian in Britain, and Alex Clare-Young.[9] One of the things that we write about is the way that churches have been having these conversations. These churches are often really well-intentioned, but they can end up perpetuating harm when they invite trans people or intersex people to come in and talk about all the things that have happened to them that were traumatic. Sara in particular noted that these conversations can be really costly if you are the person whose personhood and identity are the thing under scrutiny, much more costly than they are for the person for whom it's an interesting theological issue, but not something that is personal in the same way.

We need to push back at the idea, especially within conservative circles, that gender diversity inherently means either mental illness or self-deception—that trans people's accounts of themselves are less trustworthy—and therefore trans people need others to come along and narrate the significance of their experience. Trans people and intersex people are the experts on their own lives and their own experiences. I'd like to see a decentering of cis people's accounts of what it means and signifies to be trans. And I'm really aware of the irony of me saying that as a cis person! But at the same time, we have to acknowledge the burden, the labor that it is to ask marginalized people to do that work again and again.

Austen: Definitely. If you're going to ask people to educate or to share their story, you need to somehow account for the fact that there's a bit of a power imbalance, whether that looks like protecting them in some way or compensating them fairly or evening the playing field for all involved.

Susannah: I think the other part of why I do what I do as a cis person and as a straight person is to say we've got a responsibility to do our own reflecting on gender and sexuality. It's too easy for those of us who are cis and straight to think, "Well, I don't need to think about my sexuality. I don't need to think about my gender identity because it's the default. It's not in need of interrogation." Actually, theologies about sex and gender are in need of interrogation by all people, regardless of who you are and what identities you hold. That responsibility of reflecting on our sexuality and our gender needs to be shared.

Austen: The last thing I wanted to ask you about is the rising tide of transphobia that's especially present right now. People have heard a lot about ideas like social contagion and "rapid-onset gender dysphoria," despite the ways those ideas have been disproven.[10] That's been true in the UK, and of course we're now seeing a huge rise in antitrans legislation here in the US as well.

Susannah: When you hear stories about people being rushed into therapy, people being pushed into making decisions when they're very young, you can see how that sounds worrying, and so I think there are some really well-intentioned people who are saying, "Whoa, we need to be concerned about this. Is there really a trans lobby? Are they coming for our children?" Being able to meet some of that with actual facts—like the fact that in Britain, as I said earlier, the wait times are long, and the treatment, particularly for minors, is super, super conservative—is important. So we should be able to say, "If you've heard about this stuff and you're worried about it, what is it that worries you?" If what worries you is that people's autonomy is not being respected, that the integrity of people's bodies is not being respected and so on, those are good things to be worried about. Those are good things to be concerned about.

But let's look at the way that the rhetoric is being used against trans people. Let's not believe everything that we hear. Let's look at what is actually going on. Things are particularly vicious in Britain at the moment, and it seems to be gathering momentum among people in government, which is really worrying. Because of that, I think it's particularly important that people of faith are clear-sighted about what's happening, and are able to interrogate the media critically, and to ask what interests are behind some of the stories that are being pushed.

Austen: That need for people of faith to stand up for their trans siblings is just as present here in the US. And that brings us back to the importance of knowledgeable, compassionate, responsive spiritual care!

Susannah: Absolutely.

TEN TAKEAWAYS FOR PASTORAL CAREGIVERS

1. If your theology around bodies doesn't work for intersex, trans, or disabled bodies, it doesn't work. Interrogate Scripture and theology in light of the full diversity of human experience.
2. A good ally elevates the voices of those within the community and leverages their privilege to gain a hearing from skeptical outsiders.
3. Don't assume that all intersex and trans people seek or have had gender-related medical care. However, everyone should have the opportunity to receive medical, mental health, and spiritual care as needed.
4. Trans and intersex people may have experiences that suggest that all or most faiths are nonaffirming and may not feel safe approaching a faith leader or faith community. Work with LGBTQI2A organizations to help them direct people to safe, affirming spiritual caregivers.
5. Do the work to learn about trans and intersex people's experiences and concerns, while understanding that every individual's experiences are unique.
6. When educating yourself or your congregation, beware taking advantage of the labor of trans and intersex speakers, and make sure they are compensated fairly. Likewise, beware retraumatizing them by making them dwell on

painful experiences, especially in front of nonaffirming audiences.

7. Have resources ready to offer trans and intersex people in need: helplines, community groups, books, articles, etc. You can start with the ones recommended at the end of this book!

8. Understand both the medical and theological lenses through which intersex and trans identities may be viewed. Some people and their families find medical information reassuring, but all can benefit from theological affirmations like celebrating the diversity of creation, the joy of embodiment, and the idea of gender as vocation.

9. Cisgender and endosex people should also reflect on their gender from an analytical and theological perspective. Not to do this is to assume one's own normativity, further marginalizing trans and intersex people.

10. Have responses ready to debunk transphobic statements in the media or defuse anxiety among those unfamiliar with the reality of intersex and trans experiences. Find out which reporters and news outlets are trusted by organizations like the Trans Journalists Association (transjournalists.org) and GLAAD (glaad.org).

Small Group Study Guide

The following guide will equip you to discuss *Transforming* as a group in your congregation or community and offers flexibility to expand your study from four to six sessions, depending on the needs of your group.

The first and last sessions in the outline below can be eliminated or adapted if you need to fit the study into just four sessions. The four chapter-focused sessions each require around thirty-five pages of reading prior to the group gathering. Each session includes an icebreaker question that is somewhat personal, inviting participants to bring their whole selves to the discussion, followed by four to six questions based on the theological topics and Scriptures addressed in the assigned chapters. A weekly challenge is offered at the end of each session so that participants can practice transforming their thinking in real-life situations.

Knowing that some people are slower to speak than others, be intentional about inviting each person to respond to each question, allowing them to pass if they do not wish to speak at that time. Recognize that everyone comes to the group with different ideas, backgrounds, and perspectives. Do your best to foster an environment in which everyone feels heard and valued. It's important not to assume that gender-expansive people will want to share, but do pay particular attention to members of your group who are themselves transgender, nonbinary, or gender-nonconforming, or have family members who are, understanding that these discussions are not simply theoretical but affect real people. Assure all group members that they are welcome to step out of the room at any time to attend to their mental health.

Outline of Sessions

Session1: Why We're Here—Forewords (Optional)
Distribute books and get to know one another. Read the forewords together. Discuss participants' reasons for joining the
study and what they hope to gain from the experience.

Session 2: Introducing the Conversation—Introduction and Chapters 1–3
Explore some of the questions and challenges transgender people face and three potential lenses through which to view gender diversity. Learn the basic terminology and definitions that
will be relevant to the discussion of gender and trans theology.

Session 3: The Bible beyond Black and White—Chapters 4–6
Examine the key Scripture passages used against transgender
people and discover how expansive, diverse, and fluid the
world of the Bible really is.

Session 4: Calling All Eunuchs—Chapters 7–9
While gender diversity has always existed, it hasn't always
been visible in all cultures. Studying Scripture passages about
eunuchs—people who existed outside of the gender binary—can
help us understand biblical attitudes toward gender diversity.

Session 5: Embodied and Embraced—Chapters 10–12
Christianity sometimes creates an artificial divide between
body and spirit. But God wants to embrace every part of us—
the physical and the invisible—and calls us to embrace one
another as full, unique, beloved beings as well.

Session 6: Moving Forward—Conclusion and Afterword (Optional)
Hartke and Cornwall offer guidance for individuals and
churches to turn good intentions into action. Discuss how you
can better support the transgender community. If you have
been studying *Transforming* with the goal of making your congregation more inclusive, devote at least one session entirely to
planning your next steps for implementing meaningful change.

SESSION 1: WHY WE'RE HERE
Forewords by Matthew Vines and Jamie and Rebekah Bruesehoff

Icebreaker
Introduce yourself and what pronouns you use. Name three things that "make you *you*."

Discussion Questions
1. What do the statistics Matthew Vines shares in his foreword tell you about the significance of the work we'll be doing in this study?
2. Why do you think many Christians are not affirming of transgender people, or as Rebekah Bruesehoff says, "Some of the most hurtful and hateful things said about and to my family come from people of faith"?
3. What would it take for you or your church to be as affirming of transgender people as the community Rebekah and Jamie Bruesehoff describe?
4. What compelled you to join this study? What are you hoping to gain from the experience of studying *Transforming* with this group?

Weekly Challenge
Visit the websites of three churches about which you know nothing. (Google "churches in Springfield" or some other common town name, and randomly click on a few results!) What can you learn from those websites about how gender identity may be viewed in those congregations? What messages are they sending, intentionally or unintentionally, about how transgender people might be welcomed (or not)? For extra credit, see if the churches you find have their beliefs listed at www.churchclarity.org!

SESSION 2: INTRODUCING THE CONVERSATION
Introduction and Chapters 1–3

Icebreaker

How do you know what gender you are? How would you feel if someone insisted you were not the gender you know yourself to be?

Discussion Questions

1. Read Psalm 139:14. What does this verse mean to you? What is your response to the suggestion that transgender identities mean God "made a mistake"?

2. When did you first become aware of transgender identities? What messages have you gotten from the church about the validity and morality of being transgender?

3. What terminology in chapter 2 was new to you? How does it affect your thinking to learn that gender-expansive identities have been recognized and recorded in a variety of cultures throughout history? (See pp. 32–35.)

4. Considering the social construction of gender expression and gender roles (and even perhaps the meaning we derive from chromosomes and sex organs, according to Dr. Anne Fausto-Sterling on p. 36), what would it look like if we didn't assume gender based on genitalia?

5. Summarize the differences between the Sin, Sickness, and Specialty frameworks discussed in chapter 3. Why is the sickness (or disability) framework still problematic, even though it doesn't consider gender dysphoria or the pursuit of gender affirmation a moral failing? (See pp. 45–46.)

6. Does the idea of a specialty (or diversity) framework resonate with you? What special gifts do you see gender diverse people contributing to the fabric of society? (See p. 48.)

Weekly Challenge

Practice noticing diversity in gender expression and how it operates separately from gender identity. Notice when you find yourself assuming someone's gender identity. Ask yourself what about their gender expression makes you think that, and whether you could be wrong. (Note: you could always be wrong!)

SESSION 3: THE BIBLE BEYOND BLACK AND WHITE
Chapters 4–6

Icebreaker

Have you ever had someone use the Bible to criticize or condemn you for something? How did it feel? How do you think it would have felt if they'd offered their criticism without bringing the Bible into it?

Discussion Questions

1. Before reading these chapters, what would you have said that the Bible says about gender? Read Genesis 1:27, perhaps the most commonly cited Scripture referring to gender. What stands out to you about this verse?
2. Why do you think the writer of Genesis emphasized pairs of opposites like day and night, land and sea, male and female, when it is clear that many in-betweens exist, like dawn and dusk, marshes and estuaries, intersex and nonbinary people? (See pp. 56–57.)
3. What does it mean to you that humans are created "in the image of God"? Could there be any physical dimension of this image, when God the Creator does not have a body? (See pp. 61–62.)
4. Read Deuteronomy 22:5. What problems arise when we try to apply this law to our cultures today? Even if we assume the Scripture writer meant that "a woman shall not wear [whatever her culture considers] a man's apparel . . . ," why might this still be problematic? (See pp. 68–70.)
5. Given the examples in Scripture of celebrated people who broke with gendered norms in clothing or roles, like Joseph and Deborah (see pp. 76–78), what might we conclude about interpretations of Scripture that claim certain rules and norms are "biblical"?
6. For what reasons did people have their names changed in Scripture? What do these reasons have in common with the reasons many transgender people change their names today?

Weekly Challenge

Spend time in prayer reflecting on your identity as an image-bearer of God. When God calls you by name, what do you imagine God calls you? Is it your first name, or a name that describes you on a deeper level? Allow yourself to wonder what name or term of endearment God might want to give you to honor a particular trait you possess or transformation you've experienced.

SESSION 4: CALLING ALL EUNUCHS
Chapters 7–9

Icebreaker

How is your gender experience an asset to your discipleship or spiritual growth? If you don't feel it is, or you've never considered that possibility, why not?

Discussion Questions

1. Read Deuteronomy 23:1–6 and then read Isaiah 56:3–8. Imagine being a person condemned by the words in Deuteronomy (perhaps you actually are in one of the categories described). What would it feel like to be excluded from your faith community, and then to hear the good news that you are accepted—even celebrated—in God's house?

2. What does it mean to you that the rules changed when the Israelites' context changed? (See pp. 101–2.) Do you think God's rules continue to change?

3. Read Lawrence Richardson's quote on page 112 about seeking acceptance with all his identities—Black, trans, and Christian. How can churches grow in diversity without tokenizing those whose identities differ from the majority in the community? How can people with no (or only one) marginalized identity learn and grow from being in fellowship with multiply marginalized people? Is there a way to learn together without putting the pressure to educate on those already marginalized?

4. Read Matthew 19:11–12. Whom do you think Jesus is talking about when he references different kinds of eunuchs in this passage? What does Jesus seem to be saying about what can be learned from gender-expansive people? (See pp. 113–16.)

5. Read Acts 8:26–40. Consider the idea that the Ethiopian eunuch is doing "theology as a form of survival" (p. 132). Have you ever sought answers in the Bible with that kind of desperation? How do we reconcile that effort with the author's warning on page 130 ("Seeing ourselves in Scripture can be a tricky business . . .")?

6. When the Ethiopian eunuch asks, "What is to prevent me from being baptized?" (Acts 8:37), Philip concludes that there is nothing. What sort of implicit or explicit restrictions does your church put on becoming Christian or becoming a church member? Are there certain restrictions that do seem necessary? Why?

Weekly Challenge
Try writing a list of your social and physical identities—where you are on spectrums of age, ability, race, ethnicity, class, education level, language, orientation, and gender. This week practice looking at the spaces you're in and asking yourself, "Is there anyone here who doesn't share my identities?" If you don't see people with different identities in your space, ask yourself what invisible barriers might be at play.

SESSION 5: EMBODIED AND EMBRACED
Chapters 10–12

Icebreaker

How do you feel about the phrase "Your body is a temple"? How does your faith affect the way you think about your body?

Discussion Questions

1. The writings of the apostle Paul sometimes suggest a false separation between body and soul (see Rom. 7:5–6, 14–18, 24; 8:5–13; Gal. 5:16–21) that can make the body seem irrelevant at best and a "liability" at worst, as Asher O'Callaghan says on pages 140–41. How is Christ's incarnation a better model?
2. Why do people whose bodies have been marginalized due to color, ability, gender, or sexuality seem to understand the holiness of our physical embodiment more easily than those whose bodies are in privileged majorities? (See pp. 147–48.)
3. If our bodies are holy and precious to God in every form, color, and ability, what are the implications of making changes to our bodies, whether through cosmetic surgery, corrective vision devices and procedures, piercings and tattoos, or gender-affirming surgery?
4. While learning and sharing the knowledge that Scripture does not condemn LGBTQI2A people can be transformative and empowering, why is apologetics alone not enough? What does "abundant life" look like for trans Christians?
5. Read Galatians 3:28. What do you think this Scripture says about the importance of our individual identities? What would it look like to achieve oneness without sameness, or unity in diversity?
6. Does unity mean something different for our life on earth than it will in God's kingdom? How do you envision people coming together in the kingdom of God?

Weekly Challenge

For every person you see this week, say (silently, in your head), "You are holy and beautiful." How does it feel to affirm everyone, regardless of their physical appearance or conformity to any perceived standard? Don't forget to say it to yourself in the mirror, too!

SESSION 6: MOVING FORWARD
Conclusion and Afterword

Icebreaker

What has been the most transformative or eye-opening thing you have learned in this study?

Discussion Questions

1. Read Luke 15:4–7 (also printed on p. 175). Do you tend to see yourself as the sheep who got lost and was rescued, or one of the ninety-nine who stayed safely in the fold? How does the image of Jesus rescuing a sheep that was mistreated by the ninety-nine speak to you? (See p. 176.)

2. What steps among those listed on pages 178–82 have you or your congregation already taken? Which can you commit to start doing now?

3. Theologian Susannah Cornwall reports asking herself, "If things are a bit more complicated . . . at a biological level, what does that do to those sorts of theologies?" (p. 189). How have you found reality complicating your theology? How do you respond when lived or observed experience casts doubt on something you had previously believed?

4. How do we use our privilege to take some pressure off gender-expansive people without speaking for them? How do we balance the need to hear and learn trans people's experiences in their own words without requiring them to do additional emotional labor?

5. How can we break down the barrier to good spiritual care caused by misconceptions that all religious figures are anti-LGBTQI2A? How can pastors and other spiritual caregivers be prepared to provide care for gender-expansive people before the situation presents itself?

6. Are you prepared to counter transphobic lies and misconceptions that you may encounter in conversation or on social media? What reliable resources can you lean on if you have questions, or need to understand the arguments better?

Weekly Challenge
Outline the steps you will take this week to begin implementing a trans-affirming change in your church. Include deadlines, tasks, people to involve, and so forth. Remember to ask the gender-expansive people in your community to take positions of leadership and to offer feedback and criticism, if they'd like to, but don't pressure them. Know that these steps can change people's lives and transform your whole community for the better.

Sermon Series: The Expansive God

This four-week sermon series outline will enable you to inspire the whole congregation with the vision of God's wide-open, all-inclusive love for the world. Examining the ways that creation, law, and the Bible's example of Christian community are so much less rigid than we've been taught, you can preach the themes of *Transforming* in a way that expands your congregation's thinking about both gender and the whole of God's good world. Depending on your church's current level of LGBTQI2A affirmation, you can determine how explicitly to address gender identity as you use this series to help your congregation take the appropriate next steps toward full inclusion.

You will find insights and anecdotes in *Transforming* that will be useful in your sermons. Each sermon starter below indicates the chapters of the book most correlated with the theme of the week, starting with chapter 4. The introductory material and chapters 1–3 will be helpful for your own understanding.

— Week 1: In the Beginning (Genesis 1:1–27)
— Week 2: A God Who Changes (Isaiah 56:1–8)
— Week 3: Celebrating the Upside-Down Kingdom (Matthew 19:1–12)
— Week 4: Living as One (Galatians 3:26–28)

Week 1: In the Beginning

Focus Scripture: Genesis 1:1–27
Book references: chapters 4–5

Then God said, "Let us make humankind in our image, according to our likeness.". . . So God created humankind

217

in his image, in the image of God he created them; male
and female he created them.

(Genesis 1:26a, 27)

It's so easy to fall into black-and-white thinking: right and
wrong, healthy and unhealthy, gentle and strong (perhaps add
a few lighthearted local rivalries). Some of us are more fond of
these simple dichotomies than others. The writers of Genesis
1 and other parts of the Torah respected orderly distinctions;
think of all the clean and unclean, pure and impure categories
in Leviticus and Deuteronomy! The creation story in Genesis
1 is full of opposing pairs: light and darkness, land and water,
day and night. Yet we know from experience that dusk and
dawn fall somewhere between darkness and light, night and
day. Marshes, swamps, and estuaries are somewhere between
bodies of water and dry land. Just because Scripture names two
binary options doesn't mean that nothing exists in between
those poles.

What about that "male and female he created them" part?
Even if we love beautiful sunsets or playing in the mud,
we can often still be uncomfortable with the idea of gender
falling outside the male-female binary. Even before a baby
is born, we want to categorize the child as a boy or a girl,
based solely on what body parts are visible on an ultrasound
photo. Yet we know that intersex and transgender people
exist. (See pp. 57–58 for statistics about and examples of
intersex identities throughout history and today.) We might
feel uncomfortable when we can't easily identify someone's
gender, because our brains like to categorize things! But the
diversity of human beings God created is no less beautiful
and awe inspiring than the countless shades of color in a
sunrise.

Unlike the sun and sky and ocean and land, however, God
made humankind in God's own image. Male humans, female
humans, and humans of every other gender were all created
in God's image. Theologians throughout history have debated

what the *imago Dei* really means. (See pp. 61–64 for a few examples.) Whatever the details, we know that this divine spark is within every person we meet.

When we fail to recognize that spark, we can end up doing real damage to our fellow humans—our fellow image-bearers of God. Not only that, but when we limit our experience of the world to what we can understand, the cut-and-dried categories we embrace, we miss out on so much richness in the world God created. We miss out on much of God as well.

Week 2: A God Who Changes

Focus Scripture: Isaiah 56:1–8
Book references: chapters 6–7

> Do not let the foreigner joined to the LORD say, "The LORD will surely separate me from his people"; and do not let the eunuch say, "I am just a dry tree."
>
> (Isaiah 56:3)

This passage from Isaiah is a beautiful testament to God's loving, all-inclusive spirit. But did you know that the Bible is not exactly consistent in its celebration of foreigners and eunuchs? Deuteronomy 23 says, "No one whose testicles are crushed or whose penis is cut off shall be admitted to the assembly of the LORD. . . . No Ammonite or Moabite shall be admitted to the assembly of the LORD" (vv. 1, 3a).

Laws about organization and separation were very important to early Israelites and played a large part in their religious and community standards, but centuries later, after the nation's ordeal of exile and return, those rules weren't as straightforward as they'd seemed in the early days. Held captive in Babylon, many Israelites had intermarried with people of other nations and borne multiethnic children, and others had been castrated—made eunuchs—for various reasons. (See pp. 101–2.) Were all these returning exiles to be excluded from the restored community in Jerusalem?

The book of Isaiah was written to Israelites before, during, and after the exile; the final section, which begins with chapter 56, served to guide the Israelite people as they returned and rebuilt their community. Isaiah 56:1–8 assured those returning exiles who didn't fit the stipulations of the law set forth in Deuteronomy that they were still loved by God, had been given a name and a blessing, like their ancestors Abraham and Sarah, and were a valued part of the body. We see a similar story in the book of Ruth, where Ruth is fully embraced in Israelite community despite the fact that she was a Moabite— another group of people outlawed in Deuteronomy 23. So how do we understand these changes to the rules?

Many of us are uncomfortable with the idea of a God who changes. If God is eternal and all-knowing, wouldn't God have established a set of laws that would last the people of Israel forever, in all circumstances, no matter what happens? I don't know. The people of Israel were in a very different place as a community from where they'd been two hundred or so years before. They'd grown and developed as a nation, and endured great trials that changed the nature and needs of their community. We all struggle with the question of why bad things happen—like cancer, car accidents, or oppressive empires that destroy cities and put people in bondage for many years. We may never know the answer to that, but we do know that God works for our redemption, even in the most hopeless of situations. God is alive and active in our world, working for the good of all people, even going so far as to change or break the rules to make sure everyone is included.

Week 3: Celebrating the Upside-Down Kingdom

Focus Scripture: Matthew 19:1–12
Book references: chapters 8–9

> "Not everyone can accept this teaching, but only those to whom it is given. For there are eunuchs who have been so from birth, and there are eunuchs who have been made

eunuchs by others, and there are eunuchs for the sake of the kingdom of heaven. Let anyone accept this who can."

(Matthew 19:11–12)

The context of this Scripture passage is about divorce, but this isn't a sermon about divorce. Jesus acknowledges that it's often hard to stay married to the same person for one's whole life—and many of us can take comfort in that, regardless of how our cultural understandings and practice of marriage differ from those in Jesus' day! "Why should someone even get married under these circumstances?!" the disciples protest. Rather than extol the virtues of matrimony or the discipline of lifelong commitment, Jesus essentially responds, "Yeah, you probably can't handle it."

Jokes aside, Jesus is being pretty countercultural to say that not everyone should get married. Marriage in those times (as in many other cultures and eras throughout history) was seen as an essential duty to one's family and the community. "Be fruitful and multiply!" "Carry on the family name!" "Have kids to inherit the family business!" Also, men who got married took on extra power as head of a family. If you lived in Jesus' day and were the ancient equivalent of a cisgender, heterosexual, married man with children, then you'd carry a good deal of social power—doubly so if you were a Roman citizen. Jesus could easily encourage his disciples to conform to this model and strive to gain more power, but that's not what he does. Instead, Jesus affirms that there are people who can't or don't live their gender out in this way, and who don't follow the prescribed path of marriage and childbearing; Jesus says not only is that okay, but it is a valuable and faithful path to follow.

Jesus chooses eunuchs—the most prominent gender-expansive people in his time and place—as an example of faithful discipleship outside cultural norms. Jesus says that there are three types of eunuchs, and modern scholars have connected the first type to people who are born with differences in sex development or attraction to others, and the second type to people who were assigned male at birth but who were castrated by people in power. (See p. 114.) The third group—"eunuchs for the kingdom of heaven"—may be a reference to people who expressed their gender in ways that were countercultural as part of both their identity and their faith.

What's certain is that Jesus is celebrating all three of these groups of people whom society saw as unworthy and powerless. Instead he says that the eunuchs' ways of being are just as faithful as the ways of being of those who fit society's definition of success—or maybe even more faithful. When considering the remaining sections of Matthew 19, which celebrate childlikeness and poverty, it becomes doubly clear that Jesus is intent on lifting up all sorts of life stages and situations that were considered lesser-than in his time and place.

Two thousand years later, the categories of people "on top of the heap" really haven't changed that much. Most politicians, CEOs, and even pastors are married, cisgender, heterosexual men. Working adults are generally more valued than children, our focus is often on what those children can be or do "when they grow up," and a rich person who sells everything they have and gives the profits to the poor would be considered a laughable fool, not a role model.

But Jesus shows us that true discipleship looks like giving up power in order to be in solidarity with the oppressed, and he does that by specifically celebrating people who, by nature or by choice, do not fit into the approved categories when it comes to gender, orientation, family structure, and more. How might we follow the lead of these people in our own discipleship journey on the way to a kingdom where the last will be first?

Week 4: Living as One

Focus Scripture: Galatians 3:26–28
Book references: chapters 10–12

> For in Christ Jesus you are all children of God through faith. As many of you as were baptized into Christ have clothed yourselves with Christ. There is no longer Jew or

Greek, there is no longer slave or free, there is no longer
male and female; for all of you are one in Christ Jesus.

(Galatians 3:26–28)

As we conclude this series, I hope we've learned anew just how
expansive our God is—how wide God's embrace is, cherish-
ing every human being, each one made in God's image. We've
seen how God will expand boundaries and break rules to make
sure everyone is included, and how those seen as outliers and
nobodies in our culture may in fact be role models of faith-
fulness. Putting this expansiveness into practice, however, is a
daunting task. Diversity can be intimidating.

Differences can make us uncomfortable, especially in the
church, where we have a tendency to give our personal prefer-
ences moral weight. For example, we might be concerned that
hiring a music minister of a different ethnicity will introduce
unfamiliar songs and phase out a type of music we like. If we
feel threatened enough, our anxiety can become a moral con-
viction that certain styles of music are less pleasing to God. And
despite the overall witness of Scripture showing God's expansive love, fear can make us seek out particular verses in Scripture
to support our positions. That's not usually too hard, because
you can find Bible verses to support just about anything you
want: slavery or abolition, women keeping silent or women as
faithful leaders, cisgender-heterosexual norms or affirmation of
people and relationships beyond those categories.

Denominations in the US split over slavery in the nine-
teenth century; some of them got back together in the twentieth century, but some have not. With the exception of some
radical fringe groups, Christians can now agree that God values
and wants freedom for people of every race, and that the Scriptures approving of slavery do not hold moral weight for us. In
the twentieth century, denominations split over the ordination
of women, and in the twenty-first century over marriage and
ordination for LGBTQI2A people. Christians are still lobbing
Scriptures at one another to argue for or against the equal value
of all people.

The early church had these same sorts of debates, but instead of music styles, marriage equality, and women in leadership, it was circumcision, the status of slaves, and . . . well, still women in leadership. So many of Paul's letters to the first-century churches focus on those debates, as the apostle mediated between different factions asserting they knew the best way to follow Christ. Today's Scripture is a powerful testament to unity in the church: "There is no longer Jew or Greek, there is no longer slave or free, there is no longer male and female; for all of you are one in Christ Jesus."

This statement of oneness introduces some new complications, however. Does it mean our differences don't matter? Some people say so. You might hear someone today say, "I don't see color; I just see people." The desire to focus on commonalities can be a good thing, but in practice, it often means that minorities are expected to shed their distinctive identities and blend in with the majority. Erasing differences can mean ignoring important questions about power and tokenism. True acceptance takes work, seeing how others' identities are intrinsic to their humanity, understanding the qualities and experiences that make people who they are, in all their God-given beauty. Yes, this includes studying Scripture so that we're prepared to defend their value and belonging in God's kingdom, but we also need to work to create a church and a world where those whose worth has been debated can live fully and abundantly—no arguments needed.

God's full and vibrant kingdom is made up of beloved creations, each uniquely made in the image of God. Oneness does not mean sameness, but a place where our differences are an asset, not a source of anxiety and division. We are one in the love of Christ—Jew and Greek, male and female, Black and white, gay and straight, cis and trans, endosex and intersex, and everyone who lives beyond these binaries—all bringing beautiful facets to the shining face of God.

Acknowledgments

An incredible amount of thanks, first and foremost, to the transgender Christians and good friends who trusted me with their stories as part of this project. It was a privilege to interview you, whether we talked only one time, or once a week! You inspire me, and I'm so proud to know each one of you. I want to send special gratitude to Lynn Young, who passed away on November 18, 2020. Lynn, I never met anyone else like you. In the short time we knew each other, you taught me so much about loving all the distinct pieces of myself, even the ones with jagged edges. The sound of the drum will always remind me of you, and I hope you're dancing joyfully with your ancestors.

To Ariel and to my family, for listening to me celebrate and stress out about every single bump in the road that led to the publication of this book. Ari, I literally couldn't have done this without you, both because you kept me grounded, and because you transcribed so many of these interviews. I can't believe you've now put up with me through TWO panic-fueled manuscript submission sessions. I love you so much, and our life together just keeps getting better.

Thanks to my mom for gifting me with laughter and brilliance, and for holding my hand through the scary parts. Thanks to my dad for the hours we spent debating religion when I was a teenager, and for the truckloads of love through all the tough stuff. Thanks to Lance and Susan for keeping those other two relatively sane, and for being a huge source of goodness in my world. Thanks to Madelyn for assuring me that writers never meet their deadlines, and to Julia for the ol' razzle-dazzle.

I owe so much to so many people who have now passed on. To John and Eli Roe, whose enthusiasm and dedication to opening doors still fuels me—I think of you two whenever I look at my overflowing bookshelves—and to Liane Roe who has carried on the legacy of generosity even in their absence.

To Rachel Held Evans—this book would literally not have existed without you. You boosted my writing, you sought me out at conferences, you wrote me encouraging notes, you connected me with so many good people, but mostly you just made me feel like maybe Christianity really could be Home. You will never be forgotten.

An immense amount of gratitude is due to Deborah Jian Lee, Dianna Anderson, and Matthew Vines, my author guides who answered a bunch of my questions and pointed me in the right directions. Big hugs to Emmy Kegler, Kenji Kuramitsu, Kit Apostolacus, Allyson Robinson, Kevin Garcia, Alicia Crosby, Laura Jean Truman, Matthias Roberts, Darren Calhoun, and all the people who encouraged me, talked with me, and gave me those good, good Internet affirmations. Special thanks for support during the writing of the second edition go to my sister Madelyn, Ryan Higgins and Anna Marsh, and the AMAZING staff of Transmission Ministry Collective, especially Micah Melody Taberner, who took on extra work so that I could take time on the manuscript.

So much love to my Humble Walk church family, who took me in and reminded me what it's like to be part of the body of Christ. Your willingness to witness my renaming and your constant support throughout my transition made this book possible. And of course a special thank you to Pastor Jodi Houge for her guidance, wisdom, and knowing nods.

Thanks to all of my professors at Luther Seminary, especially Michael Chan and Eric Barreto, who agreed to look over early drafts of my proposal. Many thanks to Noa Bell for being my unofficial editor in the early stages and helping me think through how to explain theology in everyday language!

Thank you to my editor, Jessica Miller Kelley, who let me argue with her and who pretty much always had the better idea anyway. Thanks also to my agent Greg Daniel, who took a chance on me when other agencies couldn't. I really appreciate the way these two people have shaped the final form of this project.

This book would not exist without each and every transgender person who has emailed me, written a YouTube comment, tweeted me, or written me a letter asking about faith. This book is and has always been for you.

Notes

Chapter 1: Standing on the Edge

1. "A Survey of LGBT Americans: Attitudes, Experiences, and Values in Changing Times," Pew Research Center, Washington, DC, June 13, 2013, 11.

2. Jeffrey Jones, "LGBT Identification in U.S. Ticks Up to 7.1%," Gallup.com, February 17, 2022, https://news.gallup.com/poll/389792 /lgbt-identification-ticks-up.aspx.

3. "A Shifting Landscape: A Decade of Change in American Attitudes about Same-Sex Marriage and LGBT Issues," Public Religion Research Institute, Washington, DC, February 26, 2014, 19.

4. "America's Changing Religious Landscape: Christians Decline Sharply as Share of Population; Unaffiliated and Other Faiths Continue to Grow," Pew Research Center, Washington, DC, May 25, 2015.

5. "A Survey of LGBT Americans," 91.

6. "America's Changing Religious Landscape," 87.

7. See Pew Research Center, "Where the Public Stands on Religious Liberty vs Nondiscrimination," September 18, 2016, https://www .pewresearch.org/religion/wp-content/uploads/sites/7/2016/09 /Religious-Liberty-full-for-web.pdf, and Rachel Minkin and Anna Brown, "Rising Shares of U.S. Adults Know Someone Who Is Transgender or Goes by Gender-Neutral Pronouns," Pew Research Center, July 27, 2021, https://www.pewresearch.org/fact-tank/2021/07/27 /rising-shares-of-u-s-adults-know-someone-who-is-transgender-or-goes -by-gender-neutral-pronouns.

8. Emily McFarlan Miller, "Evangelical Transgender Conference Rejects Notion That Gender Identity Can Change," Religion News Service, September 21, 2015, http://religionnews.com/2015/09/21/evangelical -transgender-conference-rejects-notion-gender-identity-can-change/.

9. Bob Allen, "Conference Confronts Transgender 'Confusion,'" Baptist News Global, October 5, 2015, https://baptistnews.com/article /conference-confronts-transgender-confusion/.

10. "Dear Colleague Letter on Transgender Students," Letter from US Department of Justice Civil Rights Division and US Department of Education Office for Civil Rights, May 13, 2016, http://www2.ed.gov /about/offices/list/ocr/letters/colleague-201605-title-ix-transgender .pdf?1487962684262.

11. Liam Stack, "Religious Colleges Obtain Waivers to Law That Protects Transgender Students," December 10, 2015, http://www .nytimes.com/2015/12/11/us/religious-colleges-obtain-waivers-to-anti -discrimination-law.html?_r=0.

12. Alliance Defending Freedom, "ADF Recommends Policy to Protect Student Privacy in Restrooms, Locker Rooms," news release, December 5, 2014, https://web.archive.org/web/20150206063436/http://www .adfmedia.org/News/PRDetail/?CID=82478.

13. Rachel Percelay, "A 'Religious Freedom' Legal Powerhouse Is Leading the National Fight against Transgender Student Rights," Media Matters for America, November 5, 2015, http://mediamatters.org/research/2015/11/05 /a-religious-freedom-legal-powerhouse-is-leading/206588.

14. Peter Sprigg, "Gender Identity Protections and 'Bathroom Bills,'" Family Research Council, July 2010, https://web.archive.org /web/20150412020143/http://downloads.frc.org/EF/EF10H42.pdf.

15. Carlos Maza and Luke Brinker, "15 Experts Debunk Right-Wing Transgender Bathroom Myth," Media Matters for America, March 20, 2014, http://mediamatters.org/research/2014/03/20/15 -experts-debunk-right-wing-transgender-bathro/198533.

16. Jody L. Herman, "Gendered Restrooms and Minority Stress: The Public Regulation of Gender and Its Impact on Transgender People's Lives," The Williams Institute, June 2013, accessed July 31, 2017, https://williamsinstitute.law.ucla.edu/wp-content/uploads/Herman -Gendered-Restrooms-and-Minority-Stress-June-2013.pdf.

17. "Transgenderism—Our Position," Focus on the Family, 2008, 2015, http://www.focusonthefamily.com/socialissues/sexuality/trans genderism/transgenderism-our-position.

18. Samantha Allen, "After North Carolina's Law, Trans Suicide Hotline Calls Double," The Daily Beast, April 20, 2016, http://www .thedailybeast.com/articles/2016/04/20/after-north-carolina-s-law -trans-suicide-hotline-calls-double.html.

19. Cole Parke, "The Christian Right's Favorite New Target: North Carolina Isn't Alone," Political Research Associates, March 29, 2016, http://www.politicalresearch.org/2016/03/29/the-christian-rights -favorite-new-target-north-carolina-isnt-alone/#sthash.JyjTDsGY.dpbs.

20. John L. Rustin to Gov. Pat McCrory, Sen. Phil Berger, Rep. Tim Moore, "Why a Special Session to Repeal Charlotte's Ordinance Changes Is Necessary," March 2, 2016, North Carolina Family Policy Council, March 2016, http://www.ncfamily.org/wp-content/uploads /2016/03/160302-Charlotte-SOGI-Ordinance-Ltr.pdf.

21. "On Transgender Identity," Southern Baptist Convention, June 2014, http://www.sbc.net/resource-library/resolutions/on-transgender-identity.

22. "Gender Identity Disorder or Gender Dysphoria in Christian Perspective," Commission on Theology and Church Relations, Lutheran Church–Missouri Synod, May 2014, 8–9.

23. "Homosexuality, Marriage, and Sexual Identity," The General Council of the Assemblies of God, August 2014, https://web.archive .org/web/20150105095258/http://ag.org/top/beliefs/position_papers /pp_downloads/pp_4181_homosexuality.pdf.

24. "Vatican Says 'No' to Transsexual Godparents amid Spain Controversy," Catholic News Agency, September 2, 2015, http://www .catholicnewsagency.com/news/vatican-says-no-to-transsexual -godparents-amid-spain-controversy-54280/.

25. Heather Saul, "Pope Francis Compares Arguments for Transgender Rights to Nuclear Arms Race," February 21, 2015, http://www .independent.co.uk/news/people/pope-francis-compares-arguments-for -transgender-rights-to-nuclear-arms-race-10061223.html.

26. James Dobson, "Protect Your Kids from Tyrant Obama," World-NetDaily (WND), May 30, 2016, http://www.wnd.com/2016/05 /protect-your-kids-from-tyrant-obama/.

27. Human Rights Campaign, "Fatal Violence against the Transgender and Gender Non-Conforming Community in 2021," HRC, 2021, https://www.hrc.org/resources/fatal-violence-against-the-transgender -and-gender-non-conforming-community-in-2021.

28. Trans Murder Monitoring—TGEU, "TMM Update TDoR 2021," Trans Respect vs Transphobia Worldwide, November 11, 2021, https://transrespect.org/en/tmm-update-tdor-2021.

29. "Injustice at Every Turn: A Report of the National Transgender Discrimination Survey," National Center for Transgender Equality, Washington, DC, National Gay and Lesbian Task Force, Washington, DC, 2011, 2–8.

30. Michael L. Hendricks and Rylan J. Testa, "A Conceptual Framework for Clinical Work with Transgender and Gender Nonconforming Clients: An Adaptation of the Minority Stress Model," *Professional Psychology: Research and Practice* 43, no. 5 (2012): 460–67.

31. "Suicide Attempts among Transgender and Gender Non-Conforming Adults: Findings of the National Transgender Discrimination Survey," American Foundation for Suicide Prevention, New York, The Williams Institute, Los Angeles, January 2014, 2.

32. "New Study Shows Transgender People May Experience Substantial Problems in Public Restrooms; Some Jurisdictions Provide Protections," The Williams Institute, news release, June 25, 2013, https://web.archive.org/web/20150926201449/http://williamsinstitute.law.ucla.edu/press/press-releases/25-jun-2013/.

33. Caitlin Ryan, Stephen T. Russell, David Huebner, Rafael Diaz, and Jorge Sanchez, "Family Acceptance in Adolescence and the Health of LGBT Young Adults," *Journal of Child and Adolescent Psychiatric Nursing* (November 2010): 210.

34. Zack Ford, "Family Acceptance Is the Biggest Factor for Positive LGBT Youth Outcomes, Study Finds," ThinkProgress, June 24, 2015, https://archive.thinkprogress.org/family-acceptance-is-the-biggest-factor-for-positive-lgbt-youth-outcomes-study-finds-3da2ed7b346b/.

35. Ryan et al., "Family Acceptance in Adolescence," 210.

Chapter 2: The Beginner's Guide to Gender

1. For an easy-to-read introduction to the biopsychosocial nature of gender, see Meg-John Barker and Jules Scheele, *Gender: A Graphic Guide* (London: Icon Books, 2020), and Alex Iantaffi and Meg-John Barker, *How to Understand Your Gender: A Practical Guide for Exploring Who You Are* (London: Jessica Kingsley Publishers, 2018).

2. American Psychological Association, *APA Resolution on Gender Identity Change Efforts* (February 2021), https://www.apa.org/about/policy/resolution-gender-identity-change-efforts.pdf.

3. To learn more about the complex history and usage of the word "transgender," see Petra L. Doan and Lynda Johnston, "Under, Beside and Beyond the Transgender Umbrella," in *Rethinking Transgender Identities: Reflections from Around the Globe* (London: Routledge, 2022).

4. Julia Serano, "A 'Transsexual Versus Transgender' Intervention," in *Outspoken: A Decade of Transgender Activism and Trans Feminism* (Oakland: Switch Hitter Press, 2016).

5. The Trevor Project, *The Trevor Project Research Brief: Diversity of Youth Gender Identity* (October 2019), https://www.thetrevorproject.org/wp-content/uploads/2021/08/Trevor-Project-Gender-Identity-Research-Brief_October.pdf.

6. Stephanie Brill and Lisa Kenney, *The Transgender Teen: A Handbook for Parents and Professionals Supporting Transgender and Non-Binary Teens* (Jersey City: Cleis Press, 2016), 52.

7. Paul L. Vasey and Nancy H. Bartlett, "What Can the Samoan 'Fa'afafine' Teach Us about the Western Concept of Gender Identity Disorder in Childhood?," *Perspectives in Biology and Medicine* 50, no. 4 (2007): 481–90.

8. For a survey of research on this topic, see Luk Gijs and Anne Brewaey, "Surgical Treatment of Gender Dysphoria in Adults and Adolescents: Recent Developments, Effectiveness, and Challenges," *Annual Review of Sex Research* 18, no. 1 (November 15, 2012): 178–224. Additionally, see Marco Colizzi, Rosalia Costa, and Orlando Todarello, "Transsexual Patients' Psychiatric Comorbidity and Positive Effect of Cross-Sex Hormonal Treatment on Mental Health: Results from a Longitudinal Study," *Psychoneuroendocrinology* 39 (2014): 65–73.

9. I. H. Meyer, B. D. M. Wilson, and K. O'Neill, "LGBTQ People in the US: Select Findings from the Generations and TransPop Studies," The Williams Institute, 2021, https://williamsinstitute.law.ucla.edu/wp-content/uploads/Generations-TransPop-Toplines-Jun-2021.pdf.

10. For more on gender diversity in Indigenous communities of North America, see Will Roscoe, *Changing Ones: Third and Fourth Genders in Native North America* (New York: St. Martin's Griffin, 1998), and Sue-Ellen Jacobs, *Two-Spirit People: Native American Gender Identity, Sexuality, and Spirituality* (Urbana: University of Illinois Press, 1997).

11. For more on gender diversity in Indigenous communities around the world, see Serena Nanda, *Gender Diversity: Crosscultural Variations*, 2nd ed. (Long Grove, IL: Waveland Press, 2014); Gilbert Herdt, *Third Sex, Third Gender: Beyond Sexual Dimorphism in Culture and History* (New York: Zone Books, 1996); and Evelyn Blackwood and Saskia E. Wieringa, *Female Desires: Same-Sex Relations and Transgender Practices across Cultures* (New York: Columbia University Press, 1999).

12. Siculus Diodorus, *Diodorus of Sicily: The Library of History*, trans. Charles Henry Oldfather, vol. 1 (Cambridge: Harvard University Press, 1933), 425–26.

13. Caroline Kim-Brown, "The Woman Who Would Be King," *Humanities* 26, no. 6 (November 2005): 18–21.

14. Sabine Lang, *Men as Women, Women as Men: Changing Gender in Native American Cultures* (Austin: University of Texas Press, 1998), 67.

15. Laura Erickson-Schroth, *Trans Bodies, Trans Selves: A Resource for the Transgender Community* (Oxford: Oxford University Press USA, 2014), 502–3.

16. Elizabeth Reis, "Hermaphrodites and 'Same-Sex' Sex in Early America," in *Long before Stonewall: Histories of Same-Sex Sexuality in Early America* (New York: New York University Press, 2007), 144–63.

17. Susan Stryker, *Transgender History*, Seal Studies (Berkeley, CA: Seal Press, 2008), 32–33.

18. Martin B. Duberman, *Stonewall* (New York: Plume, 1994).

19. *Pay It No Mind: Marsha P. Johnson*, directed by Michael Kasino, USA: Frameline Films, 2012, October 15, 2012, https://www.youtube.com/watch?v=rjN9W2KstqE.

20. Stryker, *Transgender History*, 83–85.

21. *MAJOR!*, directed by Annalise Ophelian, produced by Storm-Miguel Florez, USA: Floating Ophelia Productions, 2015, http://www.missmajorfilm.com/.

22. Barry S. Hewlett, *Intimate Fathers: The Nature and Context of Aka Pygmy Paternal Infant Care* (Ann Arbor: University of Michigan Press, 1991).

23. Cai Hua, *A Society without Fathers or Husbands: The Na of China* (New York: Zone Books, 2001).

24. Jeanne Maglaty, "When Did Girls Start Wearing Pink?," Smithsonian.com, April 7, 2011, http://www.smithsonianmag.com/arts-culture/when-did-girls-start-wearing-pink-1370097.

25. Anne Fausto-Sterling, *Sexing the Body: Gender Politics and the Construction of Sexuality* (New York: Basic Books, 2000).

26. Sari M. van Anders, Jeffrey Steiger, and Katherine L. Goldey, "Effects of Gendered Behavior on Testosterone in Women and Men," *Proceedings of the National Academy of Sciences* 112, no. 45 (October 26, 2015): 13805–10.

27. Lee T. Gettler et al., "Longitudinal Evidence That Fatherhood Decreases Testosterone in Human Males," *Proceedings of the National Academy of Sciences* 108, no. 39 (September 12, 2011): 16194–99.

28. Cordelia Fine, *Delusions of Gender: How Our Minds, Society, and Neurosexism Create Difference* (New York: W. W. Norton & Co., 2011).

29. Daphna Joel, Zohar Berman, et al., "Sex beyond the Genitalia: The Human Brain Mosaic," *Proceedings of the National Academy of Sciences* 112, no. 50 (2015): 15468–73.

30. Giuseppina Rametti, Beatriz Carrillo, et al., "White Matter Microstructure in Female to Male Transsexuals before Cross-Sex Hormonal Treatment: A Diffusion Tensor Imaging Study," *Journal of Psychiatric Research* 45, no. 2 (2011): 199–204.

31. Giuseppina Rametti, Beatriz Carrillo, et al., "The Microstructure of White Matter in Male to Female Transsexuals before Cross-Sex Hormonal Treatment: A DTI Study," *Journal of Psychiatric Research* 45, no. 7 (2011): 949–54.

Chapter 3: Sin, Sickness, or Specialty?

1. A. R. Flores, J. L. Herman, G. J. Gates, and T. N. T. Brown, "How Many Adults Identify as Transgender in the United States?," The Williams Institute, 2016, accessed June 30, 2017, https://williamsinstitute.law.ucla.edu/wp-content/uploads/How-Many-Adults-Identify-as-Transgender-in-the-United-States.pdf.

2. Mark A. Yarhouse, *Understanding Gender Dysphoria: Navigating Transgender Issues in a Changing Culture* (Downers Grove, IL: IVP Academic, an imprint of InterVarsity Press, 2015), 46.

3. Robert A. J. Gagnon, "Transsexuality and Ordination," RobGagnon.net, August 2007, http://www.robgagnon.net/articles/Transsexuality Ordination.pdf, 2.

4. "The Danvers Statement," the Council on Biblical Manhood and Womanhood, Wheaton, IL, 1988.

5. See Jeremy J. Gibbs and Jeremy Goldbach, "Religious Conflict, Sexual Identity, and Suicidal Behaviors among LGBT Young Adults," *Archives of Suicide Research* 19, no. 4 (October 2015): 472–88, and John T. Super and Lamerial Jacobson, "Religious Abuse: Implications for Counseling Lesbian, Gay, Bisexual, and Transgender Individuals," *Journal of LGBT Issues in Counseling* 5, no. 3/4 (July 2011): 180–96.

6. Jack L. Turban et al., "Association between Recalled Exposure to Gender Identity Conversion Efforts and Psychological Distress and Suicide Attempts among Transgender Adults," *JAMA Psychiatry* 77, no. 1 (September 11, 2019): 68–76.

7. Yarhouse, *Understanding Gender Dysphoria*, 48–49.

8. Yarhouse, 49.

9. Luke 13:1–5.

10. Ilan H. Meyer, "Prejudice, Social Stress, and Mental Health in Lesbian, Gay, and Bisexual Populations: Conceptual Issues and Research Evidence," *Psychological Bulletin* 129, no. 5 (2003): 674–97.

11. Cathy Kelleher, "Minority Stress and Health: Implications for Lesbian, Gay, Bisexual, Transgender, and Questioning (LGBTQ) Young People," *Counselling Psychology Quarterly* 22, no. 4 (December 2009): 376.

12. Rylan J. Testa, Matthew S. Michaels, Whitney Bliss, Megan L. Rogers, Kimberly F. Balsam, and Thomas Joiner, "Suicidal Ideation in Transgender People: Gender Minority Stress and Interpersonal Theory Factors," *Journal of Abnormal Psychology* 126, no. 1 (2017): 125–36.

13. Yarhouse, *Understanding Gender Dysphoria,* 137.

14. Yarhouse, 50.

15. K. R. Olson, L. Durwood, M. Demeules, and K. A. Mclaughlin, "Mental Health of Transgender Children Who Are Supported in Their Identities," *Pediatrics* 137, no. 3 (2016).

16. Joan Roughgarden, *Evolution's Rainbow: Diversity, Gender, and Sexuality in Nature and People* (Berkeley: University of California Press, 2004), 31–33.

17. Doug VanderLaan et al., "Elevated Kin-Directed Altruism Emerges in Childhood and Is Linked to Feminine Gender Expression in Samoan Fa'afafine: A Retrospective Study," *Archives of Sexual Behavior* 46, no. 1 (January 2017): 95–108.

18. Yarhouse, *Understanding Gender Dysphoria,* 50–51.

Chapter 4: And God Said, Let There Be Marshes

1. "Timeline of Women in Methodism," United Communications– United Methodist Church, http://www.umc.org/who-we-are/timeline -of-women-in-methodism.

2. Although this idea has been talked about in many different places, I first came across it in Justin Sabia-Tanis, *Trans-Gender: Theology, Ministry, and Communities of Faith,* 2nd ed. (Eugene, OR: Wipf & Stock, 2018), 57–58.

3. Richard S. Hess and David T. Tsumura, eds., *"I Studied Inscriptions from before the Flood": Ancient Near Eastern, Literary, and Linguistic Approaches to Genesis 1–11,* Sources for Biblical and Theological Study 4 (Winona Lake, IN: Eisenbrauns, 1994).

4. Noach Dzmura, *Balancing on the Mechitza: Transgender in Jewish Community* (Berkeley, CA: North Atlantic Books, 2010).

5. Leonard Sax, "How Common Is Intersex? A Response to Anne Fausto-Sterling," *Journal of Sex Research* 39, no. 3 (2002): 174.

6. For more on intersex variations and the experiences of intersex people, see Hida Viloria and Maria Nieto, *The Spectrum of Sex: The Science of Male, Female, and Intersex* (Philadephia: Jessica Kingsley Publishers, 2020), and Georgiann Davis, *Contesting Intersex: The Dubious Diagnosis* (New York: New York University Press, 2015).

7. Megan K. DeFranza, *Sex Difference in Christian Theology: Male, Female, and Intersex in the Image of God* (Grand Rapids: Eerdmans, 2015), 66.

8. Hans Lindahl, "We Need to End Intersex Erasure in Queer Communities," *them*, June 2, 2018, https://www.them.us/story/intersex-allyship-101.

9. For more information about why these two concepts are so closely linked in Gen. 1:27, see Phyllis A. Bird, "'Male and Female He Created Them': Gen 1:27b in the Context of the Priestly Account of Creation," *Harvard Theological Review* 74, no. 2 (1981): 129–59.

10. David J. A. Clines, "The Image of God in Man," *Tyndale Bulletin* 19 (1968): 54.

11. Paul Humbert, "L' 'imago Dei' dans l'Ancien Testament," in *Études sur le récit du paradis et de la chute dans la Genèse,* Mémoires de l'université de Neuchâtel 14 (Neuchâtel: Secrétariat de l'Université, 1940), 153–75.

12. Hermann Gunkel and Mark E. Biddle, *Genesis*, Mercer Library of Biblical Studies (Macon, GA: Mercer University Press, 1997), 113.

13. Robert A. J. Gagnon, *The Bible and Homosexual Practice: Texts and Hermeneutics* (Nashville: Abingdon Press, 2001), 58.

14. James V. Brownson, *Bible, Gender, Sexuality: Reframing the Church's Debate on Same-Sex Relationships* (Grand Rapids: Eerdmans, 2013), 26.

15. Karl Barth, *Church Dogmatics, III/1–4, The Doctrine of Creation* (Edinburgh: T. & T. Clark, 1958), 193–94.

16. Claus Westermann, *Genesis 1–11: A Commentary* (Minneapolis: Augsburg Publishing House, 1984), 150.

17. John Wesley, Albert Cook Outler, and Richard P. Heitzenrater, *John Wesley's Sermons: An Anthology* (Nashville: Abingdon Press, 1991), 335.

Chapter 5: Biblical Culture Shock

1. W. Roscoe, "Priests of the Goddess: Gender Transgression in Ancient Religion," *History of Religions* 35, no. 3 (1996): 195–230.

2. Ruth N. Sandberg, *Development and Discontinuity in Jewish Law* (Lanham, MD: University Press of America, 2001), 93–94.

3. Gregory G. Bolich, *Crossdressing in Context: Dress, Gender, Transgender, and Crossdressing*, vol. 4, *Transgender & Religion* (Raleigh, NC: Psyche's, 2008), 35–36.

4. St. Thomas Aquinas, *Summa theologica*, vol. 4, pt. 3, sec. 1 (New York: Cosimo, 2007), 1877–78.

5. "Mission & Vision," the Council on Biblical Manhood and Womanhood, accessed June 25, 2017, https://cbmw.org/about/mission-vision.

6. "The Danvers Statement," the Council on Biblical Manhood and Womanhood, Wheaton, IL, 1988.

7. Rachel Held Evans, *A Year of Biblical Womanhood: How a Liberated Woman Found Herself Sitting on Her Roof, Covering Her Head, and Calling Her Husband "Master"* (Nashville: Thomas Nelson, 2012), 203–4.

8. Another important thing to notice is that Adam, the original human, is not described as male before the creation of Eve. For more on Adam as an unsexed and ungendered being, see Phyllis Trible, *God and the Rhetoric of Sexuality*, Overtures to Biblical Theology 2 (Philadelphia: Fortress Press, 1978).

9. Evans, *Year of Biblical Womanhood*, 207.

10. James V. Brownson, *Bible, Gender, Sexuality: Reframing the Church's Debate on Same-Sex Relationships* (Grand Rapids: Eerdmans, 2013), 29–30.

11. "Taiwan Yearbook 2006," Government Information Office, https://web.archive.org/web/20070708213510/http://www.gio.gov.tw/taiwan-website/5-gp/yearbook/22Religion.htm, archived from the original on July 8, 2007.

12. Annette Lynch and Mitchell D. Strauss, "Hanfu Chinese Robes," in *Ethnic Dress in the United States: A Cultural Encyclopedia* (Lanham, MD: Rowman & Littlefield, 2015), 135.

13. Theodore W. Jennings Jr., *Jacob's Wound: Homoerotic Narrative in the Literature of Ancient Israel* (New York: Continuum, 2005), 177–96; and Gregg Drinkwater, "Joseph's Fabulous Technicolor Dreamcoat," in *Torah Queeries*, ed. Gregg Drinkwater, Joshua Lesser, and David Shneer (New York: New York University Press, 2009).

14. Jennings, *Jacob's Wound*, 180.

15. Sara Järlemyr, "A Tale of Cross-Dressers, Mothers, and Murderers: Gender and Power in Judges 4 and 5," *Svensk Exegetisk Årsbok* 81 (2016): 54.

16. Ho Yi, "Something Wicked This Way Comes," *The Taipei Times*, June 30, 2014, accessed June 27, 2017, http://www.taipeitimes.com/News/feat/archives/2014/06/30/2003593988/2.

17. Ke-hsien Huang, "'Culture Wars' in a Globalized East: How Taiwanese Conservative Christianity Turned Public during the Same-Sex Marriage Controversy and a Secularist Backlash," *Review of Religion and Chinese Society* 4 (2017): 108–36.

Chapter 6: What's My Name Again?

1. "Numbers 13:16," in *Rashbam on Numbers*, Sefaria.org, Urim Publications, accessed June 5, 2017, https://www.sefaria.org/Rashbam _on_Numbers.13.16?lang=bi.

2. Stephen T. Russell et al., "Chosen Name Use Is Linked to Reduced Depressive Symptoms, Suicidal Ideation, and Suicidal Behavior among Transgender Youth," *Journal of Adolescent Health* 63, no. 4 (October 2018): 503–5.

3. "Guidelines for the Primary and Gender-Affirming Care of Transgender and Gender Nonbinary People," 2nd ed., Center of Excellence for Transgender Health, June 17, 2016, accessed June 12, 2017, http://transhealth.ucsf.edu/trans?page=guidelines-home.

Chapter 7: God Breaks the Rules to Get You In

1. For more information on the history of the book of Isaiah, specifically on Isaiah 56, see Elizabeth Achtemeier, *The Community and Message of Isaiah 56–66: A Theological Commentary* (Minneapolis: Augsburg Publishing House, 1982).

2. Joseph Blenkinsopp, *Isaiah 56–66: A New Translation with Introduction and Commentary* (New York: Doubleday, 2013), 137.

3. Benjamin D. Sommer, *A Prophet Reads Scripture: Allusion in Isaiah 40–66* (Stanford, CA: Stanford University Press, 1998), 147.

4. Mira Fox, "The First Blind Female Rabbi Is Making Sure She Won't Be the Last," *The Forward*, February 18, 2021, https://forward

.com/culture/464331/lauren-tuchman-may-be-the-first-blind-female
-rabbi-but-shes-working-not-to.

5. Clinton E. Hammock, "Isaiah 56:1–8 and the Redefining of the Restoration Judean Community," *Biblical Theology Bulletin: Journal of Bible and Culture* 30, no. 2 (2000): 51.

Chapter 8: All the Best Disciples Are Eunuchs

1. Jerome Kodell, "Celibacy Logion in Matthew 19:12," *Biblical Theology Bulletin* 8, no. 1 (February 1978): 19–23.

2. Victoria S. Kolakowski, "Toward a Christian Ethical Response to Transsexual Persons," *Theology and Sexuality* 6 (March 1997): 25.

3. J. David Hester, "Eunuchs and the Postgender Jesus: Matthew 19.12 and Transgressive Sexualities," *Journal for the Study of the New Testament* 28, no. 1 (September 2005): 33.

4. Henry Percival, *Canons of the Ecumenical Council of Nicaea I, 325 AD, and Other Early Synods*, vol. 1, *Ecumenical Christian Councils*, CreateSpace Independent Publishing Platform (2017), 4.

5. Hester, "Eunuchs and the Postgender Jesus," 34–35.

6. Hester, 20.

7. Halvor Moxnes, "Jesus in Gender Trouble," *Cross Currents* 54, no. 3 (2004): 41.

8. Justin Sabia-Tanis, *Trans-Gender: Theology, Ministry, and Communities of Faith*, 2nd ed. (Eugene, OR: Wipf & Stock, 2018), 146.

9. Hester, "Eunuchs and the Postgender Jesus," 38.

10. For more on this concept, see J. D. Hester, "Queers on Account of the Kingdom of Heaven: Rhetorical Constructions of the Eunuch Body," *Scriptura* 90 (2005): 809–23.

Chapter 9: Nothing Can Prevent Me

1. Marianne Bjelland Kartzow and Halvor Moxnes, "Complex Identities: Ethnicity, Gender, and Religion in the Story of the Ethiopian Eunuch (Acts 8:26–40)," *Religion and Theology* 17, no. 3–4 (2010): 184–204.

2. Sean D. Burke, *Queering the Ethiopian Eunuch: Strategies of Ambiguity in Acts*, Emerging Scholars (Minneapolis: Fortress Press, 2013), 19–38.

3. Justin Sabia-Tanis, *Trans-Gender: Theology, Ministry, and Communities of Faith*, 2nd ed. (Eugene, OR: Wipf & Stock, 2018), 78.

4. Sabia-Tanis, 79.

Chapter 10: Even Jesus Had a Body

1. "Quotes Misattributed to C. S. Lewis," C. S. Lewis Foundation, January 31, 2013, accessed June 26, 2017, http://www.cslewis.org /aboutus/faq/quotes-misattributed.

2. Neville Ann Kelly, "Early Contributors to Christian Asceticism: Body and Soul in Plato and Saint Paul," in *Foundation Theology 2007: Student Essays for Ministry Professionals*, ed. John H. Morgan (South Bend, IN: Cloverdale, 2007), 91–109.

3. Christina M. Fetherolf, "The Body for a Temple, A Temple for a Body: An Examination of Bodily Metaphors in 1 Corinthians," *Proceedings* 30 (2010): 98.

4. James B. Nelson, "On Doing Body Theology," *Theology and Sexuality* 2 (March 1995): 47.

5. Nancy L. Eiesland, "Encountering the Disabled God," *The Other Side* 38, no. 5 (September 2002): 14.

6. Eiesland, 12.

7. James H. Cone, "Strange Fruit: The Cross and the Lynching Tree," *Journal of Theology for Southern Africa* 148 (March 2014): 15.

8. Kelly Brown Douglas, *Sexuality and the Black Church: A Womanist Perspective* (Maryknoll, NY: Orbis Books, 1999), 117.

9. Terence E. Fretheim, *God and World in the Old Testament: A Relational Theology of Creation* (Nashville: Abingdon Press, 2005), 41–42.

10. Fretheim, 41–42.

Chapter 11: Life beyond Apologetics

1. John 10:10.

2. Justo L. González, *Luke*, Belief, a Theological Commentary on the Bible (Louisville, KY: Westminster John Knox Press, 2010), 117.

3. Robert Kysar, *John, the Maverick Gospel*, rev. ed. (Louisville, KY: Westminster John Knox Press, 1993), 120.

4. Brendan Byrne, *Life Abounding: A Reading of John's Gospel* (Collegeville, MN: Liturgical Press, 2014), 172.

5. Anneliese A. Singh, Danica G. Hays, and Laurel S. Watson, "Strength in the Face of Adversity: Resilience Strategies of Transgender Individuals," *Journal of Counseling and Development* 89, no. 1 (Winter 2011): 23.

6. Anneliese A. Singh and Vel S. McKleroy, "'Just Getting Out of Bed Is a Revolutionary Act': The Resilience of Transgender People of

Color Who Have Survived Traumatic Life Events," *Traumatology* 17, no. 2 (2011): 39.

Chapter 12: Does Gender Matter Anymore?

1. Wayne A. Meeks, "The Image of the Androgyne: Some Uses of a Symbol in Earliest Christianity," *History of Religions* 13, no. 3 (1974): 165–208.

2. Richard Twiss, *Rescuing the Gospel from the Cowboys: A Native American Expression of the Jesus Way* (Downers Grove, IL: InterVarsity Press, 2015), 104.

3. For more on "sameness and oneness," see Brigitte Kahl, "Gender Trouble in Galatia? Paul and the Rethinking of Difference," in *Is There a Future for Feminist Theology?*, ed. Deborah F. Sawyer and Diane M. Collier (Sheffield, UK: Sheffield Academic Press, 1999), 57–73.

4. Randy Woodley, *Living in Color: Embracing God's Passion for Ethnic Diversity*, rev. ed. (Downers Grove, IL: InterVarsity Press, 2004), 72.

5. Sue-Ellen Jacobs, *Two-Spirit People: Native American Gender Identity, Sexuality, and Spirituality* (Urbana: University of Illinois Press, 2005), 2.

6. Sabine Lang, *Men as Women, Women as Men: Changing Gender in Native American Cultures* (Austin: University of Texas Press, 1998).

7. Meeks, "The Image of the Androgyne," 208.

8. Meeks, 208.

Conclusion

1. This list is adapted from Virginia Ramey Mollenkott, "We Come Bearing Gifts: Seven Lessons Religious Congregations Can Learn from Transpeople," in *Trans/formations*, ed. Marcella Althaus-Reid and Lisa Isherwood (London: SCM Press, 2009), 46–58.

2. "Luisa Derouen | Profile," LGBTQ Religious Archives Network, https://lgbtqreligiousarchives.org/profiles/luisa-derouen.

3. Luisa Derouen, "I'm a Nun Who Has Ministered to Transgender People for over 20 Years. These Are Some of Their Courageous Stories," *America Magazine*, February 25, 2021, https://www.america magazine.org/faith/2021/02/25/transgender-catholics-lgbt-religious -sister-240106.

4. Stina Sieg, "Pastor Redefines 'Church' for Transgender Youth," NPR, February 21, 2016, http://www.npr.org/2016/02/21/467243382 /pastor-redefines-church-for-transgender-youth.

5. Michael Hart, "Congregation Races to Get Gender-Accurate IDs for Transgender People," *UU World Magazine*, March 8, 2017, http:// www.uuworld.org/articles/fairbanks-transgender-aid.

6. Richie DeMaria, "Transgender Community Space Opens," *Santa Barbara Independent*, March 23, 2017, http://www.independent .com/news/2017/mar/23/transgender-community-space-opens/.

7. Bekah McNeel, "Texas Pastors Vow to Protect Trans Youth, despite Abbott's Order," *Sojourners*, February 24, 2022, https://sojo.net /articles/texas-pastors-vow-protect-trans-youth-despite-abbotts-order.

8. For more information about Transgender Day of Remembrance, see https://www.glaad.org/tdor.

9. To find out more about trans-exclusionary legislation in your state, go to https://transequality.org/action-centers or https://www.aclu .org/legislation-affecting-lgbtq-rights-across-country.

Afterword

1. Esther Morris, "The Self I Will Never Know," *New Internationalist* 364 (2004): 25–27.

2. Sally Gross, "Intersexuality and Scripture," *Theology and Sexuality* 11 (1999): 65–74.

3. The PhD drew on theological work by, e.g., Victoria S. Kolakowski, "Toward a Christian Ethical Response to Transsexual Persons," *Theology and Sexuality* 6 (1997): 10–31, and Christina Beardsley, "Taking Issue: The Transsexual Hiatus in Some Issues in Human Sexuality," *Theology* 108, no. 845 (2005): 338–46, as well as foundational texts by trans scholars such as Jay Prosser, *Second Skins: The Body Narratives of Transsexuality* (New York: Columbia University Press, 1998).

4. The NHS Contract of Care 2017–2018 states that "The Provider must take account of the spiritual, religious, pastoral and cultural needs of Service Users," and that "The Provider must have regard to NHS Chaplaincy Guidelines." See NHS England, NHS Standard Contract 2017/19 and 2018/19 Service Conditions (Full Length), May 2018 edition, https://www.england.nhs.uk/wp-content/uploads/2018/05/2-nhs -standard-contract-2017-19-particulars-service-conditions-may-2018 .pdf, 14.1 and 14.2.

5. Some of the findings appear in Susannah Cornwall, "Healthcare Chaplaincy and Spiritual Care for Trans People: Envisaging the Future," *Health and Social Care Chaplaincy* 7, no. 1 (2019): 8–27.

6. Alex Clare-Young, *Transgender. Christian. Human.* (Glasgow: Wild Goose Publications, 2019), 28.

7. Justin Sabia-Tanis, *Trans-Gender: Theology, Ministry, and Communities of Faith*, 2nd ed. (Eugene, OR: Wipf & Stock, 2018), 146.

8. Rachel Mann, *Dazzling Darkness: Gender, Sexuality, Illness and God*, 2nd ed. (Glasgow: Wild Goose, 2020).

9. Susannah Cornwall, Alex Clare-Young, and Sara Gillingham, "Epistemic Injustice Exacerbating Trauma in Christian Theological Treatments of Trans People and People with Intersex Characteristics," in *Bearing Witness: Intersectional Approaches to Trauma Theology*, ed. Karen O'Donnell and Katie Cross (London: SCM Press, 2022), 111–30.

10. For more on the misinformation behind "rapid onset gender dysphoria," see Greta R. Bauer, Margaret L. Lawson, and Daniel L. Metzger, "Do Clinical Data from Transgender Adolescents Support the Phenomenon of 'Rapid-Onset Gender Dysphoria'?," *The Journal of Pediatrics* 243 (November 2021); Florence Ashley, "A Critical Commentary on 'Rapid-Onset Gender Dysphoria,'" *The Sociological Review* 68, no. 4 (July 2020): 779–99; and Arjee Javellana Restar, "Methodological Critique of Littman's (2018) Parental-Respondents Accounts of 'Rapid-Onset Gender Dysphoria,'" *Archives of Sexual Behavior* 49, no. 1 (January 2020): 61–66.

Further Reading

Helplines

Befrienders Worldwide – Hotlines in twenty-one languages. https://www.befrienders.org
The Crisis Text Line – United States: Text HOME to 741741. http://www.crisistextline.org
988 Suicide & Crisis Lifeline – United States: 988 or (800) 273-8255 (online chat available). https://988lifeline.org
Trans Lifeline – United States: (877) 565-8860; Canada: (877) 330-6366. https://www.translifeline.org

Transgender Basics

Airton, Lee. *Gender: Your Guide.* New York: Adams Media, 2019.
Barker, Meg-John, and Jules Scheele. *Gender: A Graphic Guide.* London: Icon Books, 2019.
Bongiovanni, Archie, and Tristan Jimerson. *A Quick & Easy Guide to They/Them Pronouns.* Portland, OR: Limerence Press, 2018.
Erickson-Schroth, Laura. *Trans Bodies, Trans Selves: A Resource for the Transgender Community.* 2nd ed. Oxford: Oxford University Press, 2022.

Books for Gender Exploration

Finke, Leigh. *Queerfully and Wonderfully Made: A Guide for LGBTQ+ Christian Teens.* Minneapolis: Beaming Books, 2020.
Hoffman-Fox, Dara. *You and Your Gender Identity: A Guide to Discovery.* New York: Skyhorse Publishing, 2017.
Iantaffi, Alex, and Meg-John Barker. *How to Understand Your Gender: A Practical Guide for Exploring Who You Are.* London: Jessica Kingsley Publishers, 2018.

Lorenz, Theo Nicole. *The Trans Self-Care Workbook: A Coloring Book and Journal for Trans and Non-Binary People*. London: Jessica Kingsley Publishers, 2020.

Singh, Anneliese, and Diane Ehrensaft. *The Queer and Transgender Resilience Workbook: Skills for Navigating Sexual Orientation and Gender Expression*. Oakland, CA: New Harbinger Publications, 2018.

Testa, Rylan Jay, Deborah Coolhart, and Jayme Peta. *The Gender Quest Workbook: A Guide for Teens and Young Adults Exploring Gender Identity*. Oakland, CA: New Harbinger Publications, 2016.

Triska, Andrew Maxwell. *Gender Identity Workbook for Teens: Practical Exercises to Navigate Your Exploration, Support Your Journey, and Celebrate Who You Are*. Emeryville, CA: Rockridge Press, 2021.

Trans-Affirming Faith – General Reading

Beardsley, Christina. *This Is My Body: Hearing the Theology of Transgender Christians*. London: Darton, Longman & Todd Ltd., 2017.

Cherniak, Misha, Olga Gerassimenko, and Michael Brinkschröder, eds. *"For I Am Wonderfully Made": Texts on Eastern Orthodoxy and LGBT Inclusion*. Amsterdam: Esuberanza, 2017.

Edman, Elizabeth M. *Queer Virtue: What LGBTQ People Know about Life and Love and How It Can Revitalize Christianity*. Boston: Beacon Press, 2016.

Lee, Deborah Jian. *Rescuing Jesus: How People of Color, Women, and Queer Christians Are Reclaiming Evangelicalism*. Boston: Beacon Press, 2016.

Lewin, Ellen. *Filled with the Spirit: Sexuality, Gender, and Radical Inclusivity in a Black Pentecostal Church Coalition*. Chicago: University of Chicago Press, 2018.

Mollenkott, Virginia R., and Vanessa Sheridan. *Transgender Journeys*. Eugene, OR: Resource Publications, 2010.

Paige, Chris. *OtherWise Christian 2: Stories of Resistance*. Eugene, OR: Otherwise Engaged Publishing, 2020.

Robertson, Brandan, ed. *Our Witness: The Unheard Stories of LGBT+ Christians*. Eugene, OR: Cascade Books, 2018.

Sabia-Tanis, Justin. *Trans-Gender: Theology, Ministry, and Communities of Faith*. 2nd ed. Eugene, OR: Wipf & Stock, 2018.

Smith, Taj. "Affirmation Guide for Trans & Gender-Expansive Identities." Q Christian Fellowship, 2019. https://www.qchristian.org/guides/trans.

Soughers, Tara K. *Beyond a Binary God: A Theology for Trans Allies.*
New York: Church Publishing, 2018.

Trans-Affirming Faith – Academic Works

Althaus-Reid, Marcella, and Lisa Isherwood. *Trans/formations.* London:
SCM Press, 2009.

Boisvert, Donald L., and Jay Emerson Johnson, eds. *Queer Religion:
Volume 2.* Santa Barbara, CA: Praeger, 2012.

Comstock, Gary David, and Susan E. Henking, eds. *Que(e)rying Religion: A Critical Anthology.* New York: Continuum, 1997.

Cornwall, Susannah. *Constructive Theology and Gender Variance:
Transformative Creatures.* Cambridge: Cambridge University
Press, 2022.

Goss, Robert E., and Mona West, eds. *Take Back the Word: A Queer
Reading of the Bible.* Cleveland: Pilgrim Press, 2000.

Hornsby, Teresa J., and Deryn Guest. *Transgender, Intersex, and Biblical Interpretation.* Atlanta: SBL Press, 2016.

Mollenkott, Virginia Ramey. *Omnigender: A Trans-Religious Approach.*
Cleveland: Pilgrim Press, 2007.

Shore-Goss, Robert E., Thomas Bohache, Patrick S. Cheng, and Mona
West, eds. *Queering Christianity: Finding a Place at the Table for
LGBTQI Christians.* Santa Barbara, CA: Praeger, 2013.

Stone, Ken, and Teresa J. Hornsby, eds. *Bible Trouble: Queer Reading
at the Boundaries of Biblical Scholarship.* Atlanta: Society of Biblical
Literature, 2011.

Wilcox, Melissa M. *Queer Religiosities: An Introduction to Queer and
Transgender Studies in Religion.* Lanham, MD: Rowman & Littlefield, 2020.

For Churches and Ministry Professionals

Beardsley, Christina, and Chris Dowd. *Trans Affirming Churches: How
to Celebrate Gender-Variant People and Their Loved Ones.* London:
Jessica Kingsley Publishers, 2020.

Choudrey, Sabah. *Supporting Trans People of Colour: How to Make
Your Practice Inclusive.* London: Jessica Kingsley, 2022.

Dowd, Chris, and Christina Beardsley. *Transfaith: A Transgender Pastoral Resource.* London: Darton, Longman & Todd, 2018.

Hero, Jakob, and Justin Tanis. "Guía para la bienvenida de personas
transgénero en congregaciones." Center for LGBTQ & Gender

Studies in Religion, September 30, 2017. https://www.clgs.org
/multimedia-archive/guia-para-la-bienvenida-de-personas
-transgenero-en-congregaciones.

Murray, Ross. *Made, Known, Loved: Developing LGBTQ-Inclusive Youth Ministry*. Minneapolis: Fortress Press, 2021.

Pacha, Kelsey. "Transitioning to Inclusion: A Guide to Welcoming Transgender Children and Their Families in Your Community of Faith." The Center for LGBTQ and Gender Studies in Religion. May 2, 2015. https://clgs.org/multimedia-archive /transitioningyouthresource.

Sanders, Cody J. *Christianity, LGBTQ Suicide, and the Souls of Queer Folk*. Lanham, MD: Lexington Books, 2020.

Schlager, Bernard, and David Kundtz. *Ministry among God's Queer Folk: LGBTQ Pastoral Care*. 2nd ed. Eugene, OR: Cascade Books, 2019.

Weekley, David Elias. *Retreating Forward: A Spiritual Practice with Transgender Persons*. Eugene, OR: Resource Publications, 2017.

For Parents, Partners, and Family Members

Angello, Michele, and Alisa Bowman. *Raising the Transgender Child: A Complete Guide for Parents, Families, and Caregivers*. Berkeley, CA: Seal Press, 2016.

Brill, Stephanie, and Lisa Kenney. *The Transgender Teen: A Handbook for Parents and Professionals Supporting Transgender and Non-Binary Teens*. San Francisco: Cleis Press, 2016.

Brill, Stephanie, and Rachel Pepper. *The Transgender Child: A Handbook for Parents and Professionals Supporting Transgender and Nonbinary Children*. 2nd ed. San Francisco: Cleis Press, 2022.

Bryant, Heather. *My Trans Parent: A User Guide for When Your Parent Transitions*. London: Jessica Kingsley Publishers, 2020.

Dewitt Hall, Suzanne, and Declan Dewitt Hall. *Reaching for Hope: Strategies and Support for the Partners of Transgender People*. DH Strategies, 2021.

Ehrensaft, Diane, and Norman Spack. *The Gender Creative Child: Pathways for Nurturing and Supporting Children Who Live outside Gender Boxes*. New York: The Experiment, 2016.

Green, Jo. *The Trans Partner Handbook: A Guide for When Your Partner Transitions*. Philadelphia: Jessica Kingsley Publishers, 2017.

Knox, Amanda Jette. *Love Lives Here: A Story of Thriving in a Transgender Family*. Toronto: Penguin Canada, 2019.

Maynard, D. M. *The Reflective Workbook for Parents and Families of Transgender and Non-Binary Children: Your Transition as Your Child Transitions*. London: Jessica Kingsley Publishers, 2020.

———. *The Reflective Workbook for Partners of Transgender People: Your Transition as Your Partner Transitions*. London: Jessica Kingsley Publishers, 2019.

McDonald, Greg, and Lynne McDonald. *Embracing the Journey: A Christian Parents' Blueprint to Loving Your LGBTQ Child*. New York: Howard Books, 2019.

Nealy, Elijah C. *Trans Kids and Teens: Pride, Joy, and Families in Transition*. New York: W. W. Norton & Co., 2019.

Pepper, Rachel, and Kim Pearson. *Transitions of the Heart: Stories of Love, Struggle, and Acceptance by Mothers of Transgender and Gender-Variant Children*. Berkeley, CA: Cleis Press, 2012.

Rahilly, Elizabeth P. *Trans-Affirmative Parenting: Raising Kids across the Gender Spectrum*. New York: New York University Press, 2020.

Books for Kids

Anderson, Airlie. *Neither*. New York: Little, Brown & Co., 2018.

Davids, Stacy B., and Rachael Balsaitis. *Annie's Plaid Shirt*. North Miami Beach, FL: Upswing Press, 2015.

DeSimone, Susanne, and Cheryl Kilodavis. *My Princess Boy*. New York: Aladdin, 2011.

Gonzalez, Maya Christina, and Matthew Smith-Gonzalez. *They, She, He, Me: Free to Be!* San Francisco: Reflection Press, 2017.

Hall, Michael. *Red: A Crayon's Story*. New York: Greenwillow, 2015.

Herthel, Jessica, Jazz Jennings, and Shelagh McNicholas. *I Am Jazz!* New York: Dial Books for Young Readers, 2014.

Love, Jessica. *Julián Is a Mermaid*. Somerville, MA: Candlewick Press, 2018.

Mayeno, Laurin, Robert Liu-Trujillo, and Teresa Mlawer. *One of a Kind, Like Me / Único Como Yo*. Oakland, CA: Blood Orange Press, 2016.

Pessin-Whedbee, Brook, and Naomi Bardoff. *Who Are You? The Kid's Guide to Gender Identity*. London: Jessica Kingsley Publishers, 2017.

Pitman, Gayle E., and Laure Fournier. *A Church for All*. Chicago: Albert Whitman & Co., 2018.

Pitman, Gayle E., and Violet Tobacco. *My Maddy*. Washington, DC: Magination Press, 2020.

Thom, Kai Cheng, Wai-Yant Li, and Kai Yun Ching. *From the Stars in the Sky to the Fish in the Sea*. Vancouver, BC: Arsenal Pulp Press, 2018.

Thorn, Theresa, and Noah Grigni. *It Feels Good to Be Yourself: A Book about Gender Identity*. New York: Henry Holt & Co., 2019.

Walton, Jess. *Introducing Teddy*. New York: Bloomsbury, 2016.

Autobiographies and Thoughts from Trans Folks

Andrews, Arin, and Joshua Lyon. *Some Assembly Required: The Not-So-Secret Life of a Transgender Teen*. New York: Simon & Schuster BFYR, 2015.

Barker, Meg-John, and Alex Iantaffi. *Life Isn't Binary: On Being Both, Beyond, and In-Between*. London: Jessica Kingsley Publishers, 2019.

Bornstein, Kate. *A Queer and Pleasant Danger: A Memoir*. Boston: Beacon Press, 2012.

Boylan, Jennifer Finney. *She's Not There: A Life in Two Genders*. New York: Broadway, 2003.

Clare-Young, Alex. *Transgender. Christian. Human*. Glasgow: Wild Goose Publications, 2019.

Green, Jamison. *Becoming a Visible Man*. Nashville: Vanderbilt University Press, 2006.

Jennings, Jazz. *Being Jazz: My Life as a (Transgender) Teen*. New York: Ember, 2017.

Kearns, Shannon T. L. *In the Margins: A Transgender Man's Journey with Scripture*. Grand Rapids: Eerdmans, 2022.

Mann, Rachel. *Dazzling Darkness: Gender, Sexuality, Illness and God*. 2nd ed. Glasgow: Wild Goose Publications, 2020.

Mendes, Eva A., and Meredith R. Maroney. *Gender Identity, Sexuality and Autism: Voices from across the Spectrum*. London: Jessica Kingsley Publishers, 2019.

Ming, Lei, and Lura Frazey. *Life Beyond My Body: A Transgender Journey to Manhood in China*. Oakland, CA: Transgress Press, 2016.

Mock, Janet. *Redefining Realness: My Path to Womanhood, Identity, Love, and So Much More*. New York: Simon & Schuster, 2015.

Rajunov, Micah, and Scott Duane, eds. *Nonbinary: Memoirs of Gender and Identity*. New York: Columbia University Press, 2019.

Salazar, Lisa. *Transparently: Behind the Scenes of a Good Life*. Vancouver, BC: Lisa Salazar, 2011.

Serano, Julia. *Excluded: Making Feminist and Queer Movements More Inclusive*. Berkeley, CA: Seal Press, 2013.

————. *Whipping Girl: A Transsexual Woman on Sexism and the Scapegoating of Femininity*. Berkeley, CA: Seal Press, 2016.

Twist, Jos, Ben Vincent, Meg-John Barker, and Kat Gupta, eds. *Non-Binary Lives: An Anthology of Intersecting Identities*. London: Jessica Kingsley Publishers, 2020.

Intersex Identities

Cornwall, Susannah. "Intersex and the Rhetorics of Disability and Disorder: Multiple and Provisional Significance in Sexed, Gender and Disabled Bodies." *Journal of Disability and Religion* 19, no. 2 (2015): 106–18.

————. *Sex and Uncertainty in the Body of Christ: Intersex Conditions and Christian Theology*. London: Routledge, 2010.

Davis, Georgiann. *Contesting Intersex: The Dubious Diagnosis*. New York: New York University Press, 2015.

DeFranza, Megan K. *Sex Difference in Christian Theology: Male, Female, and Intersex in the Image of God*. Grand Rapids: Eerdmans, 2015.

Reis, Elizabeth. *Bodies in Doubt: An American History of Intersex*. 2nd ed. Baltimore: Johns Hopkins University Press, 2021.

Viloria, Hida. *Born Both: An Intersex Life*. New York: Hachette Books, 2017.

Viloria, Hida, and Maria Nieto. *The Spectrum of Sex: The Science of Male, Female, and Intersex*. Philadelphia: Jessica Kingsley Publishers, 2020.

Zieselman, Kimberly M. *XOXY*. London: Jessica Kingsley Publishers, 2020.

Gender-Expansive History and Science

Bornstein, Kate, and S. Bear Bergman. *Gender Outlaws: The Next Generation*. Berkeley, CA: Seal Press, 2010.

Currah, Paisley, Richard M. Juang, and Shannon Price Minter. *Transgender Rights*. Minneapolis: University of Minnesota Press, 2006.

Devun, Leah. *The Shape of Sex: Nonbinary Gender from Genesis to the Renaissance*. New York: Columbia University Press, 2021.

Feinberg, Leslie. *Transgender Warriors: Making History from Joan of Arc to Dennis Rodman*. Boston: Beacon Press, 2005.

Fine, Cordelia. *Delusions of Gender: How Our Minds, Society, and Neurosexism Create Difference*. New York: W. W. Norton, 2011.

Gill-Peterson, Julian. *Histories of the Transgender Child*. Minneapolis: University of Minnesota Press, 2018.

Herdt, Gilbert H. *Third Sex, Third Gender: Beyond Sexual Dimorphism in Culture and History*. New York: Zone Books, 2003.

Roughgarden, Joan. *Evolution's Rainbow: Diversity, Gender, and Sexuality in Nature and People*. 10th anniversary ed. Berkeley: University of California Press, 2013.

Snorton, C. Riley. *Black on Both Sides: A Racial History of Trans Identity*. Minneapolis: University of Minnesota Press, 2017.

Stanley, Eric A., and Nat Smith, eds. *Captive Genders: Trans Embodiment and the Prison Industrial Complex*. 2nd ed. Chico, CA: AK Press, 2015.

Stryker, Susan. *Transgender History*. Berkeley, CA: Seal Press, 2008.

Stryker, Susan, and Aren Z. Aizura. *The Transgender Studies Reader 2*. London: Routledge, 2013.

Stryker, Susan, and Stephen Whittle. *The Transgender Studies Reader*. New York: Routledge, 2006.

Organizations and Community

The Center for LGBTQ and Gender Studies in Religion – Programming, research, and support for LGBTQI2A Christians. https://clgs.org/

The Center of Excellence for Transgender Health – Resources for medical professionals. https://prevention.ucsf.edu/transhealth

Church Clarity – A guide to finding churches with affirming policies. https://www.churchclarity.org/

Colage – Support for people with LGBTQI2A parents. https://www.colage.org/

Enfleshed – Expansive, affirming, anti-racist liturgical resources. https://enfleshed.com/

Gender Spectrum – Support for LGBTQI2A youth and families. https://www.genderspectrum.org/

The Institute for Welcoming Resources – An ecumenical group pushing LGBTQI2A church inclusion forward. http://www.welcomingresources.org/

The Mama Bears – Support for parents of LGBTQI2A people. https://www.realmamabears.org/

Many Voices – A Black Church Movement for Gay & Transgender Justice. www.manyvoices.org/

The National Center for Trans Equality – Advocacy and public policy organization. http://www.transequality.org/

PFLAG – Support for LGBTQI2A people and their families. https://www.pflag.org/

Q Christian Fellowship – Resources and community for LGBTQI2A Christians. https://www.qchristian.org/

Queer Grace – An LGBTQI2A faith encyclopedia. www.queergrace.com/

Queer Theology – Resources and community for LGBTQI2A Christians. https://www.queertheology.com/

Refuge Restrooms – App for finding gender-neutral, safe bathrooms. http://www.refugerestrooms.org/

The Sylvia Rivera Law Project – Legal help for transgender people. https://srlp.org/

The Trans Justice Funding Project – Grants for transgender groups and individuals. https://www.transjusticefundingproject.org/

Trans Lifeline – Crisis hotline staffed by trans people, for trans people. https://www.translifeline.org/

Trans Student Educational Resources – Trans resources by students, for students. www.transstudent.org

TransFaith – Information and community for LGBTQI2A people of all faiths. www.transfaith.info/

The Transgender Law Center – Legal advocacy and policy change. https://transgenderlawcenter.org/

Transmission Ministry Collective – Online resources and community for trans and gender-expansive Christians. https://www.transmissionministry.com/

TransParent USA – Support and resources for parents of trans and gender-expansive people. https://transparentusa.org/